AF579182

THE FALSE MESSIAHS

THE FALSE MESSIAHS

by

JACK GRATUS

LONDON
VICTOR GOLLANCZ LTD
1975

ISBN 0 575 02046 6

MADE AND PRINTED IN GREAT BRITAIN BY
THE GARDEN CITY PRESS LIMITED
LETCHWORTH, HERTFORDSHIRE
SG6 1JS

CONTENTS

PREFACE

MEN AND WOMEN who have claimed to be specially chosen by God to perform certain tasks have always attracted public attention—usually in the form of mockery and derision. If their activities have come to the notice of those in authority, they have been harshly treated. Punishments ranging from violent death to imprisonment in gaols or asylums for the insane have been meted out to them by wrathful judges, punishments which for the most part have been far in excess of any crimes they may have committed.

Yet, in spite of the dangers, they have persisted in their beliefs and have also succeeded in convincing others of the truth of their claims.

By tradition dating back to the Old Testament, claimants to divinity are called "messiahs". The adjective "false" has been added by writers to distinguish them from the true messiah who, depending on the writer's religious point of view, has either come or is still expected. False messiahs were regarded as heretics and agents of the Devil. Their histories were recorded, not so much to try to understand them, but to denounce them and to justify the actions of the authorities, religious and civil, in killing, torturing or imprisoning them.

Messiahs are no longer the exclusive concern of religion. Their extraordinary lives have been subjected to close scrutiny by psychologists, sociologists, political economists and social historians. Their religious convictions are considered of less importance than their social or political views, or the effects their movements had on their society.

Writers now prefer to start from the basis that truth, like beauty, lies in the eye of the beholder, that one man's apparently insane visions and presumptions are another's reality. This is my position. Beginning with the messianic ideology of the Old Testament, I have endeavoured to trace the history of messianism through its many claimants to the present day. Since messiahs have not lived in isolation but have been very much a heightened reflection of the mood of their times, I have also endeavoured to sketch in the historical backgrounds against which they have acted out their lives.

As there have been messiahs in every age and most countries, I have not been able to do more than sketch, and I would advise readers who are interested in any particular messiah and his period to consult more authoritative works on the subject. For instance, the influence of the Kabbalah on messianism and especially on the movement of Sabbatai Zevi in the seventeenth century is a subject of great fascination. Fortunately, it has been thoroughly documented by Gershom Scholem to whose books I have referred and which are mentioned in the bibliography. Norman Cohn's *The Pursuit of the Millennium* is a standard work on mediaeval millenarianism and deals far more extensively with the period of the eleventh to the sixteenth centuries than I have been able to do. I am indebted to Sigmund Mowinckel's *He That Cometh* and Joseph Klausner's *The Messianic Ideal in Israel* for the early history of messianism; and Abba Hillel Silver's classic study of Jewish messiahs, *A History of Messianic Speculation*, provided me with a comprehensive survey from which to begin my own research.

Causes for the sudden rise of messiahs and the flourishing of their movements at different periods in history have been hotly debated by social scientists. That the messiah fills a great need is not disputed; the problem is: what need or needs? At one extreme are Marxist writers who view the messiah as a pre-revolutionary figure responding to materialistic needs of an economically deprived proletariat. At the other are the Existentialists who consider that the messiah brings purpose and direction into the lives of those suffering from intense spiritual unease and anxiety.

The fact is that messiahs have risen to respond to both economic and spiritual deprivation; they have appealed to both the poor and the rich and even more so to those in between. While conducting my research I was struck by the recurrence of one main theme that ran like a strong current through the eddies and tides of messianic history, namely that of Exile and Return.

Followers of messiahs, for a variety of reasons, feel themselves in exile—from God, from their culture, their fellow-men and from themselves. The current word for this is "alienation". The reasons include major social upheavals such as war, pestilence, economic instability, and foreign invasions; and personal conflicts brought about by lack of faith, by fear and anxiety. They long to return to their roots which they variously identify as the Golden Age, the True Religion or the True Way, the Garden of Eden, or Paradise. Their messiahs claim that they have been elected by God to lead mankind back to these roots and that, consequently, those who follow them are also God's Elect. They are warned that they may have to fight a final, world-shattering battle against the enemies of Return, but that they will ultimately triumph and live for ever after in peace, harmony and justice.

The scenario for Exile and Return was laid down in the Old and New Testaments. Its development is summarized in the first section of this book. In the second and main section I show how the messiahs from the early Middle Ages to the present century have acted out their strange lives in accordance with that scenario. The element of play-acting appears common to most of them. They adopt, or are persuaded by their followers to adopt, the rôle of saviour. Thereafter, they follow the messianic scenario to the end, leaving their followers either to abandon their faith or to create a more comprehensive theology which in some cases has produced a full-scale, world-wide religion.

To call messiahs devils or heretics explains nothing. To dismiss them as mad or deluded is too easy. To treat them merely as victims of economic or social forces helps to place them in their historical context but does not reveal them as individuals, some of whom are evil, some good, some figures of comedy and some of tragedy.

If there is an explanation for the messianic phenomenon I suggest it lies in the relationship between the messiahs, their followers, and the outsiders. Each exists for the other. It is obvious that without the messiahs there would be no followers; it is less obvious that without the followers there would be no messiahs; and without the civil and religious opponents, who play the rôle of both spectators and participants, there would be no messianic drama.

In the concluding section of the book I attempt to analyse the relationship between these three protagonists: the messiahs, the Elect, and the Gentiles. I also bring the messianic story up to date with the latest versions of the scenario and some of the most recent protagonists.

The book is not intended as an academic study. Rather it is for readers who have seen reports in their newspapers about messiahs, who are aware that messianism has been part of our history for centuries, but who do not have access to original sources from which to study the subject. If they find the stories of the messiahs as fascinating as I have done, they can pursue their interest in works of greater depth, a number of which are referred to both in the notes and the bibliography. If I have no more than satisfied my readers' curiosity and perhaps left them with a few tentative answers to the riddles that messianism poses, then I am as content as a writer can be who is only too aware that his work does not match the magnitude of his subject.

PART ONE

In the Beginning

CHAPTER ONE

FROM KING TO MESSIAH

GOD CHOSE A man to be king, a goodly man, "from his shoulders and upward he was higher than any of the people".[1] The priest anointed the man and made him king by pouring holy oil over him. The spirit of God then entered him and he became a new man with a new heart.

The king's person was sacrosanct. To lay hands on him was sacrilege. He was the Lord's anointed, in comparison with which the ordinary man was "a dead dog", "a flea".[2]

He was a righteous man; the people loved and revered him. Invincible in battle, he protected them from their enemies. Under his vigilant eye they could find rest; safety in the power of his rule.

He governed with justice and mercy, condemning the wicked and punishing them, praising and rewarding the good. The oppressed looked to him for help; the oppressor feared his wrath.

Because he was righteous and blessed, his people were, too. They enjoyed peace and prosperity in the land. Through him God watched His People; through him, the people knew God.

Thus the ideal of kingship in ancient Israel. At different times in different cultures men have raised men to be kings or gods over them. A twelfth-dynasty Egyptian prophecy talks of the man who "shall bring cooling to the flame", "a shepherd of all the people" who will search the day long for his straying flocks, and who will "smite evil when he raises his hands against it".[3]

In 307 B.C. the Athenians bestowed divine honours on Demetrius and his father, Antigonus. They called them Saviour Gods, worshipped them with garlands, incense and libations, and praised them above other gods who were too distant or too busy to listen to their woes and answer their supplications. It is said that Demetrius accepted his deification willingly. His father, however, was not impressed. When an Athenian poet called him "god", and "child of the sun", he answered brusquely, "That's not my valet's opinion of me".[4]

The Brahman householder when performing his half-monthly sacrifices was supposed to become a deity for a period,[5] and in Cambodia, when an epidemic broke out, the inhabitants of some of the villages got together to search for a man to be temporarily incarnated. The man chosen by them was taken to the altar and made over into a god. He then received their blessings and their petitions to protect them from the oncoming epidemic.[6]

In Africa, too, there were tribal rulers who were worshipped as gods. "God made me after his own image," said the King of Iddah in West Africa to officers of the Niger expedition. "I am all the same as God; and he appointed me a king."[7] The King of Siam was also venerated as a divinity. No one could look him in the face or stand before him. His subjects had to avert their eyes and crawl on knees and elbows in his presence. The missionaries when speaking of God found that the only word they could use in Siamese was the word meaning "king".[8]

In ancient Israel the king was considered to be chosen by God. He was not crowned but anointed. He was God's anointed. In Hebrew he was *ha-mashiah*, the Anointed One. Through Aramaic, Greek and Latin the word has come down to us as *messiah*.

Samuel, when anointing Saul, says, "Is it not because the Lord hath anointed thee to be captain over his inheritance?" And when Saul failed to live up to the ideals of his office and was rejected, he was so by God. Samuel was told that he had to choose a new man even while Saul reigned.

David, the youngest son of Jesse, the Bethlehemite, was a shepherd and yet the Lord had chosen him to be king because "the Lord seeth not as man seeth; for man looketh on the outward appearance, but the Lord looketh on the heart".[9] There and then Samuel was commanded to anoint the young boy, which he did, "and the Spirit of the Lord came upon David from that day forward".[10]

In David's old age, according to the *First Book of Chronicles*, he called the congregation together and told them that God had chosen Solomon, his son, to succeed him. In due course Solomon was anointed and "sat on the throne of the Lord", not merely on the king's throne.[11]

Under David Israel achieved great power and prestige. His victories had reduced most of the neighbouring countries to the state of vassals. The Philistines had been defeated, and the other powerful nations, the Egyptians, Babylonians and Assyrians, preferred to trade with Israel than to attack it. This was in many ways Israel's Golden Age. David, with whom this age was associated, remained for all time the symbol of the great king, the strong and wise man who ruled a just nation. To what extent the symbol accorded with history is not important. What was important was the symbol. It was this that became merged with the messianic ideal, that David's strength and goodness would endure forever and be inherited by others in his line.

After David came Solomon and after Solomon other kings, none of whom matched David's glory. In time Israel's power declined. The hope remained that David, or one like him, would return. In 722 an Assyrian army conquered Israel. Its people ceased from then on to exist as a nation. Men, women and children, its leaders and soldiers, were made prisoners and led away. What happened to them is not known. They disappeared from history and into legend and myth as the Ten Lost Tribes, of whom we shall hear more later.

In Judah, the other Hebrew nation, the hope of David's return in another like him, another anointed who would conquer the enemies and return the exiled to their land, was now strengthened. Isaiah, the son of Judean nobility, prophesied: "for unto us a child is born, unto us a son is given". The child would take "government" upon his shoulder.[12] The child would become the man who would "smite the earth with the rod of his mouth", with "the breath of his lips" he would slay the wicked.[13] He would "stand for an ensign of the people".[14]

His rule would be righteous, but he would do what the kings of Israel were expected to do, in God's name "take the prey, and tread down his enemies like the mire of the streets".[15] His task, set firmly in the physical world, was to restore the people of Israel to the glory they had known in the past after destroying their enemies. By so doing, by saving his own people first, he would also bring peace to the whole world. Isaiah's prophecy that "the wolf also shall dwell with the lamb, and the leopard shall lie down with the kid"[16] has been interpreted by some commentators as referring to Israel's peaceful co-existence with other nations. "It seems to me that this idyll of the beasts of prey 'staying' with the domestic animals is intended merely as a symbol of the peace of the peoples," Martin Buber wrote. "Perhaps even a symbol in which under the name of wild beasts certain nations were to be recognized."[17]

The king-messiah, a branch of the House of David, was, therefore, a man strong in physical power and strong in spirit, too. In a time in the distant future he would bring about a complete redemption of the people of Israel, restore them to their spiritual, economic and political glory, and when this occurred the whole world would live in peace and prosperity.

"The Messianic faith developed, along with the faith in restoration, out of the longing for the future realization of the ideal of Kingship," concluded the Biblical scholar, Mowinckel, in his classic study of messianism.[18] In Isaiah's characterization the messiah was a commander of the people, but about two centuries later another prophet (or prophets) called by commentators the second or Deutero-Isaiah to distinguish him from the real Isaiah, introduced a new element into the messianic ideal. The new element was of the suffering servant of God.

"Who hath believed our report and to whom is the arm of the Lord revealed?" the Deutero-Isaiah asked. "For he shall grow up before him as a tender plant, and when we shall see him, there is no beauty that we should desire him. He is despised and rejected of men; a man of sorrows, and acquainted with grief." This man, wounded for our transgression, oppressed and afflicted, would be led like a lamb to the slaughter. Not a man of strength but a weak man; of David's line but one whom it would please the Lord to "bruise".[19] God's "servant",[20] despised and abhorred by men, he would nonetheless achieve great glory; kings and princes would worship him.[21]

Like the king-messiah he would be "just", but, according to the prophet Zechariah—a near contemporary of the Deutero-Isaiah—he would be "lowly", and would ride upon an ass, something no self-respecting king would do. Like a king, though, he would reign over the heathen but to them he would speak of peace, not war.[22]

In the period between the first Isaiah's prophecies and those of his namesake, the Deutero-Isaiah, an event of enormous consequence took place which caused the shift of emphasis from the proud to the humble, from the messiah who was king of men to the messiah who was king of peace. That event was exile.

CHAPTER TWO

EXILE AND THE LAST DAYS

IN THE NINTH year of the reign of Zedekiah, the King of Judah, Nebuchadnezzar, King of Babylon, and his army advanced against Jerusalem and besieged it. In the eleventh year of Zedekiah's reign, after a long famine, the city was "broken up". Zedekiah and his soldiers who tried to escape through the king's garden and through the gate between the two walls were pursued and captured in the plains of Jericho. They were brought before the King of Babylon. Zedekiah's sons were executed in front of him, and all the princes of Judah were put to death.

Zedekiah was blinded, put in chains and taken off to Babylon. On the tenth day of the fifth month (Ab), the Temple in Jerusalem was burnt down. The king's palace and the homes of all the nobles were also destroyed by fire. The people of Judah were sent into exile in Babylon and only some of the poor who had nothing were left to till the vineyards and the fields. "Thus Judah was carried away captive out of his own land."[1]

In historical time, these events took place between the years 598 and 587 B.C. Judah was a small and unimportant kingdom, lying uneasily between mighty Egypt, Assyria, Greece and Babylon. Yet, in spite of her insignificance, the ordeal of exile suffered by the nation during that period became, through the literature of its people, imprinted on our imaginations for all time.

The physical fact of exile was transformed through later Judaism and Christianity into a symbol of universal exile. Israel was exiled from its homeland and from the Holy City of Jerusalem. Man was exiled from God. Man was exiled from other men and from himself. Inseparably connected with the symbol of exile was the concept of the messiah. The messiah stood as the pivotal point between Exile and Return. It was through the messiah that man would be brought back to Judah. It was through the messiah that man would be brought back to the love of God. It was through the messiah that man would come to love man again and to fulfil himself in his own being.

The messianic concept cannot, I think, be wholly understood nor its universal and timeless applicability appreciated aside from its close connection with the opposing mental states of Exile and Return. Messianic movements have been categorized as social movements of a revolutionary nature, as outbreaks of nationalism, as expressions of rebellion against oppression. These some of them undoubtedly are, but all of them to a lesser or greater degree are the expressions of the need to belong.

We, in this century, do not talk about exile but about *alienation*. The meaning, I think, is the same. Wherever there has been an overwhelming sense of alienation and the longing to return from exile, whether it be physical exile as in the case of the Jews, or spiritual exile as in the case of some of the Christian messianic movements, or cultural exile as in the case of many of the messianic movements that have occurred in societies outside Europe, messiahs have arisen. Messiahs have responded to the yearning for Return, have sometimes anticipated it, but have always understood it instinctively. Through the power of their personalities they have persuaded those in need that they could bring about the wished-for Redemption, freeing their believers from the captivity imposed on them by others or by their own inadequacies.

Jeremiah prophesied that the Jews would serve Babylon for 70 years; then God would punish the king and his nation. As things turned out, he was wrong only by about twenty years. In 538 B.C. Cyrus conquered Babylon to establish the Persian empire. He permitted the Jews to return to their homeland. For a century or so caravans of exiles crossed the semi-desert to take up life again in their ravaged country. In time a population of size grew there, led in the main by those who had been in exile and whose superior education and wider culture gave them an advantage over those who had remained behind.

The reason for their return had more to do with the strong religious and cultural bond with their homeland than with politics or economics. Judah was in a wretched state. But it was essential that the sacred centre of the nation, Jerusalem, and the sacred centre of that city, the Temple, be rebuilt as it was in the glorious days of Solomon, son of David.

The man entrusted with the task of rebuilding the Temple

was the Governor of Judea, Zerubbabel. On him were pinned all the hopes of the people. It is clear from reading the two prophets of the period, Haggai and Zecheriah, that Zerubbabel was looked upon as the traditional messiah-king. The vocabulary used by these two prophets when talking about the Governor was loaded with messianic references:

"In that day, saith the Lord of hosts, will I take thee, O Zerubbabel, my servant, and will make thee as a signet: for I have chosen thee."[2]

Echoing the messianic prophecies of Isaiah, Zechariah reported God's announcement of the messiah, thus: "Behold the man whose name is the BRANCH: and he shall grow up out of his place, and he shall build the temple of the Lord".[3] Zerubbabel was to be the "branch". He was the "anointed", of the House of David, who would "sit and rule upon his throne",[4] and lay "the foundations of the house".[5]

Zerubbabel, it was hoped, would free Judah from the yoke of foreign oppression and, true to the messianic mission, once he had rebuilt the Temple, would bring back "they that are far off",[6] the exiled and the captive. But the Governor was not a monarch. He did not restore the House of David nor did he free his nation. Instead, Judah remained a pawn in the power game of the day, moving from the hands of one grasping emperor to another. Many Judeans had returned from exile in Babylon, but many were still outside. Therefore, in spite of the fact that in 515 B.C., a new Temple was dedicated, the hope that Zerubbabel was the messiah began to fade.

As the possibility of national independence became more remote so the character of the messiah became less worldly and more spiritual; less of the king and more of the servant of the Lord prophesied by the Deutero-Isaiah and by Zechariah, who pictured him riding upon an ass and speaking peace to the heathen. In Jerusalem the new messiah would not triumph like a king, but would suffer. He would be "pierced". The people would mourn him "as one mourneth for his only son". The House of David would receive a new kind of benediction, "the spirit of grace and of supplications".[7]

Jerusalem, the city, became a symbol of longing and of Return. God in his anger would punish the city for its sins by casting its people into captivity, but if they repented and went back to Him, they would be allowed to live in the city in peace, "and there shall be no more utter destruction".[8]

The way was now being made clear for the development of a messiah of the spirit as well as of the flesh. "The Servant displaces the king," wrote Mowinckel, "and himself becomes king."[9] Jewish literature still concerned itself with the physical fact of exile, with national destruction and restoration, with the messiah who could accomplish the return of the people, but more and more it concerned itself with man's inner exile, the exile from God and from himself.

When Alexander the Great dazzled the world with his conquests many Jews living in his empire hailed him as the messiah, the divinely appointed redeemer who would lead them back to their homeland, and would inaugurate that period of universal peace which the prophets had foretold.

Peace of a kind did come for a period. When he died in 323 B.C. Alexander's empire was divided up among his generals. Judea went to the Ptolemies who ruled Egypt and for a century the people lived quietly, unaffected by what was happening in the rest of the world, except that the richer among them were being strongly influenced by that culture and religion of late Greece we call Hellenism. These new ways separated the wealthy from the majority of the population which maintained its close ties with the traditional religion of the Torah.

The Syrians, ruled by the Seleucid dynasty, descendants of one of Alexander's generals, were anxious to lay claim to Judea as part of their ambition to conquer Egypt. The Seleucid emperor, Antiochus the Great, finally defeated Ptolemy in 198 B.C. and Judea now fell under Syrian rule. Within the country itself there was increasing division between those who favoured the encroachment of Hellenism and those who fought for the Torah and its laws. The priesthood had become more and more Hellenistic, identifying itself with the ruling class. The people remained conservative. The pious among them were horrified to see the encroachment of Grecian culture into their cities. Gymnasia were built in Jerusalem; wealthy young men dressed in Grecian style; the priests neglected their duties in the Temple. Finally, the Hellenizers, by now a party of strength, tried to gain control of the priesthood. Civil strife followed.

Antiochus's successor, Antiochus Epiphanes, had little patience with the Judeans and their internal squabbles over what to him was the foregone conclusion of the triumph of Hellenism over Judaism. In 168 B.C. he outlawed Judaism and its customs. Circumcision and the dietary laws were stopped and the Temple was defiled with the sacrifice of swine. A statue of the god Zeus was placed on the altar.

His efforts to destroy the traditions of Judaism were met by armed uprisings. Though the Hellenistic party continued to favour the ruler, the populace rejected his actions and his gods. They took to the hills while groups of Syrian soldiers went from place to place, forcing the people to worship strange gods. When the soldiers arrived in the small town of Modin, near Jerusalem, they were met by the family of insurgents whose name was for centuries to be associated in popular thought with the promised messiah, the Maccabees.

The origin of the name, Maccabee, is obscure. It may have been made up from the first letters of their war-cry: "Who is like unto Thee among the Mighty, O Lord". In Hebrew this spelt MKBI. Possibly the name is derived from the Hebrew word, MAKKEB, meaning "the Hammer", which, some say, their leader, Judah, was called.

The Maccabees were a family of priests. The father, Mattathias, refused to participate in heathen sacrifices. After slaying the Syrian official who came to Modin, he and his five sons collected men and arms and in 167 B.C. organized armed resistance against the Syrians. Mattathias died in 166 B.C. and his son, Judah, took command.

Judah the Maccabee was a brilliant leader and he defeated the Syrians in all their engagements. In 164 he finally performed the duty worthy of the messiah—he cleansed the Temple of defilement and rededicated it to the worship of the Hebrew God. For eight days the people celebrated the Feast of Rededication, maintained still today by Jews as the Festival of Hannukah. "Thus was there very great gladness among the people, for that the reproach of the heathen was put away."[10]

The triumph of Judah is important in the history of messianic movements, not only because the Hasmoneans, as the family was called, had messianic pretensions, but also because of the spirit of messianic fervour that Judah's resistance to foreign oppression excited. The people had been faced with exile, not from their homeland on this occasion, but from their God. They had looked for a leader, one chosen by God, to help bring them back to their religion. Judah, the Maccabee, had responded to their call.

Evidence of this fervour has come down to us in a number of contemporary books in which Judah was called "the salvation of Israel", "a prince" whose task it was to bring "peace for all the seed of the sons of the beloved".[11] The enthusiasm for the cause of the Maccabees inspired the writing of the *Book of Daniel* which, with the *Revelation of St John the Divine*, is the most important Biblical source of messianic prophecy.

The real Daniel was a prophet of the time of the Babylonian exile, but this record in his name was written in about the year 165 B.C., at the height of the Maccabean revolt against the Syrians. Its purpose was to encourage Jews not to submit to Antiochus and his religion, but to remain faithful to their own God.

The dense richness of Daniel's imagery contained secret messages of hope and courage for the people of the time, but for centuries thereafter his visions were re-interpreted to fit new times. Though the language used was precise and concrete, it referred not to an objective reality but to a vivid inner reality which could be felt if not always understood. Contemporaries read its words of rebellion against and triumph over the foe who threatened their way of life, but its appeal lay beyond the immediate. The foe was Antiochus and anyone who set up false idols of gold and forced people to worship them. The foe was also sin and evil. The triumph was that of the Maccabees over Antiochus and all righteous rulers over all tyrants. The triumph was also that of good over evil for all time.

Daniel had a vision in which he saw beasts come up from the sea. The four beasts referred at the time of writing to the kingdoms of the Babylonians, the Medes, the Persians and, of course, that of the Seleucids with whom the Maccabees were then at war. Since then these "beasts" have symbolized different kingdoms to suit different periods of history, the point being that their power had to come to an end before the age of the messiah could be ushered in. Early Christians considered Daniel the "prophet and witness of Christ" and appropriately they interpreted his vision of "the Son of Man" who "came with the clouds of heaven" as Jesus Christ.

The Book was filled with cryptic references to people, places and times when certain events would occur, and these have provided mystics, visionaries and successive claimants to the messianic title with endless interpretative possibilities. There is the reference to the ten horns of the fourth beast and the additional "little horn" with "eyes of man and a mouth speaking great things"[12] which has been interpreted as the Anti-Christ, the arch enemy of the Church. Time periods abound like "seventy days to make an end of sins",[13] "seven weeks from the command to restore and to build Jerusalem to the coming of the messiah",[14] and the ever-puzzling "a time and times and the dividing of time",[15] or again, "a time, times, and an half".[16] By various methods of computation based on Daniel's hints, the pious of all periods have tried to arrive at the definitive moment in history when the messiah will come.

Of great significance for all future messianic claims was the close connection between the coming of the messiah and the drawing to an end of the world as it was known. The messiah was conceived by Daniel's writers as being both of this-world and of the other-world, a man and something more than a man. He would be an intimate part of God's judgment on the world, a judgment that was certain and unavoidable. He would reign with those judged to be the "saints of the most High",[17] and his reign would last for ever.

The atmosphere of the *Book of Daniel* is one of hope, but hope tempered by a sense of foreboding. Ultimately the world would prosper and the righteous triumph over sin, but before that happened there would be "troublous times". Throughout, there is a pervading awareness of time drawing to a close, of time, ticking away like a bomb, to explode with universal destruction, of time being marked for us by God, the judge, of time waiting to be released from itself into timelessness which only the "wise" who have recognized the messiah would enjoy.

The messiah would come, that Daniel prophesied, but his coming would be preceded by destruction, flood and desolation. Before joy there would be great sadness; before triumph more defeat and greater exile. Only in the future beyond the future would there be life everlasting.

The present world was evil; kings did battle; they worshipped false gods; the people suffered. But this was destined to end. From the hints Daniel gave, the "wise" would know when this was to be so that they could prepare for it.

Historically, Daniel's sense of foreboding was wholly justified.

Judah the Maccabee turned out not to be the messiah as some believed he was. He was killed in battle in 160 B.C. and his leadership passed to his other brothers, to Jonathan who was acclaimed High Priest in 152 B.C. and to Simon who in a great assembly was confirmed as the hereditary ruler of Judea, thus establishing the Hasmonean dynasty.

The Hasmoneans, as time went by and prosperity of the nation increased, became themselves inclined to strange and unholy ways which their forebears had fought so bravely to defeat. The immense popularity which they had enjoyed with the common people was gradually disappearing. Civil strife and dissension began again in Judea.

Then came the Romans. They conquered Syria and took Judea under their control and into their empire. What Daniel had foreseen in his vision of the four beasts had come about. This Roman "beast" was every bit as "dreadful and terrible, and strong exceedingly" as the prophet had foretold.[18] The people of Judea hated their new rulers and those they had put over them to govern their unruly province. As in the days of Judah the Maccabee men banded together into guerilla groups to cause the Roman authorities constant problems. To them they were "bandits"; to the people, however, they were freedom fighters.

To a few, they were messiahs.

CHAPTER THREE

SIMON, JUDAH AND JOSHUA

"NOW AT THIS time there were ten thousand other disorders in Judea," wrote the historian, Flavius Josephus.[1] The need for the messiah to set his face against the enemies of the Jews grew more desperate. The Romans were the hated infidel, demanding sacrifices to their emperors in the sacred Temple in Jerusalem. They were the occupying army with soldiers who treated the inhabitants with cruelty and contempt.

As the enormity, the impossibility, of the task of over-throwing the oppressors became more apparent with the passing years so the concept of the messiah, growing out of the longing for release from oppression, became less man-like and more god-like, less physical, more spiritual until to those few who followed Jesus of Nazareth he became a god-man, a divinity in the form of a man.

Contemporaneous with Jesus, as Josephus showed, there were a number of men who manifested little divinity but who claimed the role of messiah. Since Josephus was, though a Jew, a member of the noble class and a friend to the Romans, he saw these messianic claimants as no more than robbers and upstarts. The whole notion of a messiah was summed up by him as, "an ambiguous oracle, likewise found in the sacred Scriptures, to the effect that at that time one from their country would become the ruler of the world".[2]

Herod the Great died in 4 B.C. One of his former slaves by the name of Simon rose up as a messiah. Josephus described him as being "a comely person, of a tall and robust body". Superior to the other slaves, he was given important administrative duties while the king was still alive. In the confusion that followed Herod's death, Simon, the slave, "was so bold as to put a diadem on his head, while a certain number of people stood by him, and by them he was declared to be a king, and thought himself more worthy of that dignity than anyone else".

Simon burnt down the royal palace at Jericho, and plundered the treasures there, and, according to Josephus, he would have committed even greater violence had not the commander of Herod's soldiers, one Gratus, taken an army and defeated the messiah. Simon's own disordered troops fought a brave but hopeless battle and were destroyed. Simon escaped, but Gratus tracked him down, caught him, and cut off his head.[3]

The greatest of the folk heroes of the period, and the leader of the militant patriots fighting against the Romans, was Judas of Galilee. Judas, called by Josephus a "robber", had gathered together a large band of "men of a profligate character" about Sepphoris in Galilee. He attacked the palace and seized all weapons and money. With his army, now armed, "he became terrible to all men, by tearing and rending those that came near him; and all this in order to raise himself, and out of an ambitious desire of the royal dignity".[4]

Judas, too, was finally caught.

The messiahs of the time were not all homebred; some came from far off, attracted, no doubt, by the confused and confusing social conditions. One arrived from Egypt. "He was a cheat," declared Josephus firmly. "He pretended to be a prophet, and got together thirty thousand men that were deluded by him. These he led round from the wilderness to the Mount of Olives." From there they overlooked the walls of the Holy City which the Egyptian messiah promised would fall down before them. Felix, the procurator, dealt quickly and decisively with the prophet: he and his followers were put to death.[5]

In the time of the procurator, Fadus, about A.D. 45, a man whose name was Theudas proclaimed himself a messiah. This "magician" persuaded a large number of people to take their effects with them and to follow him to the River Jordan. Like Moses and the Red Sea, Theudas told his people that, at his command, the Jordan would divide and afford them a passage over it. The procurator overtook Theudas and his followers as they made their way towards the river with all their belongings. Many were killed and others taken prisoner. Theudas was captured alive, then beheaded; his head was carried back to Jerusalem as a warning to others not to be deluded by "false" prophets.[6]

Of the many Jewish sects of the period perhaps the best known to history is that of the Essenes. Even Josephus, by no means sympathetic to sectarianism, admired their ascetic way of life, their disciplined community and their strict piety. Instead of immersing themselves in the political activity of the day, the Essenes withdrew from society into a monastic existence to wait for the End of Days and the coming of the messiah. In their literature they spoke of two messiahs, the one who would lead his people to victory, defeat the enemy and bring in the kingdom of God. He was of the Davidic line and was a Prince of the Congregation. The other messiah was of the family of Aaron. He was represented as the High Priest of the kingdom, the one who knew the Torah and revealed its wisdom to the people.

The Essenes practised ritual purification, believing that the sins of men could be washed away by the act of daily ablutions in spring water. One who was either an Essene or very close to the sect and who was a well-known figure of his time was a man named Jonathan, or John. He lived on locusts and wild honey and wore the clothes of the ancient prophets: a cloak of camel's hair and a leather girdle.[7] By many this man, John the Baptist, was thought to be the prophet Elijah, who by tradition would come to earth to announce the messiah. "Ye yourselves bear me witness," he told his followers who had asked him if he was the messiah. "I am not the Christ, but that I am sent before him."[8]

John's successful preaching aroused antagonism. He was arrested, imprisoned and later beheaded. Josephus mentioned him and his ministry, acknowledging him as a prominent Jewish personality, but failed to mention his most famous disciple, Jesus of Nazareth, possibly because Jesus was not of much importance to his immediate contemporaries.

The facts known about Jesus are few. His name, the Greek form of the Hebrew, Joshua, was one of the most common of the period. Josephus mentioned about twenty men by the same name.[9] He was born in Bethlehem, somewhere about the year 4 B.C., the son of Joseph, who was possibly a joiner by trade, and Miriam, his wife. His home was in Nazareth.

In order to substantiate a claim to messiahship it was essential that Jesus was the "son of David", that is, of the Davidic line of king-messiahs. In the Gospels written long after the death of Jesus, Matthew traced the descent of Jesus through Joseph, his father, his grandfather, Jacob, to Solomon, the king, and from Solomon to David, and beyond that to Abraham, the father of his people.[10] Luke went even further and traced Jesus's genealogy directly to Seth, the son of Adam, the son of God.[11] It is interesting to note that in both genealogies, the line to David is traced through his father, Joseph. The writers of the Gospels apparently found no inconsistency between this necessary link to David and the statement made by Matthew (in the very same chapter) that Jesus was of virgin birth.

There is some evidence in the Gospels that Jesus was at variance with his family as he grew up. At the marriage feast in Cana, as recorded in the Gospel of St John, he turned on his mother in annoyance if not anger when she asked him to produce wine for the feast. "Woman," he said, "what have I to do with thee? Mine hour is not yet come."[12]

Luke recorded Jesus as commending those who left their homes and families, their wives and their children, "for the kingdom of God's sake".[13] In even more uncompromising terms, according to Luke, Jesus told his disciples, "If any man come to me, and hate not his father, and mother, and wife, and children, and brethren, and sisters, yea, and his own life also, he cannot be my disciple".[14]

This rejection of ordinary family life, of the society and companionship of those uncommitted to the messiah, is a feature common to messiahs and their relationship with their followers. The followers, in order to be of the community of the chosen, the elect, have to give up all intimate connection with their past, and their past, of course, includes their parents and also usually their wives or husbands and children unless these have joined them in the community. Family life which binds the followers and holds them back from total absorption into the community as demanded by the messiah has to be rejected.

When he was in his late twenties, somewhere between 27 and 29, Jesus was baptized in the River Jordan by John, who believed himself to be the "messenger" of the messiah and who apparently saw in this young man the one "that cometh after" him and who was mightier than John. John told Jesus that it was he, Jesus, who should baptize him and not the other way around, but this Jesus refused to do, insisting on his own baptism.

When this took place, Jesus came out of the water, "and lo, the heavens opened unto him, and he saw the Spirit of God descending like a dove, and lighting upon him". Jesus heard himself "called" by God: "This is my beloved Son, in whom I am well pleased".[15] From then on he knew that he was set aside from ordinary mortals; that he had a task to perform beyond the task given to other men; and that he was chosen directly by God to do God's bidding.

What Jesus experienced on the banks of the Jordan, all claimants to messiahship experience—the awesome and awful moment of being "called". It is a moment filled with great joy and terror. There is joy because the recipients are aware that they have been selected, and they recognize the tremendous significance of the election. At the same time they are terrified by the uncertainty whether the election is of their own doing or of God's. If the former, they know they are doomed; if the latter, they realize that they are no longer like other men, that their way is now alone, and their destination a mystery. They sense that they will suffer dishonour, perhaps physical torture, certainly mental torment, and finally a martyrdom of some kind. They are aware that, once they have been chosen, they are required by the choice to reach out for the impossible, to do things on earth that no man has ever done before or at least not within their own time. They know this very reaching out for the impossible will stretch them beyond their humanity so that either they will soar up to the heavens and be higher than all men in honour and glory or they will plummet to the earth and be destroyed.

Whatever their fate, once they have been "called" they become new men; like Saul on his anointment by Samuel, God gives them "another heart". Jesus regarded spiritual rebirth as an essential pre-requisite for entrance to the "kingdom of God". The second birth is "not of blood, nor of the will of the flesh, nor of the will of man, but of God".[16] Nicodemus, the Pharisee, asked Jesus, "How can a man be born when he is old? Can he enter the second time into his mother's womb, and be born?" Jesus replied: "Except a man be born of water and of the Spirit, he cannot enter into the Kingdom of God".[17]

Rebirth, whether through baptism or not, has an elemental character that is found in the myths and dreams of men throughout the ages. I shall touch on this subject further in chapters fifteen and sixteen. For the present it is enough to mention that immersion and rebirth have an ancient association. Modern psychologists who have examined patients claiming to have gone through the experience of being born again have noticed the recurrence in these patients of dreams of being under water, of drowning or floating at the bottom of a body of water, then re-emerging as a new person into a new and more intense life.[18]

Jesus died to his old self in the River Jordan and emerged strong enough to counter the temptations of wealth and power offered to him in the wilderness. His ministry began. He gathered his apostles together and he went about Galilee, teaching in the synagogues and healing the sick, his fame spreading rapidly. People came to him and he performed miraculous cures, such as of the leper, of the two men possessed by devils, and of the man sick with palsy. He raised from the dead the daughter of Jairus, and when the multitude gathered to hear him speak and had nothing to eat, he took the five loaves and two fish given to him by his disciples and he turned them miraculously into sufficient to feed "five thousand men, beside women and children".[19]

There is in Jesus's life—as opposed to his teachings—little to distinguish him from other preachers and miracle-workers whose deeds have been lauded and glorified by their faithful followers. Whether he was wholly a man of peace or whether he had connections with some of the anti-Roman militants as did other messiahs of the period is beyond our knowledge. Matthew does record Jesus as saying: "Think not that I am come to send peace on earth: I am come not to send peace, but a sword".[20] This one phrase, however, does not make a war-cry.

He rebuked the Pharisees for their insistence on strict adherence to the Torah, and called them hypocrites, but in many respects his way of life was that of a middle-of-the-road Pharisee rather than of a strict sectarian. Unlike the Essenes he did not live a monastic existence, secure in the closed community, but went out to preach to the people, confronting them in the midst of their daily lives.

There is evidence in the Gospels that he acted contrary to the Law and was, for this, understandably condemned by the Pharisees who saw themselves as the guardians of that Law. There is, however, no evidence that he ceased to be accepted as a Jew at any time in his life, or that he belonged to any one sect that either denied the Law in its entirety or the *de facto* authority of Rome. The Gospels, written many generations after his death and with the purpose of publicizing his life, teaching and the Church that was rising in his name, tended to treat him as a god-man, belonging to the whole world and not as the Jew he was, belonging to his own time. If he was noticed at all by the majority of his fellow-Jews it was probably as the bright young rabbinical student who had involved himself in some of the current and unreliable enthusiasms and had consequently gone astray.

Whether Jesus claimed to be the messiah or not is also open to question. He made frequent references to the messianic phrase "the Son of Man". Originally this was applied impersonally to the Jewish people as the messianic nation, but by his time it had definite associations with a personal messiah. His references, however, were in the third person. After hearing God "calling" him His "beloved Son", Jesus cautioned his disciples to "Tell the vision to no man, until the Son of Man be risen again from the dead".[21] He also told his disciples, not that *he* would die, but that, "The Son of Man shall be betrayed into the hands of men; and they shall kill him, and the third day he shall be raised again".[22] The people call you the Christ, the Messiah, Peter told him. He forbade him to mention this.

If Jesus thought of himself as the messiah it was as the "suffering servant" of sectarian Jewish thinking and not as the king-messiah of orthodox Jewish tradition. Deutero-Isaiah had predicted the coming of "the despised and rejected man of sorrows", "wounded for our transgressions" who, because he had "poured out his soul unto death" and borne "the sin of many", would receive "a portion with the great" and be exalted and extolled.[23] It was this fate that Jesus predicted for himself. He told his disciples that the Son of Man had to suffer many things, be rejected of the elders, the chief priests and the scribes, and be killed. But he added that he would rise again after three days.[24]

When he went to Jerusalem he might well have known that if he had to die, that was the place where his death would occur. The city, according to Luke, had a reputation for killing its prophets. Commentators have suggested that his actions were a deliberate acting out of the messianic rôle. If this is the case then it confirms that he did—at least by the end of his life—come to see himself (as did his followers) as the messiah.

All messiahs finally have to face the consequences of their claims. All have to confront the challenge which their deeds and words have issued to the rest of society. If they are the specially chosen of God as they claim to be, and their beliefs are the specific intentions and wishes of God, then they finally have to prove this, with their lives if necessary. Otherwise, they will be seen to be deluded or, worse still, frauds and false prophets.

Jesus was prepared. The priests, Sadducees and not Pharisees, were already incensed by his triumphant entry into their city. They had heard how many had spread their garments in the path of the holy man who had meekly ridden in on an ass as prophesied by Zechariah; how others had cut down branches of trees and had strewn them along his way. How people had gone in front of him, believing him to be the promised Son of God, crying out, "Hosanna!"

Now the time had come for the messianic scenario outlined by the prophets to move to its final scene. Judas had to betray Jesus to the priests and show them the man who claimed to be the messiah. This he did.

After his arrest, Jesus was asked directly whether he believed himself to be the messiah. For his interrogators this was the crucial question because they alone had the knowledge to challenge and judge his claims. According to Matthew and Luke, the answer Jesus gave was cautious and equivocal. "You used the words, Son of God," he said, "not me."[25] According to Mark, however, his reply was a simple: "I am". Then he switched to the third person in his customary manner and spoke of "the Son of Man sitting on the right hand of power and coming in the clouds of Heaven".[26]

The priests, worldly Sadducees though they might have been, knew from their own religious traditions that Jesus, by saying he would sit on God's right hand, meant he believed he would not suffer death like ordinary mortals, but would be raised up to God. His fate from then on was virtually decided. "What need we of further witnesses?" they asked. He had condemned himself out of his own mouth.

Jesus was delivered to Pontius Pilate, the Roman Governor, who sent him to Herod who returned him to Pilate. No one seemed to know what to do with him. He was an embarrassment, as all messiahs have always been. He was not a soldier who invaded with arms. He invaded with the spirit. He forced a new reality or a different reality onto that accepted by the majority and by their leaders. For this he had to be put out of the way. But how and by whom?

Pilate wanted to have none of this Jewish business. "Art thou King of the Jews?" he asked. Jesus turned the question aside by answering again, "Thou sayest".[27]

It was customary for the governor of the province to grant

to a Jewish prisoner an amnesty on the Passover. Barabbas, the insurrectionist, was also awaiting death. A cruel game then ensued, played out between Pilate, the priests and the crowds gathered before the governor's palace. The crowds wanted Jesus to die. Pilate would have preferred the revolutionary, Barabbas, who was much more of a threat to his authority than the preacher.

But the Jews, difficult at the best of times, were even worse at the Passover when they celebrated their victory over the Egyptians and their release from captivity. Pilate let them have their way. The popular hero, Barabbas, was saved. After washing his hands, Pilate ordered Jesus to be crucified.

The Roman soldiers stripped him and dressed him in a scarlet robe, plaited a crown of thorns on his head, gave him a reed in his right hand and bowed before him. This mock ceremony of the crowning of a king was more than a charade directed at a deluded and pathetic preacher from the countryside. It was a deliberate gesture of contempt against the whole Jewish messianic ideal. It was not just Jesus who was spat upon but the whole concept of a Jewish national saviour.

When the soldiers called Jesus "King of the Jews" they were mocking not only him but his fellow-Jews also, pouring abuse upon their longing for a king and for sovereignty in their own land. When they crucified Jesus and callously watched him die under the placard carrying his sentence: "This is Jesus, the King of the Jews", they thought they were crucifying, in the man, Jewish, or more accurately, Judean nationalism and religious pride.

The priests at the end joined the others in the mocking. "If thou be the Son of God," they called out to the man on the cross, "come down." He who had talked about saving others could not even save himself. They wanted Jesus to prove objectively what they knew was beyond his powers, what they might even have suspected was beyond his aspirations, namely, his divinity. Their reality and his reality had long ago parted ways. When he talked about "saving" he had meant not the bodies but the souls of men. To the priests brought up in the orthodox tradition such an act belonged not to man at all, not even to the messiah when he eventually came, but to God alone.

The Jewish messiah was not divine. He was a superb man chosen by God for his attributes to act out human tasks: to restore the Jews to their independence under the perpetual government of the House of David. Through this physical accomplishment, the spiritual return of the people to their God would follow. All Jewish messiahs who have arisen over the centuries have, as shall be shown, acknowledged as their first task that of returning the Jews to Israel. Christian messiahs, when they have spoken about Exile and Return, about banishment from the Holy Land and the restoration of the elect to Jerusalem have, in the main, used these terms metaphorically.

Jesus died, having conspicuously failed to bring about any change in the political situation in Judea. His messianic drama was played out, but the world went on. In fact, things grew worse. In A.D. 66, pushed to the limit of their patience by a greedy and cruel procurator named Florus, the political extremists in Jerusalem seized the Temple and put a stop to the daily sacrifices to the emperor which so disgusted the populace. This was an act of outright rebellion and the Roman fist, always poised threateningly above Judea, now smashed down hard.

For the next seven years the Judeans resisted, but they were no match for the might of the Roman empire. On 10 May 70, Jerusalem was invaded. In August of the same year the Temple was burnt down. A month later, after 139 days of siege, the city fell. Pockets of resistance persisted; the last to succumb was the fortress at Masada. After a siege lasting two years Masada was finally captured. The Jews of Judea were about to enter the longest exile of their history.

With the thousands forced to leave Judea were members of the Jesus-sect. There had been perhaps a hundred or so living in Jerusalem and about 500 in Galilee.[28] They had gone on believing that Jesus had come as the messiah and had delivered a new and inspiring message directly to them. He was still among them in spirit and it was in his spirit they lived.

"And all that believed were together, and had all things in common; And sold their possessions and goods, and parted them to all men, as every man had need. And they, continuing daily with one accord in the temple, and breaking bread from house to house, did eat their meat with gladness and singleness of heart."[29]

The sectarians regarded themselves as Jews and continued to observe the Torah and the traditions of their ancestors, but as time went on and the memory of the living Jesus faded so the sect changed its direction. New influences were brought in that must have seemed strange if not blasphemous to some of these early followers. The Hellenized Jew, Paul, said that whether you were a Jew, circumcized according to ancient custom, or an uncircumcized pagan, it mattered not so long as you believed in the divinity of Jesus Christ. "For there is no difference between the Jew and the Greek: for the same Lord over all is rich unto all that call upon him. For whosoever shall call upon the name of the Lord shall be saved."[30] In time the original sect diminished in importance, being replaced by the growing Church of Christ that believed in Jesus as divine. After the tenth century no more is heard of these first followers of Jesus, the man.

Both the Jewish sectarians and the Christians who replaced them shared a belief in the return of Jesus, in his Second Coming, in their own lifetime or in time to come. During the terrible persecutions suffered by the young Church this belief was necessary for its survival. On the barren, rocky island of Patmos in the Aegean Sea lived a man, probably a Jewish Christian, well versed in the Scriptures and the apocalyptic books written by his contemporaries and near contemporaries in Judea and elsewhere who had prophesied in these the approaching End of the World. It is thought that this man, John Mark, was the author of the last book of the Christian Bible, the *Revelation of St John the Divine.*[31] This extraordinary account of a series of visions was composed sometime between A.D. 54 and 95; it was addressed to the seven churches of Asia, encouraging them to be faithful to the new religion in spite of persecution.

Like the *Book of Daniel*, and for similar reasons, the *Book of Revelation* has been and is still, nearly 2,000 years later, one of the main sources of messianic inspiration. Both Books described the messianic age; both were worded in such a way that they could be interpreted to suit all times and all situations. If anything the *Book of Revelation* is even more difficult to unravel than *Daniel*. Myth, symbolism and metaphor cloak its meanings; numbers such as "seven" and multiples of twelve and 1,000 are used to convey hints and warnings of things to come.

The one message of *Revelation* that is not ambiguous is that Christ will return. "Behold, I come as a thief. Blessed is he that watcheth."[32] Christ would rule for 1,000 years: the Millennium, during which Satan would be bound up and "cast into a bottomless pit". After the end of that period, Satan would be freed, once again to "deceive the nations", and, with the aid of Gog and Magog, "do battle against the saints". But fire from God out of heaven would destroy them and Satan would be cast into the lake of fire and brimstone.[33]

After the final judgment of the living and the dead, the world would begin again; but it would be a very different world, "a new heaven and a new earth". The New Jerusalem, the Holy City, would come down from God out of heaven. Mankind's wanderings, isolation and exile would be over. God would dwell with men and they would be His people. All tears would be wiped away. There would be no more death, sorrow, crying or pain.[34]

Whether in the name of Jesus, the Christ, or David, the King of Israel, it is this promise that all messiahs and their followers have continued to believe in. It is this hope they pursue to this very day.

PART TWO

The Anointed Ones

CHAPTER FOUR

CREATION TO ADAM + X YEARS = MESSIAH

IN ONE OF the books of the Apocrypha written in the second century B.C. there is a story of how Rabbi Joshua ben Levi was privileged to see the Seven Compartments of Paradise. In the Fifth Compartment dwelt the messiah and the prophet Elijah. The Compartment, according to the Rabbi, was magnificent: it was twelve myriads of miles in width and twelve myriads of miles in length. The walls were of silver and gold, and a perfume wafted through the air more exquisite than all the perfumes of Lebanon. The beds were made of silver and gold, and decked with violet and purple covers woven by Eve herself.

The messiah lay in his abode, anxiously waiting his call to go to the people on earth. Every Monday, Thursday, Saturday and on all the sacred holidays the patriarchs visited the messiah with Moses and Aaron, David and Solomon, all the kings of Israel and of the house of Judah. They wept with him and comforted him. They told him: "Be quiet and wait and depend on God, for the end draws near".

Then the Rabbi himself ventured to approach the messiah. The messiah turned to him and asked, "What is Israel doing in the world from which you come?" "Everyday it awaits you," the Rabbi replied.

The messiah raised his voice and wept.[1]

Such was the longing of the Jews for their messiah. No less anxious was the longing of the early Christians for the return of their Lord, as evidenced by Paul's letters to the Thessalonians. He would come, Paul assured them, of that there was no doubt. The task of the faithful was to remain awake, "to watch and be sober". Let the rest of the world, the children of darkness, sleep and remain "drunken in the night", but "let us, who are of the day, children of light, put on the breastplate of faith and love, and for an helmet, the hope of salvation".[2]

While Judea suffered the death and agonies of her nationhood and while the early Christians suffered persecution at the hands of the pagans, the yearning for peace, comfort and a reward for their patience remained constant. But then matters changed for them both.

For the Jews, once their nation was dead, they had to learn to survive as a dispersed people. For the Christians, recognition, and with it power, was now coming to them. As a result this longing for the messiah or for the return of Christ was becoming something of an embarrassment to the leaders of both Jewish and Christian communities.

For the Jewish rabbis there seemed no point in yearning for what might never take place, or take place only in the far distant future. It made living in the present more difficult and people in exile more restless to return to their homeland. They, therefore, regarded speculation about the coming of the messiah as a threat, possibly justified, to the stability and faith of the communities under their religious authority. Wrote Rabbi Jonathan, who lived between the second and third centuries, "Perish all those who calculate the end of the world, for men will say, since the predicted end is here and the messiah is not come, he will never come."[3]

For the Christian priesthood, the longing for the return of Christ indicated a lack of proper respect for the great achievements of the Church. The Christ had come; the Church had been founded and spread throughout most of the known world; the Millennium had arrived. For that every believing Christian ought to be thankful.

St Augustine, the greatest of the Latin Fathers of the Church, said that the *Book of Revelation* was only a spiritual allegory and ought not to be taken literally. The Millennium had started with the birth of Christianity and was fully realized in the Church. The Church itself went even further in its condemnation of millennial speculation, declaring it, at the Council of Ephesus in 431, a "superstitious aberration".[4]

A modern churchman has expressed a similar view that "this Jewish idea" of a Millennium on earth, "with Christ reigning here . . . is not only a gross and unspiritual idea, but is quite inconsistent with the rest of New Testament thinking. I find it quite hopeless to try to fit it in." Concerning the prophetic images of the *Book of Revelation* the same writer has written: "Its pictures are *pictures*, and should be treated as pictures. Any other method of interpretation leads, as it has so often done, to fanatical absurdities.... The one thing we can always rule out, even in the prophets, is mere long-distance *prediction* about future generations."[5]

Yet, in spite of official opposition and condemnation, both of churchmen and rabbis, there have been men who have attempted by various methods "long-distance prediction" of the End of the World and of the coming of the messiah or of his Second Coming as the case may be. These "forcers of the End", as the rabbis called them, could not wait for the messiah but wanted to do something personally to hasten his arrival.

While the scoffers, "walking after their own lusts", asked: "Where is the promise of his coming?" and when they showed that all around things were as they always were, that nothing ever changed,[6] the mathematicians of the messiah worked with an obsessiveness bordering on the fanatical to determine beyond doubt the exact year of his coming.

Joachim of Flora, a visionary of great influence in the twelfth and thirteenth centuries, was born in 1132 in Calabria, Italy. As a young man he went on a pilgrimage to the Holy Land and thereafter enjoyed a successful monastic career, first as a monk then as an abbot. He gave all that up to his prophetic calling and lived as a hermit. He calculated that there were 42 generations between Adam and Jesus, each lasting 30 years. This equalled 1,260 years. A similar span of time lay between the coming of Christ and the blessed era of the Holy Ghost, less the last two generations, namely, the year 1200. At that date Christendom would be overthrown by Antichrist, the trumpet of the archangel would sound, all the mysteries of the Scriptures would be explained, and the time of peace and truth for the whole earth would have arrived.

"If the last day finds me still living," he said, "may I have the strength to fight the good fight for the faith of Jesus Christ and, in company with those confessors of Jesus who are still living, ascend to the kingdom of heaven."[7]

Joachim saw the year 1200 ushered in; but no messiah. He died two years later, whether disappointed or still expectant we do not know.

The method Joachim employed to find the start of the messianic age was a version of that used by others who speculated on the question. Basically the idea was to take passages from the Old or New Testaments, or both, and to interpret them in various ways so as to arrive at a date or dates for the messiah's appearance.

Interpreters were drawn particularly to *Daniel* and *Revelation* because of their complex imagery, hints of times and seasons, and references to successive epochs. They treated the books as intricate puzzles that contained the final mystery. *Daniel*, for instance, hinted at six dates at least which raised many questions in the minds of the messianic calculators. Were the periods mutually exclusive? Were the "days" years? What did "weeks" mean? How long was a "season", and how long was "time"? Once these problems were solved, so it was believed, all would be revealed.

Biblical works other than these were source material for speculation. Hippolytus based his computations on *Exodus*, 25:10 which told of God's commandment to Moses to build a sanctuary and an ark of wood: "two cubits and a half shall be the length thereof, and a cubit and a half the breadth thereof, and a cubit and a half the height thereof". The total number of cubits was five and a half. This number, said Hippolytus, was equivalent to the five and a half millennia, that is, from Creation to the birth of Christ. "From the birth of Christ, then, we must reckon the five hundred years that remain to make up the six thousand (years) and then the End shall be."[8]

The *Book of Genesis* was preferred by a near contemporary of Joachim of Flora, Abraham ben Hiyya. He was a Spanish-Jewish astronomer who had read and absorbed all the writings on the subject in the belief that messianic speculation strengthened faith and raised the morale of the people in exile. According to *Genesis* God took six days to make heaven and earth. On the seventh day He rested. According to ben Hiyya, each day was equal to a thousand years, or more precisely by his calculations, 857 1/7th years. From the beginning of Creation to the Flood was two Days or 1,714 years. At the close of the third Day the Law was given to Israel, that is, by the year 2448. Three more Days had to pass before the messiah would come, or another 2,448 years. The astronomer's prediction was for the year 4896, or the Christian year of 1136,[9] or more probably 1230.

Perhaps the most complex system used to calculate the coming of the messiah was that known as Gematria, or numerology, the interpretation of a word according to the numerical value of its letters. Gematria was developed to a high art in the late Middle Ages onwards, but its use dates from early on in the Christian era. Devised by Jews for the Bible in Hebrew or Aramaic, it was also applied by Christian interpreters to the Latin Bible.

To the devout Jew the words of the Bible were the words of God Himself. They had their literal meaning, but more than that each letter of every word was the "visible revelation of invisible truth". Words did not only convey thought, they were thought itself.[10] They possessed a life and spirit of their own. A wise man did not merely interpret their meaning, therefore, he "played" a sacred game with the words. He changed them about, altered their letters, took letters out, contracted the words, substituted one word for another, made anagrams and acrostics, but most of all he calculated with Gematria.

A simple example of how this very complicated method worked is found in the battle that raged between the supporters and opponents of Sabbatai Zevi, the Jewish messiah of the seventeenth century. Zevi's followers said that the value of each letter of Zevi's name added up to 814. This was the same as the numerical value of the name of God and also of the phrase in Hebrew: "And my year of redemption is come", thus proving his messiahship. Opponents, however, pointed out that Zevi's name had the same numerical value as the Biblical phrase: "And he (Esau) was a cunning hunter, a man of the field", and that his first name, "Sabbatai", bore the numerical equivalent of "Balaam, the wicked".[11]

Such calculations could lead thought up strange and perhaps dangerous paths, and it was this temptation that worried the practical-minded community leaders. They argued that if a man started with the determination to find the date of the coming of the messiah, it was more than likely that he would end up with the answer he sought. Once he had that answer, he could easily persuade himself against all argument that his methods were based entirely on objectively provable data, namely, his pages and pages of figures in arithmetic combinations. Such a conviction might easily lead a man into fanaticism.

The argument was not without some foundation. Gematria was arithmetic and much more. The determined calculator who computed with the numerical value of words did so in the spirit of religious fervour. His aim was to become so totally absorbed by the calculations that eventually reason and thought itself were taken over by another force, the force of faith. "The less understandable the names (words) are," said a teacher of Gematria to his pupil, "the higher their order."[12]

The pupil in question was Abraham Aboulafia, one of the most outstanding numerologists of his time, a man of great learning, piety and discipline, who also claimed to be the messiah in the year 1284. He was born in Saragossa, Spain, in 1240. Like most male children of an orthodox father, he was early led into the study of the Scriptures and their commentaries, the Talmud. After the death of his father when he was eighteen, Abraham went on a pilgrimage to the Holy Land. He reached Acre, but could get no further because of the war between the Muslims and the Crusaders.

"Then the spirit of the Lord roused me and I took my wife with me," he wrote in an autobiographical account, "and set my face to reach my people."[13]

His pilgrimage was long. He travelled between Spain and Italy, settling finally in Messina. Along the way he was both student and teacher, but nothing he read in the natural sciences, in philosophy and logic, in medicine and even in the Bible and the Talmud moved him spiritually. They gave him knowledge, but not the gift of prophecy which he felt he was destined to receive.

Aboulafia's travels took him along the same route as the Kabbalah—the works of Jewish mysticism—at the same time as its influence was beginning to spread from Spain to Italy and from there to the rest of Europe. In Barcelona, at the age of 31, he read an early work of the Kabbalah, the *Book of Creation*, and he felt himself about to undergo a profound conversion. "The spirit of the Lord reached my mouth and worked through me so that I manifested many dread and awful sights with signs and wonders."[14]

At last he was experiencing the beginnings of a mystical awakening, but because of this he found himself cut off from society. For the next decade he was "like a blind man groping about at noon", searching for the true way with Satan at his right hand, trying to lead him astray. He could not decide whether his dreams and visions were truly from God or whether they were the manifestations of madness.

Alone and isolated from others Aboulafia began producing books in which he developed a system of thought and practice that in time exerted a considerable influence on Jewish mysticism in general and the Kabbalah in particular.

Then he conceived of a remarkable plan of converting the Pope, Nicholas III, to Judaism. He set out for Rome on the day before the Jewish New Year with this in mind, but the Pope, hearing of his impending arrival, "arranged for a stake to be erected near the inner gate of the town so as to be spared the inconvenience of an audience" with him.[15] Aboulafia turned back when he heard of these preparations on his behalf and went to a lonely room where he received more visions and composed another of his books. When he set out the following day, he was told that the Pope had died the previous night. He was seized by some Franciscan monks and thrown into gaol, but his luck held out and his life was spared.

He returned to the safer occupation of mysticism, working to develop his system further. This was one of rigorous discipline and asceticism, combining physical exercises and stances with deep meditation, not unlike Indian Yoga. Gematria was an essential part of it. He learnt it originally from an old Kabbalist who had given him a book containing hundreds of combinations of words and letters, of names and mystic numbers "of which nobody will ever be able to understand anything for they are not composed in a way meant to be understood".[16]

After a while he began to be aware of something strange happening within him. For three nights, without telling his instructor, he sat over the figures and letters, meditating on their combinations and their meanings. On the third night, with quill-pen in his hand and paper on his knee, he began to doze. He awoke suddenly and noticed the candle was going out. As he got up to put it right, he realized that the room was growing not dark but light; the light was emanating not from the candle but from himself!

He walked about the house, unable to believe his eyes. He lay on his couch and covered himself up. The light remained bright. He knew this was a sign of great significance.

He continued his calculations with letters and numbers for another fortnight with even greater enthusiasm. During the second week he was so strongly moved by the power of his meditations that he could barely manage to write down all the combinations that came to him. Quickly he filled page after page until he had completed more than ten men could do in the same time.

Now he felt himself ready to turn his attention to the most absorbing and inspiring challenge of all—the 72 names of the Almighty. He began combining their letters until they assumed different shapes in his mind. He saw them as vast mountains, and a trembling overcame him. He fell down, and lying on the floor in abject terror, asked himself: Was this madness?

The following day he went to his instructor and told him what had happened. "My son," the old Kabbalist replied, "you have done well. You have reached a high stage in the degrees of prophecy." Aboulafia was encouraged but he felt that unless he could harness the energy he had created through his meditation and through the combinations, he would lose it all.

"Only God can give you the power to control that force," his instructor warned him.

Aboulafia returned to his studies. For two days and two nights he meditated and worked the Gematria. He lost all feeling of his body; he was only thought and soul. He felt his forehead was about to burst. He knew then that he was ready to approach the most holy name of all, the name that the rabbis forbade anyone to speak, that could only be pronounced "Adonai" and written with four consonants YHWH—the Ineffable Name of God.

But as soon as he thought the thought, he heard a voice saying: "You will die for this! Who are you to touch the Ineffable Name of God?" He fell to the floor and prayed to God for guidance. As he was praying he felt "oil like the oil of anointment" cover him over from head to foot. He was seized by an indescribable joy. God had answered him. He had anointed Abraham as the messiah!

When he came to broadcast to his fellow Jews his messianic mission most of them rejected his claim out of hand. The rabbis objected vehemently to the way he criticized them and their traditional approach to the Scriptures. He had told them that it was barren, that Israel suffered in exile because it had forgotten God's true name and only through the Kabbalah and the techniques of Gematria could His Name be recalled and the Redemption brought about. They particularly objected to being called "apes" by him in contrast to the Kabbalists who, he said, were real "men".[17]

For his pains the rabbis pronounced a ban on him, forbidding him to teach. They accused him of being a scoundrel and they persecuted him whenever the opportunity arose. They scorned his ideas, his spiritual exercises. They mocked the way in which he would pronounce the Name of God in a variety of different ways, write it down in many forms, and accompany these activities with bows and twisting movements until, so he claimed, his body became quiescent, his mind filled with ecstacy, and his soul was united with the divine.[18]

Officially rejected by his own community, Aboulafia addressed and found favour with many Christians who accepted his messiahship and followed his esoteric methods. He prophesied on the basis of the *Book of Daniel* that by 1290 the king of the south—the Muslims—would slay the king of the north—the Christians—but that he in turn would be killed by the king of the east—the Mongols. Doubtless some could read into that a very long-distance prediction of the fate of the Christian West overtaken by the Communist East. However, to Aboulafia, when that event had finally taken place the joyful messianic age could be expected to begin.

Christians believed this; the Jews were forbidden to, but some did, and in 1286 there was a large migration to Palestine in anticipation of the messiah's rule on earth.

Abraham Aboulafia's influence on the Kabbalah and on religious thinking in general was considerable. He left behind many disciples who worshipped his memory and followed his system. The exact date and circumstances of his death are not known, but it was believed that he died sometime after 1291.

Within a few years two disciples predicted the new age of the coming of the messiah—1295. As the appointed day approached, the people made ready with white garments they were to wear on the great occasion. They left these in the synagogue where they would gather to receive the messiah. The day of his coming arrived. The crowds collected in the house of worship, dressed in their new white robes; but to their consternation, they noticed small crosses on their robes. How had they got there? Had they been sewn on or was it a miracle of God to warn them where their enthusiasm might lead them?

After they had waited for the messiah in vain for many hours, their rabbi, who had not been caught up in the general hysteria, lectured to them on the proper precautions that had to be taken before accepting a messianic claimant or prediction. Every case, he told them, had to be thoroughly investigated by scholars, the prophecies and miracles given the severest tests, and the character and motives of claimant or forecaster scrutinized.[19]

For most of the congregation the words made sense. Sadder but wiser they returned home. For others, however, the disappointment was too profound to be endured. They would not go back to being Jews in exile; instead, they chose to be and were converted to Christians.

One of the outstanding fifteenth-century messianic calculators was Isaac Abravanel who lived through some of the most terrible years in Jewish history when exile once again confronted settled communities and drove them into more strange lands. The end, he thought, was not far off and now was the time to reveal it. "Our life is so hard and our fortunes so unhappy that we are constrained to enquire after the hour of our release and Redemption."[20]

Abravanel was no fanatic. Born in Lisbon of a distinguished family, he served as finance minister to a series of royal rulers—of Spain, Portugal and Naples—all of whom repaid his services by confiscating his possessions and sending him into exile. Abravanel's knowledge of messianic speculation was encyclopaedic, and he regarded the task as one of the utmost importance. Redemption, he said, had already begun. Events in Europe—the decay of the Church, the advance of the Ottoman Turks, the expulsion of the Jews from England, France, Germany, Spain and Portugal—all these were strong indications of the "birth pangs" preceding the messiah who would be superior to Abraham and more elevated than Moses. Possible dates for his coming were 1503, 1505 and 1534.[21]

Abravanel used various methods of prediction including astrology, which was well grounded in Jewish tradition, having been adopted from Canaanite and Assyrian practices. Like Gematria it was officially frowned upon. Moses exhorted his people neither to worship nor serve "the sun, the moon, the stars and all the hosts of heaven".[22] To do so was thought to be negating free will and individual moral responsibility. The Church similarly opposed it. Yet astrology persisted and even gained in popularity. "Life, offspring and sustenance do not depend upon merit," said

Raba in the fourth century, "but upon the planets."[23] Contact with Arab thought in the early Middle Ages further influenced both Jews and Christians towards astrology.

Abravanel based his astrological predictions on the forthcoming conjunction of Jupiter and Saturn which by tradition was regarded as being of great significance to Jews. Christians, too, considered it of importance because six years before Jesus was born such a conjunction had taken place.[24]

The sixteenth and seventeenth centuries were periods of great religious upheaval for both Christianity and Jewry. In the former, the Reformation had split the Church apart and the Reformed Church itself was splintering into fragments. In the latter, the Kabbalah was developing doctrine and practices that were rivalling orthodox rabbinical thought. In both religions there was a distinct shift in emphasis from dogma to individual belief, from official and traditional interpretation of Holy Scripture to a direct and more personal revelation of the meaning of the texts. Bible translations into the vernacular meant that each man with a little education was able to read what the prophets had written, to interpret them for himself and come to his own conclusions without the help of priests or rabbis.

From the sacred texts numerous messianic forecasts were produced over the next four centuries and the practice continues into the present century. Throughout Europe people waited for the messiah whose coming preceded the Millennium. Both Old and New Testaments and now the Kabbalah also, since it had been enthusiastically received into certain esoteric Christian circles, all gave hints of dates and times. The *Zohar*, or *Book of Splendour*, regarded as the "Bible" of Kabbalah, predicted 1648 as the messianic year. In 1648 the Thirty Years War ended. Could this mean, people asked themselves, that the age of universal peace was about to be ushered in? Puritan sects in England speculated that 1666 was the crucial year for had it not been said in *Revelation* that the number of the beast was "six hundred threescore and six"?

At the close of the eighteenth century, Nathaniel Brassey Halhed, considered the most brilliant linguist of his day, turned his attention to messianic speculation and produced an extraordinary calculation of the date of the Millennium which, I suspect, only a modern computer could verify.

> Now admitting the common solar year to consist of 365 days 5 hours 48 minutes 54¾ seconds [he wrote] and multiplying 5,913 [the age of the world in A.D. 1794] into quarters of seconds, we shall find, on dividing this quotient by 360, a produce amounting to 5,999 such divine years and a fraction; which fraction, deducted from the sum total of one year, leave a deficiency, at the end of the year of our Lord 1794, equal to 322 days 6 hours 40 minutes 23¼ seconds, being so much wanting at the opening of the present year, to the full completion of 6,000 *divine* or *prophetical* years; and shewing that the Millennium will commence on the 19th day of November next, or about sun-rise in the lattitude of Jerusalem.[25]

Speculation was not confined to Europe. In the nineteenth century the American, William Miller, set alight the hearts and hopes of men and women in the eastern states with his predictions of the End of the World, the Second Coming, and the consequent start of the New Era. He was born in 1782 and became a prosperous farmer. A devout Baptist, Miller spent years in the study of the Bible with such intensity that it eventually began to reveal its mysteries to him. The difficult and apparently contradictory passages served only to puzzle and inspire him "to persevere the more in penetrating its beauty and mysteries".[26]

He concentrated his attention on the *Book of Daniel* which he took literally and he drew up intricate charts of calculations. In May 1832 he wrote: "I am satisfied that the end of the world is at hand. The evidence flows in from every quarter."[27] By that time he was a prominent and popular preacher, delivering powerful sermons to churches of different denominations throughout the east. In so doing he had acquired a large and devoted following that had formed itself into the Millerite sect. A plain, simple and somewhat ingenuous man, Miller suffered from continuous ill health that tended to make him appear much older than he was. He dressed in simple country style and, as one congregant observed, "No one can hear him five minutes without being convinced of his sincerity".

Miller drew up a number of different calculations, all of which arrived at the same conclusion: the End of the World preceding the messianic age would begin in 1843. Thus:

From the full term of Daniel's vision	2300
Subtract 70 weeks of years to Christ's crucifixion	490
	1810
Add to this the term of our Saviour's life	33
End of the world in	1843[28]

The hysteria Miller's predictions incited grew as the year 1843 drew on. People demanded to know the exact month, the exact day of Christ's Second Coming. April came. "We are commanded to occupy ourselves until Christ comes," wrote the committee that had established itself to conduct the affairs of the Millerite Church. "We are to do good as we have the opportunity, and by no means spend our time in idleness."[29]

People took no notice of the stern injunction. Shops shut, businesses ceased trading. Read one notice posted on a shop door: "This shop is closed in honor of the King of Kings who will appear about the 20th October". A farmer gave his land and livestock to his son who did not accept Miller's predictions. When the prediction was not fulfilled, the son refused to return the farm and left his father destitute.

Men and women went about with umbrellas to facilitate their ascendancy to Heaven. One man put on a pair of turkey wings, went up into a tree, and after praying to God to take him, leapt off. He fell to the ground, breaking an arm. Others jumped off roofs to their death. One wealthy woman sat on a large trunk into which she had placed all her valuables and which she had buckled to her so that when she ascended her trunk and its contents were sure to go with her.

Not everyone was caught up in the excitement. The story was told of the Millerite who came across the philosopher, Ralph Waldo Emerson, walking with his friend, Theodore Parker, on the anticipated Day of the Lord. They seemed very calm and undisturbed in spite of the momentousness of the occasion. "Gentlemen, don't you know, don't you realize that the world is coming to an end today?" the Millerite said. Parker shrugged and replied: "It doesn't much concern me. I live in Boston." Emerson, too, was unmoved. "The end of the world doesn't bother me," he said philosophically as befitted his profession. "I can get along without it."[30]

April passed; then May, June, July, the whole summer. Miller hesitated. He was not quite sure that in his calculations the Christian year was meant. Possibly it was the Jewish year, in which case March 1844 was the moment.

But March 1844 came and the world went on without the End and without Christ's re-appearance. "Every one felt lonely, with hardly a desire to speak to any one," an elder of the Millerite Church wrote. "Still in the cold world! No deliverance—the Lord not come!"[31]

By now Miller was tired and old and sick. He frankly admitted his error. He blamed his mistakes on Pride and Fanaticism, and said that he had been swept up in the prevailing hysteria. Another elder blamed the hysteria on mesmerism and—though he did not use the term—mass hypnosis.

> The great point which gave power to that movement [said the elder with considerable psychological insight] was the positiveness with which we cried, "The Lord will come in the clouds of heaven" on the tenth day of the seventh month. Take away that positiveness and the event which that positiveness referred to, and no one believes the excitement that existed would have come into being. We were deluded by a mere human influence [he concluded] which we mistook for the Spirit of God.[32]

Miller's following quickly fell away, from 50,000 at its height to a mere handful. Those who continued in their beliefs said that the coming had not been a material one but one of the spirit. They were thereby able to withstand the shock of disappointment.

Miller, however, would have none of that. Before he died in December 1849 he summed up for one of his closest associates his view on what had happened. "I do not wonder that the world calls us insane; for I confess it looks like insanity to me to see religious, candid men spend their time and talents on questions of so little consequence to us here or hereafter."[33]

CHAPTER FIVE

MESSIAHS OF THE FIRST MILLENNIUM

"THIS IS THE king-messiah!"

With this announcement the celebrated Talmudist, Rabbi Akiva, greeted Simon Bar Kochba who rose up with an army of insurgents against the Romans in A.D. 132. The revolt had begun in Judea; it spread rapidly to Galilee and Transjordan. There had been rumours that Emperor Hadrian was going to rebuild the Temple in Jerusalem. The rumours gave rise to religious excitement. The people were about to be restored to their true religion; perhaps the foreign oppressor would leave, and the unhappiness that had been the lot of the Judeans since the destruction of the Temple 62 years before would come to an end.

The rumours were false. Hadrian intended to build a temple; that was true; but the temple was to be Roman and dedicated to Jupiter. That he was to build such a temple in Jerusalem was insulting enough to the populace but that he intended to do so on the site of the ancient Temple was much worse.

Once again civil strife threatened, and as Antiochus Epiphanes had done before, so now the Romans attempted to suppress not only the people but their religion as well. All Jewish practices including circumcision were banned. Armed bands rallied to the leadership of Simon Bar Kochba. His family or his father's name was probably Bar Koseva, but during the revolt he came to be identified with the prophecy of Balaam who saw "a Star (*kokhav*) out of Jacob" rise to smite and destroy the enemy.[1]

Simon Bar Kochba took upon himself the mantle of the messiah. The leader of the rabbinical party, Akiva, accepted him as such. On coins minted at the time Bar Kochba is shown bearing a pot of manna and the rod of Aaron, unmistakable symbols of the messiah[2] in whose name the insurgents seized towns and villages from the Romans. They built fortifications and inflicted heavy losses on the occupying army, as had Judah the Maccabee centuries before.

Bar Kochba was a harsh and imperious leader who built up his army on uncompromising discipline. To be one of his soldiers a man had to be able to uproot a cedar tree or be prepared to have a finger lopped off. Land captured by the insurgents was regarded as liberated territory and taken by Bar Kochba into his own possession.[3]

Since A.D. 73 when the Romans had destroyed the last Jewish resistance, the people had languished under their rule. Now the chance presented itself once again for independence under the leadership of a Jew, one thought to be chosen by God. The struggle that followed was fierce and politically important enough for the emperor to order from Britain one of his most experienced and successful commanders, Julius Severus. Severus recognized the difficulties of trying to confront an army largely made up of civilian guerillas. Instead, he surrounded and besieged the rebels wherever he found them. By forcing them into starvation, he finally restored Roman supremacy. In the course of this, the last Jewish war against the Romans, 50 fortresses were destroyed, 985 villages razed to the ground, and over half a million people killed, not counting those who died of starvation and disease during the various sieges.[4]

The war lasted about three and a half years. Bar Kochba and the remainder of his rebel army were forced to take refuge in the fortress at Bethar, south-west of Jerusalem. There Bar Kochba was killed and Bethar captured—by tradition on the ninth day of the month of Ab, when the First and Second Temples were also supposed to have been destroyed. Jerusalem was recaptured and Emperor Hadrian made sure that there would be no further uprisings. The city as an explosive symbol of revolt was rendered harmless—or so he hoped—by renaming it Aelia Capitolonia and by driving all Jews from within its walls. Judea was now called Palestina.

"Oh, Akiva," said a fellow-rabbi in answer to the venerable old man's support of Bar Kochba's claim to messiah-ship, "grass will grow out of your cheeks and the son of David still will not have come!"[5]

So disappointed were the Jews and their leaders in Bar Kochba's failure that messianism as an inspiration for the future Redemption was ended for centuries. Had some rabbis their way, they would have put a stop to all speculation on the subject forever. Many things, they said, were hidden from men. These included the day of a man's death, what was in his neighbour's heart, but above all when the kingdom of David would be restored. Only God knew that and it was tampering with the forbidden to enquire too deeply into such knowledge.[6]

For at least 300 years no Jews presumed to take up the vacant rôle. Then came a man out of Crete who appeared before the community there, promising that, like Moses, he would lead the people back to the Promised Land by commanding the sea to part and make way for them. Hundreds gathered with their belongings on the seashore. Moses raised his arms and ordered the sea to separate. At the same time he told his followers to stride forward. They obeyed but the sea did not. Many were drowned and when those remaining looked about to revenge themselves on their leader, they found that he had disappeared, never to be seen again.

In 645 another claimed that the messiah had come. Anticipating some of the Christian social revolutionary movements led by messiahs from the twelfth century on, he gathered about him disaffected tradesmen and artisans: weavers, carpet makers and launderers, altogether about 400 men. In the wave of messianic excitement they attacked and destroyed three Christian sanctuaries and killed the chief of the locality. This craftsmen's messiah was caught and crucified and his followers and their families were massacred.[7]

In the eighth and ninth centuries there were three more claimants. During this period the Jewish communities had been confronted and overtaken by a new religious power—Islam. By the time of their founder's death in 632, the followers of Muhammad were in control of all of western Arabia, and soon after his death north and eastern Arabia, too. All Syria and Iraq were also brought within the Muslim empire and Egypt was made a tributary. A century later saw parts of Africa, Spain, France, and Central Asia right up to the border of India taken into the hands of the Muslim.[8] In all these countries there were settled Jewish communities.

The confident, conquering young religion absorbed other cultures quite readily and the Jews who lived in the empire found themselves, if not the equals of their new rulers, at least not oppressed by them. They were given the status of "protected" subjects, as were Christians. For the most part they were permitted to carry on their own religious practices without interference.

The yearning for the Holy Land, however, was still too strong for many, who responded when men rose up to lead them back from exile. In 720 a messiah from Shirin in Syria promised to restore them to what was now Palestine, after throwing out the Muslims. Serene, the messiah, quickly accumulated a large following of Spanish and French Jews who left their homes and their possessions and set out to meet him.

Serene practised and preached a doctrine that challenged traditional religious views and authority—in common with almost all messiahs, whatever their religion. He rejected many of the prayers; he neglected the strict laws relating to the eating of forbidden food; he did not celebrate all the holidays laid down. It was also suggested that he permitted men and women to live together without the proper formalities of marriage. As his movement grew, so the authorities became strengthened in their opposition. Finally he was captured by the officers of the ruling Caliph, Yazid II. As he had not broken any Muslim law or directly challenged the rule of the Caliph, Serene was handed over to the rabbis for punishment.

It is interesting to compare the treatment of this Jewish messiah with that of Christian messiahs who attacked the authority of the priests. The latter were generally done to death or cruelly punished. Their followers, too, usually found themselves facing the executioner's sword or firebrand unless they recanted and repented. Serene and his followers were not allowed to escape entirely. Their goods were confiscated and the leaders were whipped. They were also required to swear solemnly in the synagogue that they would never relapse. But the main object was to "rehabilitate" them, not to destroy or repudiate them. Once they had mended their ways they were welcomed back into the fold.[9]

Abu Isa Isfahani, who founded a sect in Persia in the middle of the eighth century was killed, not because he advocated anti-rabbinical laws, but because he formed an army against the Caliph. He was an illiterate tailor and called himself the Fifth and Last Messenger of the Messiah. He believed that he was sent to free Israel from the yoke of the Gentile, and his efforts to do so lasted a number of years. At the time a great power struggle was taking place within Islam between the Umayyad and the Abbasid dynasties—won eventually by the latter—and it is not unlikely that this and the general upheaval gave the tailor the idea that the End of Days was about to arrive with the coming of the Messiah and the return of the Jews to Israel.

Messiahs are invariably (though not always) thrown up by social unrest because of the sense of fear, of doom anticipated, and most of all because of uncertainty that such periods in history bring about. The messiahs respond to this uncertainty by presenting their followers with absolutes, with distinct and definite commands, with clear goals or at least goals that can be grasped with the imagination if not with the hand. Abu Isa promised the Persian Jews freedom in the Holy Land and they followed him. He also gave them a certain degree of freedom from rabbinical laws. Tolerant of Christianity and of Islam, he advocated the study of the Gospels and the Koran. He accepted that Jesus, the son of Mary, was a prophet and so, too, was Muhammad, and that their followers' faith was as valid in guiding their behaviour as was that of the Jews.

The army he set up against the Caliph was defeated in 755 and Abu Isa was killed, though his people believed either that he had entered a cave and disappeared or that he had protected himself and those closest to him by drawing a magic circle about them with a myrtle branch. His sect, the Isunians or Isfahanians, lived on after him for more than a century.[10]

Yudghan, the Shepherd of Hamadan, was Abu Isa's principal disciple and led a separate Persian sect called the Yudghanites who accepted him as the messiah. The sect practised vegetarianism and teetotalism. They observed all the Jewish traditions except for the most important—the keeping of the Sabbath. This was abolished. Yudghan died in the second half of the ninth century.[11]

It was during this period that a doctrine not dissimilar to Judaeo-Christian messianism was being developed within Islam by numerous Muslim mystical sects. The Caliph was regarded as the political head of the community, but the spiritual head was the Imãm. Muslim mystics believed that the occult interpretation of the Koran was possible only by the line of hereditary Imãms. In time these Imãms acquired more than human qualities; they were thought to be the incarnations of the Divine Light which had passed through generations of prophets since Adam. Some radical sects regarded the Imãm as the manifestation of God

Himself. A tradition began at the end of the ninth century that Mohammed al-Muntazar, the Expected One, was the twelfth and last Imãm and that he would return after his death. His return is still awaited by some.

As the year 1000, the end of the first Millennium, approached so Europe began to be seized with messianic excitement. In 960 the Jews of the Rhine sent a letter to the rabbinical school in Jerusalem asking the rabbis if it was true that the messiah was coming. The rabbis answered impatiently: "You do not even deserve a reply. The signs identified by the Sages for the time of the Messiah have not yet come to pass. If you believed in their words, you would know this."[12]

But these anxious enquirers were reflecting an expectancy that originated not from within their own communities but from within the Christian communities since it was for the latter that the year 1000 was of greatest significance. The 1,000 years prophesied by the *Book of Revelation* was about to end. During this time Satan had been bound, cast into the bottomless sea, and shut up so that he could deceive nations no more. But after 1,000 years he would be loosed again out of his prison and would gather together Gog and Magog to do battle against the saints. All this was to happen before the Final Judgment, the Resurrection of the Dead, and the advent of the New Jerusalem, "coming down from God out of heaven".[13]

The prophecies were made more potent by a number of strange events that had occurred in the last years of the tenth century. In 922, Good Friday, the day of Christ's Crucifixion, fell on Lady Day, the festival of the Annunciation of the Virgin Mary. This, the prophets of the day believed, was ominous. Numerologists, working on their texts, considered 955 as the possible year of the End of the World. The year passed uneventfully but not the anxieties that had accompanied it and when in the next few years there followed in rapid succession an eclipse of the sun, one extremely severe winter, plague, an eruption of Vesuvius, and the invasions of Magyar, Norman and Saracen, the portents seemed too numerous to ignore.[14] Something terrible was going to happen, so terrible that it could only be followed by the hoped-for age of the messiah, the awaited Second Coming.

What, in fact, followed the year 1000 was not universal peace but more pain and sorrow for practically everyone. In the name of Christ, the Prince of Peace, there began a series of wars, battles, skirmishes and general shedding of blood that has been honoured by the name of the Crusades. The aim of the Crusaders was to free the Holy Land from the Muslim infidel, but it appeared that there were a great many infidel to kill before that could be accomplished.

The first Crusade began in 1096 and lasted for three years; the eighth and last was in the thirteenth century under Louis of France who died of fever in 1270. Between those years, wave upon wave of Christians crossed and re-crossed Europe, burning, pillaging and looting, destroying ancient communities, and bringing havoc to nations.

So gripped were men by the need to move for the sake of moving, to fight for the sake of fighting, to die for the sake of dying, with apparently little to show in the way of real and lasting conquests, that the Crusades could well be described—as indeed they have been by modern social psychologists—as "mental epidemics".[15]

It requires only a small leap of the imagination to connect these holy "epidemics" with the anxieties and fears that preceded the year 1000, or to see that they were partly the outcome of a terrible human desire to find some purpose, some activity, no matter how fruitless, to help assuage the anxiety of uncertainty.

Before the Crusaders began their pilgrimages of war, there had been a period when men and women seemed altogether transfixed by their fears that the world was about to be engulfed by nameless catastrophe. Churches were filled with congregations offering up prayers for safety. Crucifixes were erected on hills around which crowds gathered and waited—for death or deliverance. In Germany people dug shelters and lay breathing in dust and fear. In the Middle East they sat in terror with the rats in cellars. The Emperor in Constantinople had the windows of his palace walled up, and in England the Archbishop of Canterbury proclaimed a national fast to divert the expected tragedy.[16]

Then this helpless and hopeless immobility gave way with explosive violence to a desire to act. To kill infidels and to free the Holy Land was a much more worthwhile task for a Christian to undertake. After all, had it not been prophesied many times in the Bible that the messianic age was to be preceded by a final war between good and evil, and that Jerusalem would have to be restored before peace would reign forever?

Historians have pointed out that the time of the Crusades was also one of social and economic change, when large numbers of peasants, of journeymen and unskilled workers roamed about central Europe in search of a place in which to live and to work in security. The Crusades gave to many of these homeless wanderers a purpose in life; they also gave them the opportunity to accumulate from the spoils of looting the goods and possessions that were otherwise denied to them. From the eleventh century to the thirteenth century, the poor of over-crowded Europe found in holy wars an answer to their needs, at least in part.

When fear is in the air, when countries are seething with internal strife, when life holds out little hope and death seems imminent, then people seek a leader who will give them something to believe in, to hold on to. The greater the fear, the greater the anxieties about how to earn a living or how to keep family and home together, the more desperate the need is to project onto one individual all the power and omnipotence required to solve seemingly insoluble problems. Tanchelm was such a man.[17]

This prophet and messiah of the poor started humbly as did most of those who had come before and followed after him. He was a notary at the court of Robert II of Flanders. Like other prophets he was not recognized in his own city, Bruges; in fact he was expelled from there. Outside of Flanders, however, his success was assured. All the basic socio-economic conditions for a messianic movement were in existence: over-crowded towns, uncertainty caused by an upsurge in commercial activity, restlessness and frustration.

In about 1110 Tanchelm began preaching to masses of these aimless folk with great success. At first he dressed simply in the robes of a monk. His speech was colourful and fluent. People came to him, seeing in him an Angel of the Lord. They listened to his sermons, at first shocked by what he preached, then enraptured by the freedom his words offered. The priests, he said, were unworthy to administer the sacraments. In Antwerp lived a priest in open concubinage! The Church was no better than a brothel. The more one despised it, the greater one's morality.

As a final, and perhaps most devastating attack on the Church, he told his followers that tithes—the compulsory one-tenth annual tax on the products of land and cattle—which, like all taxes were hated and resented by the poor, need not be paid.

His following increased and so, too, his self-aggrandizement. He discarded the monk's habit for robes of gold. He no longer travelled alone but with a retinue bearing his banner and sword. His hair bound in a gold band, he appeared before his adoring followers like a king. King he said he was, Holy Spirit and a god, like Christ. According to contemporary witnesses he had a terrifying bodyguard of some 3,000 men and no prince of the region dared come near him.

As is common with messianic claimants, Tanchelm appointed twelve apostles, including one woman who represented the Virgin Mary. Before one vast gathering he had himself betrothed to a statue of the Virgin Mary. The "wedding" was celebrated by offerings from his people: one coffer was for gifts from the men, one for gifts from the women. Tanchelm stood up and asked which of them had the greater love for him and his "bride". There was a rush of people with money and jewellery to prove their adoration. Tanchelm also "sold" his bathwater, which his followers drank instead of the wine of the Eucharist, a sacrament, he said, which no longer filled any purpose.

Tanchelm's reign of glory lasted only about five years. A priest murdered him in the year 1115.

"Sing with the gladness of Jacob, saith the Lord, and shout among the chief of the nations. Behold I will bring them from the north country and gather them from the coasts of the earth, a great company shall return hither." Thus had Jeremiah prophesied. "He that scattered Israel will gather him and keep him, as a shepherd doth his flock. Then shall the virgin rejoice in the dance, both young men and old together: for I will turn their mourning into joy, and will comfort them, and make them rejoice from their sorrow."[18]

Some rabbis had calculated with Gematria that this beautiful vision of the future would come to pass in the 1,028th year of Jewish exile which corresponded to the Christian year of 1096. Some had said it was to be the year of the messiah. In fact, for the Jews "it turned into sorrow and groaning, weeping and lamentation".[19] The Crusades had begun.

The delicate balance that existed between Christian, Jew and Muslim was completely destroyed by these soldiers of Christ. There had been religious hatred and violence before the Crusades but it had been confined to specific localities. Men in power had come down heavily on communities, stealing from them, forcing them to convert to Islam, driving them out of their territories; but then the minorities would be welcomed in other areas and would begin their lives again with some semblance of normality and security. The Crusades ended that.

Now ravening hordes drove communities from one part of Europe to another. Though freeing the Holy City was their ostensible aim, they had a more convenient and accessible victim in the Jew. "We hoped for peace and there was none," wrote Eliezer ben Nathan of the year 1096, "for a time of healing and, behold, dismay!"[20]

Unscrupulous priests like Peter the Hermit preached sermons of hate against the Jews, accusing them of being the killers of Christ, of being destroyers of the Christian religion, of being the dreaded Antichrist. So long as they were permitted to live in peace Christ's Second Coming would be delayed. They had to be killed, their property grabbed; their houses and shops and schools razed to the ground. Pilgrimages of *pauperes*, "the poor", stirred up by these rabble-rousers, set out from centres like Rouen in Normandy, and from towns all along the Rhine. Jews were at first saved from death if they agreed to convert to Christianity since conversion and not plain theft was the prime motive; but for the looter the rewards in this life were more important than the possible rewards in the life hereafter, and Jew, rich or poor, was relieved of his possessions whether or not he was prepared to change his religion.

The Crusades destroyed a spirit of independence and of enquiry that had grown up in the Jewish communities during the respite from violence in the course of the first 1,000 years of the Christian era. This spirit was typified by the great philosopher, Moses Maimonides, who died in 1204 and whose works on ethics, law and medicine influenced not only Jewish but Western thought also. Maimonides wrote at some length about messianic movements and, being a rationalist, had little patience with those who consoled themselves in their times of trouble with the hope of the coming of the messiah. In his own life time he had twice barely escaped forced conversion (not at the hands of Christians, but of the fanatical Moorish sect of Almohades), but he cautioned that to hope for the messiah was beside the point. There was no knowing when the messiah would come; tomorrow or in 1,000 years, no man could foretell. What was important was to observe the Law and to follow the Commandments. To be a good Jew had nothing whatever to do with the messiah and those who advised doing nothing but waiting and praying for him might well be leading their co-religionists astray.[21]

By way of further caution and elucidation for the benefit of would-be messiah worshippers, Maimonides listed a number of claimants who had appeared before various communities during the previous century and a half. The messiah who had particularly stirred the philosopher to write on the subject had risen in the Yemen in 1172. What worried Maimonides was not the impiety of the man's claims but the effect these had on his followers and Jews in general. The Yemen messiah he dismissed as "beyond doubt demented". He diagnosed the man's problems as might a modern psychiatrist. "His actions are the effect of his disease over which he has no control," he wrote. If the man had been perfectly sane, his irresponsible conduct might have deserved death, but since he was mad he should be locked away for a while, informing all, including the Gentiles, that he was insane. If he were then set free, neither would he be hurt for making his claims, nor would the Jewish community be mocked for believing them.[22]

The Yemen messiah was finally caught and brought before the Caliph, who questioned him about his claims. He said that he had spoken the truth and was obeying the word of God. "A sign," the Caliph said. "Give me a sign." "Cut off my head," replied the messiah, "and I will return to life again." "There can be no greater sign than that," said the Caliph. "If you can do that all the world will believe you, including myself."[23]

The ruler ordered the messiah's beheading. The messiah died and the Jews who had followed him—and many who had not—were heavily fined. Yet many went on believing in him and in his imminent return from the grave.

Maimonides read his people a firm lesson on how to recognize the messiah when eventually he did appear. First he had to be of the House of David; second he had to have the qualities of wisdom, strength and wealth, that is, the wisdom of prophecy, the strength of self-control, and the wealth of a great mind.[24] He did not have to perform miracles like reviving the dead. Instead he had to practise the Commandments of the Law and encourage his people to do the same. Finally he had to be powerful enough to conquer the enemies of the Lord and lead the scattered tribes of Israel back to the Holy Land where he would accomplish the re-building of the Temple. "Let no one think that in the days of the Messiah anything of the natural course of the world will cease or that any innovation will be introduced into creation. Rather," the philosopher warned, "the world will continue in its accustomed course."[25]

One man who was thought to have possessed many of the qualities of the true messiah was Menahem ben Solomon, or David, King of the Jews: David Alroy. He was born in 1147 in Kurdistan and was regarded by all who came into contact with him as strikingly handsome and of great personal charm. He studied at the Baghdad Academy where he excelled. He also became skilled in mysticism and magic. Most of what is known of Alroy is legendary but in the first half of the twelfth century he started a movement in his name and called himself messiah. A letter was sent to Jewish communities throughout the Middle East, announcing his claim and telling his people to prepare for the return to Jerusalem with fasting and praying. A hostile apostate to Islam, Samuel al-Maghribi, told of how the Jews of Baghdad, supposedly so astute in worldly matters, collected their money and jewellery together and prepared themselves for the angel who would carry them on his wings to the Holy City.

While they waited on their rooftops, dressed in the green of Alroy's colours, two thieving impostors relieved them of the bulk of their wealth. The mothers sat unconcerned that they were now paupers, worrying only that if they and their babies did not travel together on the angel's wings, the children might miss their regular meals.[26]

Alroy's movement was finally suppressed, but he survived persecution to set up a centre in Amadiya, in the mountains of Azerbaijan. From there he began his revolt against the Persian ruler. In an attempt to storm the citadel, he was defeated and probably killed though there is a tradition that his father-in-law was bribed by the governor of the town to murder him.[27]

Benjamin Disraeli, himself a convert to Christianity, was intrigued by the Alroy legend and wrote an unremembered romance based on the messiah's exploits.[28] The novel reveals something of Disraeli's ambivalent attitude towards his Jewish origins. One cannot help feeling that in Alroy he perhaps allowed the secret side of himself, the lone Jew among hostile Gentiles, to surface, if only for a brief moment.

"And He is there, the Chosen One," wrote the future Prime Minister of England and Queen Victoria's favourite, "the Chosen One that leads his race to victory, warriors of Judah! holy men that battle for the Lord!"[29]

CHAPTER SIX

EVERY MAN HIS OWN MESSIAH

THE HUSBAND HAD been suspicious for a long time. His wife told him that she went to church. She even had her Prayer-book with her. But he had heard stories that it was no ordinary church in which she prayed. One day he followed her down a road which led by twists and turns to some steps. The wife descended these, unaware that her husband was close behind her in disguise. They entered a crowded underground cavern where everyone wore tunics cut away in front downwards from the belt, and short hoods. The women covered their heads with cloaks.

A man stood at a stone altar. He told the congregation to choose partners and at his signal they began to dance. When they were exhausted of that, food appeared and wine. The leader joined them in eating and drinking, then he stood up to harangue them. He told them that man was the king of the world and of all he surveyed. "If you follow our Way," he said, "you can attain such perfection that you will all be beyond sin. No longer will you be subject to the rules and authority of the Church. You will be greater than any Church and any prince. They are imperfect; you will be perfect.

"Where the Spirit of the Lord is, there is liberty![1] To the soul that is perfect everything is permitted. Nothing is forbidden. Since everything belongs to such a soul, it may take of whatever it pleases. The perfect man may lie with another man's wife; he may lie with his own mother; or his own sister. He may do so, not in a bed, but on this very altar. A virgin thus taken by a perfect soul is perfect also. Even if she lies with ten men and the last man is free in spirit, she will still remain a virgin.

"Every man can become perfect, every woman, too. The perfect being is no longer separated from God but is united with Him. His body is completely penetrated by the Divine Light, so that he ceases to be an ordinary man but becomes Divine himself, becomes God himself.

"Those who wish to become God need only follow our Way. Our Way is not easy. All worldly goods must be renounced. Family, home, friends, warmth, comfort, all these things must be cast away. You must learn to depend on what you can steal or borrow or beg for sustenance. Many will hate you. Many will try to kill you. The priests will denounce you and if they find you out, you will doubtless be tortured and burnt at the stake. For the Church above all hates us. We do not take of the Body of Christ nor of his Blood, nor do we stand up when his Body is elevated because He is no more perfect than we. We, like Him, are at one with God. We, too, are God."

The priest then took a young woman by the hand and led her to the altar. Slowly they both undressed. The priest bade the congregation do the same. "This," he said to them, pointing to the girl, "is the Virgin Mary and I am Jesus. Now watch what we do and follow us."

The girl lay down on the stone altar and the priest covered her with his body. The congregation danced around them, then each pair lay down on the ground. The husband, who had all the while remained close by his wife's side, caught hold of her hand before she lay down with her partner, and quickly slipped her wedding ring from her finger. So intent was she on following the priest's bidding that she did not notice what had happened. The husband fled the scene.

When later that day she returned from "church", he confronted her with what he had discovered. She denied it all. "Do you really believe I have become a heretic?" she asked. "With all our wealth and possession that I would go into the streets to beg?"

Rather than argue with her, the husband asked her to show him her marriage ring. She looked down at her finger and went pale. When she raised her eyes and saw the expression on his face, she knew she had been found out. She thought herself fortunate later that he had only whipped her within an inch of her life. He might have reported her to the Church along with the others he had informed on, and she, too, might have been burnt at the stake.

The story was current popular mythology in the late Middle Ages. The ideas expressed by the "priest" were typical of the people who were called collectively the Brethren of the Free Spirit.[2] The Brethren were not one Church but were loosely related sects with separate though similar ideologies. All were condemned as heretics by the Catholic Church and persecuted with severity. Much of what is known about them is from hostile sources, from the evidence of people who had been "free in spirit" but then under pain or threat of torture had retracted and recanted.

The aspect of Free Spirit ideology that most attracted popular attention concerned their supposed sexual permissiveness and their general attack on accepted morality. Many lewd stories were told about orgies in the nude and mass fornication. The stories may have been true; they may also have been the inventions of enemies, the kind of fantasy projections of sexually frustrated individuals that social outcasts always seem to attract.

In the main, however, they lived very simply. Some, like the *beghards* and *beguines*, roamed the country, begging for their food rather than stealing it, aspiring to what they believed was the ideal apostolic life of poverty and prayer. The Adamites, who also fell into the category of Free Spirits, called their church Paradise and in imitation of Adam in the Garden of Eden went about in the nude.

The perfection these "free in spirit" desired was not a state easily achieved. It could come only through self-denial and prayer. However, once that state had been reached, they believed they were freed from all conventional duties and responsibilities. They were united with God and were themselves god-like.

Not surprisingly it was this that most disturbed the Church. When a man or woman arrogated to himself the divinity of God, when he claimed that because he was perfect he could disregard all idea of morality, that he was above sin, then this was blasphemy of the highest order that could be cured only by the stake. John of Brunn, for twenty years a Free Spirit, said that those who had reached through self-abnegation a state of perfection could steal and grasp "with the hands all that the eye sees and desires". If a perfect man desired a perfect woman, he could have her. If the woman fell pregnant, she could drown the child like a worm, with a clear conscience.[3] The Lord's Prayer, according to their belief, should have read, "lead us *into* temptation".[4] Though few brethren actually behaved in this manner, what was important from the standpoint of conventional morality was that their ideology permitted them to do so. It went further —it encouraged them to be cruel and depraved for it was believed that the more the perfect individual sinned, the more proof he gave of his perfection.

The Brethren, men and women, were not the poor and the unskilled but were comfortably placed in society. They regarded poverty as the ideal. They lived in groups, each one under a prophet or messiah who might have been a former monk or priest. The messiahs were mostly literate men, able to express their ideas forcefully and coherently. Walter was a priest who was defrocked and burnt at the stake for his Free Spirit activities which were supposed to have included midnight orgies in underground hideouts. He called himself Christ and claimed that he would rise again three days after his death.[5]

It was a characteristic of Free Spirit ideology that the only sin was to disobey the leader and that disobedience was much worse than murder or fornication. In this way the messiahs wielded absolute power over their people.[6] Nicholas of Basle was a Free Spirit messiah who taught that he understood the Gospels better than all the Apostles, including St Paul. "So great was his power and control over us," said one of his disciples, "that he could order us to do whatever he wanted—to kill or to fornicate. He taught that only he could release us from our vows of obedience to the Church and return us to our state of innocence." Nicholas, like Walter, was burnt at the stake.[7]

"The heart of the heresy was in fact not a philosophical idea at all but an aspiration," concluded the historian, Cohn. "It was a passionate desire of certain human beings to surpass the condition of humanity and become God."[8] To do so nothing was allowed to hold them back, not the Church nor the Bible. They regarded their own inspiration as much more vital and "true" than the Bible. What the perfect individual "heard" in his inner ear was the clear voice of God speaking directly to him, ordering him to live his life and to conduct his affairs in a particular way. This order was to be obeyed whatever the Church thought or taught.

Being above ordinary men and women, being the direct recipient of God's message, the only one who can understand and interpret God's intentions places the individual in the category of the messiah. This direct relationship with God is, indeed, a pre-condition of messiahship. Accordingly, each Free Spirit was a messiah to himself or herself.

The Brethren disappeared by the end of the fifteenth century, but as every century has had its messiahs, so every century has seen a resurgence or recurrence of their form of spiritual anarchy.

In the sixteenth century radical anti-Catholics like the Anabaptists attacked both the traditions of the Catholic Church and the ideologies of the newly created Protestant Church. Apart from their specific rejection of the practice of infant baptism, the Anabaptists claimed (or at least some did since they were not in thinking wholly uniform) that the adult baptized believer "might do what he liked, because, if he sinned, it affected the body alone, with which his soul had no more to do than with any of the things of this world".[9]

Claus Ludwig, who had once belonged to the Anabaptists, rejected all the sacraments, saying that the one and only true sacrament by which a man or woman could be admitted into his church was the sexual act. Ludwig's church—the Chriesterung or Community of the Sacred—existed clandestinely in the vicinity of Mühlhausen in northern Germany in the mid-sixteenth century. It owed its allegiance to Ludwig only. He said he was Christ, Son of God; that it had been revealed to him that the "time and times and the dividing of time" prophesied by Daniel had come to pass and that he was sent to exterminate the godless with Gideon's sword, free the faithful, and establish the divine kingdom.[10]

Man was Bread, he taught, and Woman was Wine. Together the two were in Holy Communion. The woman who had sex with a liberated *Bloodfriend*, as the members called themselves, would herself be liberated and made pure. Children born of such union would be holy. *Bloodfriends* were immune; they could not be killed by the sword or made sick by the plague; and the women would have children without pain.

Ludwig selected twelve judges to help administer the Community, and a woman "clothed with the sun" who would lie with him and from his loins bear the future judge of all the world. All other women members were also required to lie with Ludwig as part of their ceremony of initiation.

At each meeting of the Chriesterung, Ludwig read from the Bible and interpreted the Scriptures, completing each dissertation with the appropriate words: "Be fruitful and multiply", which command the couples would instantly obey. Since, according to Ludwig, all desires and what others called "sins" were but the sacred promptings of the Holy Ghost, whenever any member of the sect felt thus prompted, it was perfectly permissible for him to go to the wife of another member and sanctify their communion. One Bloodfriend who had been frequently prompted in this way confessed at his trial that he had celebrated such rites with at least sixteen sisters of the Community.

Aware that their beliefs and practices would be condemned by the Church, Ludwig cautioned his people to live outwardly in the manner of their neighbours, to attend church and take part in Holy Communion to avoid suspicion. Nevertheless some of the groups were discovered; in 1551 three Bloodfriends were executed, the others quickly recanted. Ludwig himself was never caught.

In the seventeenth century the heretical notions of the Free Spirit emerged once again. The names had changed and many of the beliefs, in keeping with changed social and religious conditions, but the underlying themes and motivations remained the same. Some men and some women felt the need to raise themselves up and beyond the conditions of ordinary humanity with its pain, suffering, its disappointments, despair, its frustrations and boredom, and become so close to God as to be godlike.

When the Familists and later the Ranters, as these people came to be called in England, denied the separation of the material and the spirit world, of God in heaven and sinful man on earth, when they said that God dwelt among them as a member of their communities as He existed in all things that were created, they were harking back to the Brethren of the Free Spirit. When the Ranters denied the necessity of having to obey civil and moral laws and stated that acts of adultery, drunkenness, swearing and theft were not in themselves sinful or shameful, but were expressions of godliness, they were echoing beliefs which had been practised in the late Middle Ages.

In the same century, the spectre of spiritual nihilism again rose up to afright the orthodox guardians of morality, but this time the guardians were Jewish. In much of the Turkish empire and parts of central and eastern Europe the theology of the messiah, Sabbatai Zevi, spread like a forest fire through many of the communities. On Zevi's death in 1676 his followers, the Sabbataians, were attracted to other messiahs who advocated even greater freedom from conventional morality.* The Free Spirit perversion of the Lord's Prayer, "lead us *into* temptation" was echoed in the Sabbataian prayer, "Praised be to Thee, O Lord, who permits the forbidden".[11] One Sabbataian sect averred that whoever committed a sin and did evil was good in the eyes of God because by defiling himself before the world he was brought into direct contact with the spirit of holiness.[12]

In the eighteenth century the radical Sabbataian messiah, Jacob Frank, who formed his own sect of Frankists in Poland, went to the extreme of spiritual anarchy, deliberately turning upside down all notions of acceptable social behaviour. He claimed that he had come into the world not to build but to destroy and annihilate, to end all laws and customs so that the Good God could emerge into a world of innocence.[13]

The Free Spirits of the thirteenth century, like the Ranters of the seventeenth century, believed that only by sinning to the utmost could the world be cleared of sin. The Sabbataians of the eighteenth century maintained that man had to stretch himself to the furthest point of temptation in order to destroy temptation, to sink into the deepest abyss in order to be raised into unity with God. Again in the nineteenth century, in the peace and quiet of an English countryside, Brother Henry Prince gathered his followers around him and, in his church, had intercourse with a young virgin "as it was—ignorant, indifferent, independent, at enmity against God, and having nothing to commend it to Him" so that "the whole order of living men might be saved—their bodies like their souls; the whole man . . . purged from sin, received into grace, and fused into the Holy One for ever".†[14]

In this century, the Hollywood messiah, Charles Manson, preached to his "family" ideas that were not far removed from the mediaeval heresy of the Free Spirit‡ In this century, too, we have witnessed the ultimate expression of moral anarchy on a vast scale. Hitler also offered his followers—in his case a whole nation—the way to become one, not with God as such but with the nation as God through deliberate rejection of "the dirty and degrading modifications of . . . conscience and morality". To be merciful was weak; to be cruel was good. "Unless you are prepared to be pitiless you will get nowhere," he maintained. "If a

* See chapter eleven.

† See chapter thirteen.

‡ See chapter sixteen.

people is to become free it needs pride and will-power, defiance, hate, hate, and once again hate."[15]

Perhaps if man is freed from all sense of sin and wrongdoing, what results is not total innocence and sinlessness as the Brethren and their successive incarnations have maintained from century to century, but the concentration camps and the gas chambers of the Third Reich.

Yet there exists an interesting paradox. Elements of spiritual nihilism are found in many of the important religious and social reform movements from the sixteenth century onwards. They were toned down and adapted to suit the circumstances, but they were still recognizable. Anabaptism begot Familism which begot Ranterism which begot early Quakerism. Sabbataianism begot Frankism which begot early reformed Judaism. Frankists welcomed the French Revolution with joy and enthusiasm. A leading Frankist and one of Frank's nephews who called himself Junius Frey was executed along with Danton during the Reign of Terror in 1794.[16] The revolutionary Young Turk movement which revitalized the Turkish nation in the early part of this century had a number of Sabbataians in its front rank. One Sabbataian, Djavid Bey, a descendant of a messiah named Russo, became a member of the first Young Turk government.[17]*

The paradox can be explained. In the very act of releasing their followers from the burden of sin and guilt and by encouraging them to defy morality, the radical messiahs who advocated spiritual anarchism brought about a re-examination of traditional values expressed by the religion of the society in which they had grown up. Their deliberate opposition to all accepted customs led to a questioning and a revaluation. If they could not always find new answers themselves, their heirs sometimes did, and it is these new answers that provided the impetus for the reforms that we now take for granted.

*See also chapter sixteen.

CHAPTER SEVEN

DAVID AND SOLOMON

SAINT LOUIS, OR Louis IX, King of France, set out at the age of 33 on his first Crusade. He had with him an army of 40,000 and the hopes of the Christian world in the final triumph of Christ over the infidel. But he was captured and ignominiously released for a ransom. His failure brought with it a deep sense of disappointment. The nobility, many felt, had let down their king.

A year later, at Easter 1251, three men preached to a gathering of shepherds in Picardy, exhorting them to arm themselves in aid of Louis. Their message spread throughout the country and a new and very different Crusade began—the Crusade of the Shepherds, the Pastoureaux. They were soon joined by the flotsam and jetsam of town and country, murderers, thieves, prostitutes, who also clothed themselves in simple shepherd's garb. They were led by one of the three original preachers, a man who claimed to have received a direct call from the Virgin Mary to summons the Crusade. He was said to have come from Hungary and was known as Jacob, the Master of Hungary.[1]

A tall man with a pale, bearded face, Jacob was an ex-monk. Articulate and eloquent, fluent in French, German and Latin, he held his audiences with his imposing bearing and fiery speech. So quickly did he rise in power that he was able to attack the clergy with impunity. He assumed to himself the right to marry and divorce members of the Pastoureaux, and in one case was said to have married a woman to eleven men. He claimed that his elect would never go hungry or in need because he had the power to increase their provisions indefinitely.

In fact, the Pastoureaux provisioned themselves by going into towns and villages and taking what they wanted. The main target of their forays were the Jews and in a short time the Pastoureaux were said to have sacked over 100 of their communities.

No one stood in Jacob's way. As his followers grew in force so his power increased. Town after town welcomed his people as holy and Jacob as Christ himself. In awe the populace watched him, dressed as a bishop, grant absolution to sinners and sprinkle holy water over the blessed. Blanche, the Queen Mother, received him in Paris with expensive gifts.

The authorities did nothing to stop the Pastoureaux from killing and looting so long as no one of importance was bothered. Jews and the less well-off were perfectly permissible targets for attacks. But when Jacob, in his arrogance, turned his attention to the nobility and the landowners and proclaimed them the enemy of the people, the Queen Mother outlawed the movement. During one of the many frenzied meetings conducted by Jacob he was challenged by a spectator. Jacob struck down and killed the man. That was the last straw. He and his followers were chased from the town. Jacob was caught and cut into pieces and his followers were killed wherever they were found. Some fled as far off as Shoreham in England where they were summarily despatched. None ever reached the Holy Land, and the Crusade of the Shepherds came to a dismal end.

In the Old Testament Moses had prophesied that the Jews, because of their disobedience to the Lord, would be scattered from one end of the world to the other. They would serve other gods and among the nations would know no ease nor resting place, but would know only fear and sorrow. "And thy life shall hang in doubt before thee; and thou shalt fear day and night, and shalt have none assurance of thy life."[2]

For Jews living in the late Middle Ages this prophecy must have seemed to have come true in all its terrible detail. Jacob and his Pastoureaux was the last Crusade to bring devastation to the French Jews, but a few years later they were forced to leave France altogether. Edward I of England, having drained his Jews dry of their wealth, expelled them from the country and from all his dominions in 1290, taking their last few possessions as the price of their freedom. In Germany anti-semitic riots occurred in 1298 and again in 1336.

The Black Death which attacked Europe from the East in 1348 spared neither Jew nor Christian, but the former was made by the latter to pay for the sickness which killed them both. As one recent historian has noted, "For anyone who had lived through the Black Death, hysteria could never be far away".[3]

That hysteria was to a large extent directed against those who could least defend themselves. Jews were accused of poisoning the wells and the very fact that their methods of hygiene protected them to some degree against the plague was turned against them. They were said to practise witchcraft and for this, too, they were made to suffer. "In every country where Jews still existed, immense burnings took place, sometimes of entire communities. Tens of thousands of Jews perished, and in many places ancient communities were utterly destroyed and never rebuilt."[4]

The allegation that Jews murdered non-Jews in order to obtain their blood for the Passover, which had its origins in the reign of Antiochus Epiphanes, spread through Europe and gave cause—if cause were needed—for more riots and expulsions. This "blood libel" was joined by yet another: the Jews, whenever they could, stole the Body of Christ as symbolically represented by the Host—the consecrated wafer—in order to avenge themselves on Christianity. In Germany and France in particular, men were accused of both libels and whole communities perished for their alleged crimes no matter how hard their leaders argued to show that these accusations were absurd in the extreme.

One area was seemingly free of the sickness of violent anti-semitism and that was the Iberian Peninsula. Under Islam the Spanish and Portuguese Jews had, with the Christians, enjoyed protected status; there were no large-scale pogroms or expulsions. In peace they could look forward to as long a life as their non-Jewish neighbours and in war they suffered with them as the inhabitants of a place and not as Jews.[5] When the Christian invaders began their *reconquista* of the peninsula, Jewish life and culture expanded, especially in the northern parts of the country where the Christian invaders welcomed them. Barcelona became their cultural centre. In Toledo they were given power over the Muslim communities; in Tortosa they were granted land. Settlement of Jews was especially encouraged in so-called "frontier communities" where Christian-held territories bordered on Muslim areas. Christian rulers even protected the Jews against the Crusaders and, as late as 1212, Spanish knights prevented a massacre of Jews in Toledo by French troops.[6]

So long as the peninsula remained half-Muslim, and the Jews were seen as a necessary buffer between the main antagonists, the Christians and the Muslims, their freedom was assured. Their communities flourished. They were the principal transmitters to the Western world of Eastern philosophy and science and were hard put to keep up with the demand for translations into Latin of Arabic classics. But as Christian supremacy over Islam was confirmed by successive conquests so the Jews lost their favoured position. Christian animosity against them increased. They were accused of a variety of terrible atrocities, such as roasting babies on spits.[7] The "blood libel", like a virulent infection, once again began to spread.

In 1391, stirred up by Fernando Martinez, a leading cleric in Seville, the mobs gathered and on Ash Wednesday, 15 March, riots broke out. The mobs were at first held back by the authorities, but by 4 June they had broken free and attacked the Judería. As many as 4,000 people were killed; others were forcibly baptized. The violence spread to Cordova, Toledo, Valencia; and in Barcelona, in spite of its being protected by the authorities, the community was utterly destroyed. Even the stretch of sea separating the mainland from the Balearic Islands did not save the communities there; in Palma alone 50,000 people perished.[8]

The massacres were terrible, but what brought lasting shame to the survivors was the fact that so many of them lived—as Christians, or as they came to be called (with great contempt) *Marranos*. In Spanish the word means "pig". More politely these converts were also known as New Christians.

Conversions of so many had almost certainly never before occurred in Jewish history—in Aragon and Castile alone something like 200,000 people became Christians.[9] The phenomenon was to have a lasting effect, not only on the Jewish community as a whole throughout Western Europe, but also on Spanish and Portuguese life (since the experience was to be repeated in Portugal).

Anti-semitic riots followed by death or conversions occurred unabated throughout the fifteenth century. Vincente Ferrer replaced Martinez as the leading opponent of the Jews. In 1411 he travelled from one end of Castile to the other, breaking into synagogues, carrying a scroll of the Law in one hand and a crucifix in the other, and, with the aid of the mob, forced the congregations into Christianity. In one day 4,000 Jews of Toledo submitted to baptizement. Within a century 850,000 Castilian Jews had been reduced to a mere 50,000.[10]

The fate of the remainder was finally sealed in 1491 when King Ferdinand ordered their expulsion. The community was still sufficiently intact to try to prevent or delay their exile and the great Don Isaac Abravanel whose messianic speculations were touched upon in chapter four was sent to bargain with the King. Three times he begged him to spare his loyal subjects who had done no harm to anyone; he also begged his friends at court to intercede on their behalf. "But his ears were closed as though he were stone deaf."[11] The Queen, sitting on the King's right, was even more adamant that the decree go forward. 300,000 ducats were offered as a bribe and, according to witnesses, the King was about to accept this when Torquemada, the Grand Inquisitor himself, interrupted the proceedings with an impassioned speech. Holding up a crucifix, he cried, "Behold the crucified whom the wicked Judas sold. Now you want to sell him again. Take him and sell him. I resign my power and you will answer to God for your deed!"[12] The King backed down. The decree of expulsion was issued on 31 March 1491.

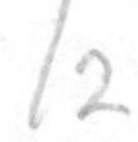

The greatest Jewish community in the world was destroyed, its people killed or forced into a strange religion, the remnant sent into exile as Moses had prophesied would happen to those who did not heed the word of God. The sense of sin and of guilt fastened on to those who remained and would not let them or their descendants rest for centuries to come. Exile and forced conversion were seen as punishment; homelessness symbolized Godlessness; and the longing to return to God who had turned His back on His people never left them. The yearning for the messiah who would lead them back to their own faith and to their homes once again asserted itself.

Expelled from Spain, many thousands fled to Portugal, but there a similar fate awaited them. The Portuguese King's wife was the daughter of Ferdinand and Isabella of Spain. She had refused to enter the country until all heretics were driven out.[13] Jews in her eyes were the arch heretics. In the name of Christ and national unity, the Forced Conversion of all Portuguese Jews was decreed in 1497.

Three million or so Marranos or *conversos* from now on became an important element in both nations. Freed from their former civil disabilities as Jews many achieved great power and eminence in every sphere of life not excluding the Church itself. Numbers of leading clerics had Jewish parents. Pablo de Santa Maria, the Bishop of Burgos, was formerly Rabbi Solomon ha-Levi. Rabbi Jehoshua ha-Lorqui became Gerónimo de

Santafé, a rabid anti-Jewish polemicist,[14] and even St Theresa de Jesus, the joint patron saint of Spain was of Jewish descent.[15] Marranos also made themselves felt in government, business, in art and in literature. An historian has said of these New Christians that the "entire fabric of Spanish culture was thus deeply permeated by New Christian influences";[16] and the same was true of Portugal.

But this influence did not in the end serve to protect them. Marranos were used by the authorities for one of the least popular but most profitable occupations—tax-gathering. As a result of concessions granted to them, some became very rich and at the same time the objects of hatred. In Lisbon in 1506 this hatred, aided and abetted by rising food prices and severe pestilence, led to riots which killed up to 4,000 Marranos. Though Emanuel had the ringleaders executed—and earned for himself the pejorative title of the "Jewish" king—the animosity against the Marranos continued and grew.[17] By the time the Inquisition came to Portugal the Marranos were already established in the minds of the general populace as fuel for the hungry Inquisitorial fires.

The Inquisition was established in Spain in 1481 and in Portugal 60 years later. Statistics which have come down to us show quite clearly that the Marranos were its main concern. Other heretics were caught up in its net but Judaizers, as they were called in Inquisitorial language, were the prime sufferers. In the Toledo Inquisition, for example, of about 1,100 cases tried during the years 1648 to 1794 more than half were charged with "Judaism",[18] the charge covering almost any act which might connect the accused with his former religion, no matter how remotely.

The Marranos's religion was a strange and confused admixture of Catholicism and Judaism, with a liturgy consisting only of 40 pages repeated over and over again in the vernacular and passed down from generation to generation. In it the messianic ideal held a prominent place.[19] The messiah would come and he would relieve them of their misery, of the terrible guilt they suffered for turning their backs on their true religion. He would return them to the Holy Land where they could live as complete men and women in the full knowledge that God had accepted them back as true sons and daughters of Israel.

The riots, the expulsions, the Inquisition, these were seen as the "birth pangs" of the messiah, the period of terrible calamity which by tradition preceded his coming. The more the Marranos suffered, the more they came to believe in the imminence of the messiah's appearance. Shut off from the rest of society by their own secret lives and by the animosity of the populace, their messianic excitement grew like an exotic plant in a hothouse, feeding on despair and hope.

Then, as if in answer to their prayers, they heard a whisper: the messiah had come. He was now in Rome, at the very heart of the Holy Mother Church, conversing with the Pope himself. Soon he would come to them. Soon he would deliver them from their enemies.

David Reubeni was a short, stocky man, very dark in complexion. One morning in Rome in 1524 he mounted his white palfrey with the ease of an expert horseman and, with his servant before him and a crowd of curious spectators behind him, rode in state towards the Pope's palace. The visit was a formal one. He came—so he claimed—as the ambassador of his brother, King Joseph, who ruled over "thirty myriads of the tribe of Gad and of the tribe of Reuben and of the half-tribe of Manesseh"[20] in Khaibar, north of Medina. Some historians have said that he was an out-and-out fake and that he was from Germany; others that he was from the Cochin province in India.[21] No one knows for sure exactly who David Reubeni was, whether his brother was a tribal chief or not. What is known is that he arrived at the Pope's palace and asked, demanded, to see the Holy Father. He had an important message for him.[22]

The cardinals and the princes of the Church came to look at this strange visitor. It was not every day that a Jew, claiming not only to be the brother of a ruler but also a direct descendant of Jesse, and therefore of King David, entered the Pope's palace. Cardinal Egidio received him with courtesy and promised he would pass on his request for an audience; then he spent the rest of the day talking to Reubeni. They spoke through an interpreter since Reubeni had no Latin or Italian and the Cardinal no Hebrew or Arabic. At the end of the day the Cardinal took leave of his visitor who found himself once again mobbed by well-wishers, Jew and Christian alike, as he rode back to his lodgings.

At eight o'clock on the following Sunday morning, Reubeni and twelve respected Jews of the city went to the Pope's palace.

He was graciously received by Clement VII, a distinguished-looking man, a nephew of Lorenzo de Medici, and like all Medicis, a patron of literature, art and music.[23] Clement was also a man of esoteric interests, which may account for the manner in which he received Reubeni whose qualifications as an ambassador were, to say the least, doubtful. Clement dabbled in astrology[24] and enjoyed conversation with men of learning. Of these a significant number were rabbis, learned in the Kabbalah, who crowded his court and engaged him and his cardinals in long and elevated discussions. "This Pope is the most secretive in the world, and I have never spoken with one whose sayings were so hard to define," said one of his retinue.[25]

Reubeni put an extraordinary proposal to the Pope. He wanted arms and men in order to mount a Crusade to the Holy Land and wrest it from the Turks. Would the Pope give him assistance? The Pope listened with interest. Preposterous though the idea might have sounded, it was not impossible. The power of the Vatican was under attack from all sides. The forces of the Reformation were threatening the Church; that rebel Luther and his followers were stirring up anti-Catholic feelings throughout large parts of Europe which previously had been totally loyal to the Pope. A successful Crusade which would restore the Holy Land to the Christians, even if led by a Jew, might help considerably to restore papal authority.[26]

Clement promised that he would do what he could. He suggested that Reubeni go to Portugal to elicit aid from that loyal son of the Church, King John, but that in the meantime he remain in Rome where he would be treated with the utmost respect and dignity as became the ambassador of a reigning monarch.

A fine house was prepared for Reubeni and for the next year he stayed in Rome, one of its most unusual and respected residents. When he became ill after one of his many long fasts—since he was by nature an ascetic who prayed and fasted often—he was attended by the best physicians. Nevertheless he grew worse and it looked as if he was about to die. "I will not die," he told his worried doctor, "until I have brought Israel to Jerusalem, built the altar, and offered sacrifice there."[27] Soon after this, he recovered. Everyone was astonished. Could Reubeni be more than just the simple man, the "sinner and man of war" he said he was? Might he not be the messiah himself? After all, was he not of the House of David whose Son was appointed by God with the task of returning Israel to Jerusalem. Only the messiah had the power and glory sufficient to rebuild the Temple and offer sacrifice at the altar as Reubeni said he would do.

The word went about Rome. Reubeni was the messiah. Reubeni denied this emphatically, especially to the Christians. To the Jews he was ambivalent. He said he was of the House of David; he talked about bringing the Jews back to the Holy Land. He must have known the effect these words would have on a people brought up to expect the messiah. He even went about performing miraculous cures associated with the messiah. A girl, sick from the plague, was brought back to health by his prayers.[28]

The people most affected by his presence in Rome were, not surprisingly, the Marranos who had escaped from Spain or Portugal. Here was a man, avowedly Jewish, claiming for himself the status of a prince, walking freely and undisturbed in the very centre of the hostile Catholic world. Such courage could only be the attribute of the one they so fervently expected to save them.

Because of the secret life they led, the Marranos were perforce required to build up a very efficient system of intelligence—a system which, by the way, helped some to achieve brilliant careers in international diplomacy and trade. The word quickly spread that the long-awaited messiah had come knocking at the Pope's door, demanding his people be freed. It was heard wherever there were Marranos—in Italy, England, France, Holland, Turkey, and especially in Spain and Portugal.

By the time the Pope finally gave Reubeni a letter of safe conduct—which, as a Jew, he needed to permit him to travel through the Iberian Peninsula—the Marranos in Portugal were eagerly expecting his arrival. The Pope also gave Reubeni 100 golden ducats, which the latter refused. "For your servants," said the Pope. Reubeni took the gift and rewarded those who had taken care of him in Rome. Then he departed the city. "Be strong and of good courage," the Pope had said to him; "fear not for God is with thee." Reubeni had replied: "I will serve you all the days of my life. There is none before me but the Almighty and thou",[29] diplomatic if somewhat curious words for a would-be messiah, but then, at that stage, Reubeni had refused the rôle others were eager to thrust upon him.

It needed a man of great determination or great madness to walk directly into the lion's den in the manner and garb of the lion's favourite dinner. Reubeni, the Jew, arrived in Portugal from which all his co-religionists had been expelled, in a ship boldly flying the Star of David; and with a retinue composed entirely of Jews—armed, what is more—he travelled in pomp and ceremony to meet Portugal's King, the safe conduct given him by Clement in Rome being all that stood between him and death. He went, moreover, not as supplicant begging for mercy, but as the brother of a king, an ambassador of the Pope, a military leader of his people intent on negotiating an arms' deal with another king.

Little wonder that the Marranos lost their heads over him, whether he called himself messiah or not; that wherever he went he was followed by crowds, bowing low before him and kissing his hands. The Christians looked on in amazement. There were mutterings that only the King's hand should be kissed. These were to grow in strength as time went on, but for the moment David Reubeni's arrival produced an immediate cessation of anti-Marrano persecution and possibly even delayed the formal introduction of the Inquisition into Portugal which finally took place in 1531.[30]

On the way to the King, Reubeni was challenged by a priest who said that there were no Jewish kings and that they had no sons of royal seed as Reubeni claimed he was. The small man grabbed hold of the large priest and flung him to the ground in front of a crowd of Christians who applauded his courage.[31]

Then came a messenger from King John with 500 ducats and a scribe to assist the visitor. This gesture of welcome sent the Marranos wild with exctement, but Reubeni realized that their enthusiasm, rather than helping, might hinder his cause. He tried to cool their ardour but chose the wrong words with which to do so. He told them that he did not come with a sign or a miracle or a mystery. He was the son of King Solomon, a man of war from his youth, and came "to help our King and to help you and to go in the way he shall lead me to the land of Israel",[32] which was just what they expected to hear from the lips of the messiah.

In Almeida the auspicious meeting with John III took place. Reubeni, accompanied by a procession of 50 men and fifteen horses, rode up to the King's palace. He came before His Majesty with his retinue who stood by proudly, their hands resting on their swords. As they were all Jews, this was an act of unprecedented provocation and impudence in the eyes of the court, but so great was Reubeni's reputation by this time that the King received him and his men with great honour instead of clapping them all immediately into gaol.

The meeting went well. King John promised him eight ships and 4,000 firearms for the proposed invasion of Palestine. Reubeni was satisfied; the Marranos were ecstatic. For them no further proof was needed that Reubeni was, in fact, the messiah. "The hour of redemption after which they had yearned so ardently in their deepest soul had come at last," wrote the historian, Graetz.[33]

In Spain a woman known as the Maid of Herrera had visions in which she saw and heard Moses and the angels promising to lead the Marranos back to the Holy Land. Later she and about 90 of her followers were rounded up and put to death. Young Marranos, suddenly released from their fears of their oppressors by Reubeni's presence, planned daring escapades into Spain to rescue out of the gaols of the Inquisition a number of Marrano women who were being held and tortured there. Their efforts to do so failed, but the spirit that had driven them continued to exist so long as Reubeni remained in the peninsula.

None of this escaped the notice of the authorities. When the Portuguese ambassador to Rome returned to tell the King that he had heard that it was Reubeni's desire to bring the Marranos back to Judaism, no assurances to the contrary from Reubeni convinced the Christians that he was not a messianic pretender with subversive intentions.

Finally an event took place which horrified Reubeni as much as it disturbed the Portuguese court. A young, romantic and brilliant Marrano named Diego Pires, who while still in his early twenties had been appointed to serve as a secretary to the King in the Courts of Justice, made known his wish to revert to the religion of his ancestors. Moved by the plight of the Jews, borne along by the messianic ecstacy, Pires sought out Reubeni and told him what he intended to do. Reubeni immediately realized how dangerous the young zealot could be and he tried unsuccessfully to dissuade him. "I have had a vision," Pires told him. "I have seen myself circumcised as a Jew. I ask you or one of your servants to perform this act for me." Reubeni refused. "Stay in your duties to the King," he told him, "until the Almighty opens the door."[34]

Pires was too far gone in his enthusiasm to listen to the older man. He performed the painful operation himself, changed his name to Solomon Molcho, and made it known that he was now a Jew. The King heard about this and it confirmed for him his worst fears: Reubeni was about to turn the Marranos away from Christianity and back to Judaism. He sent for him.

"You have circumcised my secretary," he said.

"God forbid," replied Reubeni. "I have come only for my business and thy service."

The King pointed out that when Reubeni appeared all the Marranos bowed to him and kissed his hand. "Only the King is entitled to such honour."

Reubeni promised that he would put a stop to the practice, but it was too late. Pires's circumcision was proof enough.[35] King John withdrew his offer of aid. He also suggested that it would be healthier for Reubeni to leave Portugal while he could. Reubeni took the hint, but not before he spoke again to Pires, now Solomon Molcho. "Get out of here," he warned him. "You have caused enough trouble. Go to Jerusalem or they will burn you."[36]

Reubeni took his leave of the Portuguese Marranos. They wept in anguish to see him go. "Trust in God and do not fear," he told them, "for you will be privileged to behold the rebuilding of Jerusalem. First we must wage great battles around the Holy City before the land will be ours, and before we can offer sacrifices there. After that is done we will return and take you there, but now I only came to announce that the time of your deliverance is near at hand."[37]

Reubeni went on his way; his destination being Leghorn in Italy. He and his attendants were thoroughly searched before boarding their ship to see if they were taking with them any Marranos. A storm drove them to the coast of Spain and they were immediately taken into custody, but a speedy letter from Reubeni to Emperor Charles, whose Empress was the sister of the King of Portugal, secured them their release.[38] Even so, his star was now on the wane while that of Solomon Molcho, his disciple, was in the ascendancy.

Molcho took Reubeni's advice and left Portugal; he certainly would have been arrested by the Inquisition so long as he called himself a Jew. But there was another reason for his leaving—he wanted to steep himself in Judaism, and especially in its mystical form of the Kabbalah which was then beginning to achieve enormous importance in Jewish religious thought—and soon, thereafter, in Christian thought, too. The Kabbalah, strongly messianic in mood with its poignant themes of Exile from and Return to God, of spiritual separation and unity, had an especial appeal for Marranos like Molcho who had suffered both spiritual and physical exile and longed for restoration and redemption.

After much fasting, prayer and meditation as became an aspiring Kabbalist, Solomon Molcho had a vision in which a heavenly wise man told him to go to Turkey. This he did and in Salonika, which had a large and important Jewish community, he was received with great enthusiasm. Not only was he an inspired and inspiring orator, but he was also handsome and engaging. He attracted large audiences who listened to his sermons with rapt attention. He had with amazing speed absorbed Kabbalistic and Talmudic lore and could dispute and discuss both with the best rabbis in Turkey. One famous Kabbalist, Joseph Karo, called Molcho, "my beloved, my dearest Solomon".[39]

Wherever he went he spoke not of himself but of his master, Prince David Reubeni; yet there were many who were saying that not Reubeni but Molcho was the expected messiah. "From his lips came words of grace, for the spirit of the Lord was upon him and His word was constantly on his tongue," wrote a contemporary. "He continually drew forth marvellous words from the deep fountain of the Kabbalah and he wrote them upon tablets."[40] None of his works, unfortunately, has survived.

From Turkey Solomon pursued his master to Italy, all the while gathering a following and popularity of his own. In Italy on his journey to Rome he preached to ever more enthusiastic audiences. Like Reubeni he intended to visit the Pope. While still in Salonika, which was then part of the Turkish empire, and was known as the Jerusalem of the Balkans because of all the Marrano refugees who had fled there,[41] Solomon had predicted that the reign of the messiah would begin in the year 1540. Rome was in danger of attack by the armies of the Reformation and this he interpreted as an important event preceding the messiah's appearance.

The city was, in fact, sacked in May 1527 and when Molcho arrived there it was in dire straits. "Hell has nothing to compare with the present state of Rome," wrote a Venetian visitor at the time.[42] The mood of its inhabitants was gloomy, almost morbid. They had been beset by plague and by war. Now every unusual event such as a particularly vivid flash of lightning was regarded as a portent of new disaster. When men are oppressed by anxiety, when they are transfixed by a sense of hopelessness and feel that time has come to a stop for them, they look to one who can offer them solace, and more than that, a sense of the future : in a word, hope. For many, both Jew and Christian, Solomon Molcho was such a man. They flocked to hear him speak and he had little difficulty in reaching the Pope whose problems were manifold. Clement gave him a letter of safe-conduct in his own signature; this valuable document permitted Molcho to live as he pleased.

Solomon entered the Jewish community wholeheartedly, but the welcome given him was more circumspect. The rabbis were suspicious of this Kabbalist who predicted events from the stars, who had audience with the Pope, who went about not in the clothes worn by other Jews but in the adornment of non-Jews.[43] Most of all they disliked the way he preached the Law to the people in the synagogues, he who only a few years before had been a Christian.

Eventually he was betrayed to the Inquisition as an apostate Catholic and it seemed as if his doom was sealed. But he had so endeared himself to Clement that the Pope, against the advice of his cardinals and to the anger of the judges of the Inquisition, tried to intervene in his case. Even the Holy Father himself could not stop the Inquisitorial machinery once it had begun, so he hid Molcho in the Vatican and arranged for some poor innocent to be seen abroad in Molcho's clothes. The man was arrested and quickly burned by the Inquisitors. They rushed off to the Pope and gleefully told him, "The man in whose honour you delight is now a burning fire." Then Molcho appeared. The judges were confounded. "You've made a mistake," Clement told them, "now you had better enter into your judgment book that the victim you burned had reviled and cursed his God and King so that no one shall know you have erred, otherwise trouble will follow." They hastened to do the Holy Father's bidding while Solomon's followers rejoiced that their master had been saved by a miracle.[44]

Through astrological calculations, Molcho predicted that Rome would suffer flooding and soon afterwards, on 8 October 1530, the Tiber threatened to inundate the city. Again by astrology, he foretold of an earthquake in Portugal, and Lisbon was almost destroyed by one on 26 January 1531. These events and his "miraculous" escape from the Inquisition confirmed in the minds of many that Solomon was the messiah.

Some time during his stay in Rome, the exact date is not known, Solomon met up again with David Reubeni. What happened at this meeting can only be conjectured, but it must surely have been a strange and poignant moment. Both men had been hailed as messiahs; they both had followers who were prepared to go to the stake if need be for their faith in their leaders. Reubeni, some ten or more years older than Molcho, was now a faded figure whereas his young disciple was at the height of his fame. Judging by what happened next it would seem that they were able to settle their differences. They decided they would travel to see the Holy Roman Emperor, Charles V, and elicit his aid to drive the Turks from the Holy Land so that the Jews could return to their ancient home. Whether Reubeni had urged Molcho or Molcho Reubeni, they had now both assumed the sacred task assigned to the messiah.

In that year, 1532, the Emperor was holding a Diet at Ratisbon (Regensburg) on the Bavarian Danube. Jewish leaders warned David and Solomon that Charles was no friend to the Jews and they were endangering their lives and those of their followers by approaching him. The two, however, were already beyond such advice. Their messianic inspiration—or vaunting ambition—held them enthralled. They prepared themselves, and bearing a banner, they entered the city. The banner displayed the Hebrew word, MKBI, an acrostic for the Biblical quotation: "Who is like unto Thee among the Mighty, O Lord"—the battle cry of Judah the Maccabee.* Whether or not Charles had heard of this former messianic revolutionary leader, the choice of emblem was provocative in the extreme. Emperors do not like to be reminded of their inferiority in the eyes of God, and ill-tempered Charles was no exception. He refused to see or hear the messianic pair and had them and their people put in irons.

There they remained until the Emperor closed the Diet and moved with his court and his prisoners to Mantua where Solomon was handed over to the Italian Inquisition to be tried

* See chapter two.

as an apostate Catholic. The Pope, a dying man himself, could no longer help Solomon. He was found guilty and condemned to death by burning at an auto-da-fé.

To prevent the young messiah whose fame was widespread from speaking to the crowds at the stake, the judges had his jaw bound in a bridle. Just as he was about to be fed to the flames a noble arrived from Charles. He ordered the executioners to remove the bridle. The noble spoke to Solomon. "My message from the Emperor is this: recant and you shall live. You will be received back by him and shall be one of his court. If not . . ." The heat of the flames eloquently finished the sentence for him. Molcho remained still. "I repent only of one thing," he said in a voice so quiet that the eager spectators had to strain forward to hear him. "That I was ever of your religion. That I spent my youth as a Catholic."[45]

Solomon was flung into the flames and those followers who were arrested with him were also executed. An adoring disciple wrote of his death afterwards: "He was as a burnt offering to the Lord Who smelled the sweet savour and took to Him Solomon's pure soul".[46]

In Italy and Turkey the remainder of his believers continued to maintain that Solomon did not die in the fire, but that through his great wisdom and understanding of Kabbalistic magic escaped the flames. Some even took an oath that he was in his home eight days after the auto-da-fé, and that he had left there, never to be seen again.[47] There were others, Kabbalists as Solomon had been, who predicted that he would rise again and take revenge on those who had killed him.[48]

David Reubeni's end was much less dramatic. He had always been a Jew and was therefore not subject to the laws of the Church or the Inquisition. He remained in prison in Italy and was then sent, bound in chains, to a prison in Spain. His ultimate fate is not known for certain. It is said by some hostile to him that he was poisoned after he had divulged under torture the names of many Marranos who were practising Judaism in secret and who were subsequently arrested and executed.[49] Whether true or not, he was never released and he died in gaol two or three years after Solomon, in about 1537.

Were Reubeni and Molcho right in raising the hopes of the Marranos in the way they did? This is a question always posed by a messiah and his mission to the hopeless and dejected. One answer is that to live in hope is better than to live in continued despair. Another—the more orthodox view—is that it is cruel and callous to raise men's hopes and then to dash them. There is a third view and that is that hope is good and necessary so long as it does not prevent men from acting realistically in the present or prevent them from living out their lives to the furthest of their potential given the circumstances in which they find themselves.

Promises of a better world "removed in space and time are", said Karl Mannheim, "like uncashable cheques".[50] If a man sits holding his cheque postdated for the future and meanwhile allows his life to fall into disarray around him, then the messiah and his mission may be said to have been failures. If, however, the cheque, though uncashable in the present, gives him a sense of security and of purpose, so that he can come to realize his potential, can it then be said that the messiah has wholly failed? Judging by what the Marranos who had believed in their David and Solomon felt after the death of their heroes, the answer surely must be "no".

CHAPTER EIGHT

WARS AND RUMOURS OF WARS

IN ITS ORIGINAL conception the idea of the messiah was closely associated with that of warfare and the struggle against the forces of evil and oppression. The "anointed" of the House of David was not primarily a man of peace but of war. Only when the might of the adversaries had been overcome would he administer mercy and justice and inaugurate the kingdom of the righteous.

The Old Testament is filled with accounts of great leaders and of conflicts between the people of Israel and their enemies. Gideon, for instance, and his glorious "three hundred", as told in the *Book of Judges,* defeated the Midianites by coming upon them in their camp in the middle of the night, blowing trumpets and causing them to flee in terror.[1] When David praised God in the Psalms for teaching his hands to war, for providing him with the shield of salvation, for girding him with strength, and subduing those who rose up against him, he was talking about real war and real enemies.[2]

Later, when the Jews ceased to be self-governing and most of them were living in exile, the battles of the messianic saviour were shifted from a worldly to an other-worldly plane. The messiah's rôle shifted, too, from that of the military prince to the Prince of Peace, the conqueror of cosmic evil.

The New Testament which adopted and developed this concept referred to battles, to defeat and triumph, but these were of a spiritual nature even if they were spoken of in physical terms. The *Book of Revelation* talked about "a place called in the Hebrew tongue Armageddon". This was where Christ would "gather them to the battle of that great day of God Almighty".[3] The place itself may have existed on earth, but the battle was of an universal order between the forces of darkness and the forces of light, between evil and good.

Yet, in spite of the Christian insistence on the spirituality of the messiah, many Christians who aspired to the messianic rôle did so more in the Old Testament manner than in the New. They were not men of peace but of war, not spiritual but military leaders. Their ultimate aim, however, was the same: the creation of a state of perpetual peace and plenitude on earth and an end to injustice and oppression.

Fra Dolcino in 1300 gathered together more than 1,000 men in Piedmont to wage war against the armies of the Pope. He was defeated and burnt as a heretic. In England John Ball, a former priest, denounced the abuses of the Church and joined Wat Tyler in leading the Peasants' Revolt in 1381. He was captured and executed at St Albans.[4]

The sixteenth century saw the advent of two outstanding messiahs whose exploits were separated by one decade. The first was Thomas Müntzer; the second Jan Bockelson. Both deliberately harked back to messianism in its early Old Testament form. Unlike Jewish messiahs they could not lead their people back from a physical exile to Jerusalem, there to build the Temple, but they used the same metaphors to achieve the same results—the galvanizing into action of a people who were seeking a way out of seemingly hopeless circumstances. When they spoke of the children of Israel they meant their own followers. When they talked of battle they meant the final, world-shattering war between the elect and their religious and economic oppressors. The New Jerusalem was the place where they could live without priests, ritual, or onerous tithes, in freedom and justice.

Thomas Müntzer was a man of learning. In a period when few men could read he was an exception. He absorbed whatever he could lay his hands on, German, Greek, Hebrew, theology, philosophy, mysticism.[5] His knowledge of the Bible was formidable, especially of the prophets Isaiah, Jeremiah and Ezekiel, the men who had spoken of exile, of the fate of Israel and of its ultimate triumph.

He was born in 1488 into an age of spiritual turmoil. He was 29 when his contemporary, Martin Luther, nailed the theses against indulgences on the church door at Wittenberg. Three years later Luther presented his address on Church reform to the Christian princes of Germany and launched the German Reformation. Müntzer, a Catholic, become a devoted follower of Luther. He took up a ministry in Zwickau, a small city in Saxony, south-west of Dresden, which was by then becoming an important industrial centre, rich in silver. There Müntzer saw the oppressive social conditions that afflicted a large portion of the population: heavy taxation, economic uncertainty, inflation. He preached to the weavers who were suffering greatly from the new industrialization. He heard their complaints; he sensed their confusion. But it was not till he met the mystic Nicklas Storch that he began to formulate the world-view that was to dominate his actions for the rest of his short life.

Storch preached the Apocalypse—that the End of the World was at hand. He said that first the Turks would conquer the world and the Antichrist would rule over it. Then God's elect would rise up and destroy the godless. This final battle would be followed by the Second Coming of Christ and the Millennium.[6]

In addition to his apocalyptic message, Storch spoke of the mystics' belief in the indwelling of the Christ in man, the living Christ through whose spirit each man could redeem himself from his state of exile and become at one with God. The Cross upon which the historical Christ had been crucified was the symbol of suffering and despair. When each man reached the point where he was crucified by his own despair then, like Christ, he would come into direct communication with God.

Müntzer was quick to absorb and extend Storch's teachings. Not only could the individual be united with God through his sufferings; he could become as God. The Brethren of the Free Spirit were all long dead and gone, but through Thomas Müntzer there coursed the heady wine of their spiritual anarchism. Man could free himself from his material self and become more than man, become god-like. He could soar above this world which hemmed him in; he could with a sweep of his godly might destroy his enemies and establish a glorious kingdom, the New Jerusalem.

Such inflammatory words from the mouth of a young minister did not suit the authorities in Zwickau and when there occurred riots in the town, Müntzer was summarily thrown out. He travelled from place to place and in 1523 took up another ministry in the town of Allstedt. Here he married. Here he created the first liturgy in the German language and translated Latin hymns into the vernacular. His name spread rapidly. The workers in the silver mines, the peasants from the neighbouring farms and villages flocked to hear him. They looked upon him as more than a preacher, as a leader of men, and they rallied to his call when he created his own League of the Elect.

By that time he had broken with Luther and with the newly formed Protestant Church. "I preach such a Christian faith," he told his followers, "as does not agree with that of Luther, but which is in conformity with the heart of the elect of this world." Faith, he said, was what mattered most, not Church or doctrine. Those who had faith in God were godly, no matter how they prayed to him. Rather than debate theology with priests, "I would sooner talk with the Heathen, Turks and Jews about the very smallest of all the words of God".[7]

His preaching was bound to attract the attention of the authorities once again, and Duke John of Saxony, a convert to Lutheranism, ordered Müntzer to deliver a sermon on his beliefs. Müntzer did so with alacrity. He preached the End of Days, the final destruction of all world empires. Priests, monks and all godless rulers would die by the sword. The messianic reign was about to be ushered in but only the elect would live in it, only the poor would inherit the new kingdom.

In spite of its revolutionary message, John received Müntzer's sermon with tolerance, insisting only that he remain in Weimar and not preach again until his case could be considered. Müntzer was not prepared to be muzzled for the shortest space of time. His sense of election weighed too heavily on him. He escaped to nearby Mühlhausen where he started a new League of the Elect.

The line between messianic fervour and armed rebellion is sometimes very thin. The would-be messiah whose mission is conceived in purely religious terms of bringing about the kingdom of the elect soon finds that his way is blocked by Church and State. The final war between good and evil, between the elect and the godless that he has preached with such certainty and passion now becomes more than a mere metaphor. The restlessness of his followers and his own impatience to destroy the old and create the new demand action. Either he is to act on his words and redeem his promises or he must concede the emptiness of his message and withdraw in ignominy. Usually, by the time this crisis is reached, he had gone too far along the way towards confrontation with the authorities to back down. He must go on because he now believes absolutely in the reality he has created for himself and his followers. He *is* the messiah; he *is* god-like; he *is* almighty; he *is* invincible. Those who believe in him, who have projected on to him all their wishes and their desires, believe that because they have accepted him they are the elect; that they, too, are god-like and invincible.

In Mühlhausen, Thomas Müntzer reached that crisis. A red crucifix and a sword were carried before him by his followers who were now armed to the teeth. They patrolled the town until the civil administration had Müntzer expelled. When he returned soon afterwards, he found himself in the midst of social upheaval. The peasants who had been in rebellion against the nobles and the clergy and who had risen up unsuccessfully from time to time since the beginning of the sixteenth century were about to enter into the final phase of their revolt. Müntzer saw the opportunity so far denied him to enter into history and possibly to change it.

In April 1525 he set up a white banner in a church in Mühlhausen upon which was emblazoned a colourful rainbow, symbolizing God's covenant with mankind. Beneath this banner, he announced, he would march into battle against the godless. The final war between the elect and the forces of darkness was about to take place. This was Armageddon.

The peasants flocked to him, the leader they had been seeking. After a few brief and successful skirmishes, Müntzer established his rule. By May 8,000 men were under his command, a formidable army. At Frankenhausen he ordered all the other peasant groups to link up with his. "I am like Gideon," he told them, "and you are the elected three hundred. Together we will destroy the Midianites in their camps. The Lord will deliver them into our hands."

"Wretched shabby bag of worms," was how one of the German princes addressed him in a letter challenging him and his army to battle. "Thievish, murderous peasants" was Luther's scornful opinion of them.[8] Philip of Hesse, a young commander who had chalked up a number of military successes, realized that if Müntzer was brought down the whole revolt would collapse. He, therefore, offered the peasants their lives for the life of their "saviour". In reply Müntzer addressed the peasants.

"I am the shepherd, David, appointed by the Lord to feed you," he said to them. "The Lord will cause the evil beasts to cease out of the land and we will live safely. No more shall we be prey to the heathen; nor shall the beast of the land devour us. The Lord has made with us a covenant of peace. The tree of the field shall yield her fruit, and the earth shall yield her increase and we shall be safe in the land."[9]

He told them of the coming of darkness, of the time of tribulation when the sun and the moon would give off no light and the stars would fall from the heaven and the powers of the heaven would be shaken. But then he promised them that the sign of the Son of Man would appear, "coming in the clouds of heaven with power and great glory".[10]

At the height of his harangue a rainbow appeared in the sky —his very own symbol! The peasants saw and were convinced. Müntzer was the saviour! "Go into battle," he commanded them, seizing on this chance event. "It is the time for the final battle. At them! At them! I will catch their cannonballs in my sleeves!"[11]

The most fanatical of the elect were now so persuaded of their immunity to death that they needed no further prompting. They quickly convinced those who still held back to charge into battle against the Prince's army. The two armies confronted each other. The Prince, not having had a reply to his offer, ordered his cannons to fire. The peasants, more like the Midianites than Gideon's men, broke rank in panic and fled right into the Prince's cavalry. They were cut down in their thousands and the few who were left surrendered.

Müntzer escaped to Frankenhausen, but like Mühlhausen it had been defeated by the Prince. He was caught in a cellar, dragged out and tortured. On 27 May 1525 he was beheaded.

The fire Thomas Müntzer had begun raged even more fiercely after his death, touching all who came near it with the heat of religious fervour and, as it turned out, consuming many. Müntzer has been called "the father of Anabaptism".[12] He held to the central tenet of that group of radical Protestants, namely, that infant baptism was of no religious significance whatever. Only the baptism of an adult able to make a proper profession of his or her faith could be considered a sacrament. All Anabaptists, as the name implies, in order to become members of the sect, were re-baptized, or baptized "anew" as adults. In so doing they cut themselves off from Catholics and from other Protestants who believed in infant baptism as the signal initiation into the Church.

Müntzer's rebellion coincided with the growth and spread of

Anabaptism. It attracted what one historian has called "the disinherited classes of the time", the peasants, the poorer artisans and journeymen living in the towns, "to whose oppressed position, economically and politically, it powerfully appealed".[13]

The Anabaptists rejected all ceremony except such simple rituals as bread-breaking which symbolized the renewal of the covenant with God and the confirmation of brotherly love. A contemporary wrote of them: "They brake bread with one another as a sign of oneness and love, helped one another truly with precept, lending, borrowing, giving; taught that all things should be in common and called each other, 'Brother' ".[14] It was mainly for their attitude to the ownership in common of their worldly goods that they have been regarded as the first communists.

Bible reading was becoming more and more the concern of the day as translations began to come off the printing presses. And as people read so their dependence on the priests for interpretation weakened. Now they could see for themselves what God had said and what Christ had taught. Now they could go straight to the Bible without the intercession of the Church for what spiritual comfort and guidance they needed. It was Scripture not Church that was the final authority.

The Anabaptists steeped themselves in the Bible, both Old and New Testaments. They saw themselves not as part of the continuing history of the Church but as the direct descendants of the first Christians, like them a brotherhood of baptized believers, separate from the worldliness of the Church, indifferent to the affairs of State.[15]

The movement began in Zurich in about 1523; Müntzer's example and the general upheaval, economic and religious, of the times gave it impetus. It spread throughout the Netherlands and southern Germany, provoking the anger of the Church and the princes wherever it appeared. With the memory of Müntzer still fresh in their minds, they, the bishops and the princes, quickly brought all their power to bear on the Anabaptists. The Church objected to their rejection of the sacrament of infant baptism, to their belief in the transforming power of faith to bring each individual into direct oneness with God, to the freedom from sin and freedom to sin claimed as a right by each true believer. The State objected to their communism, to their pacifism, to their refusal to take oaths.

In 1525 persecution against the Anabaptists began, but it was not until 1527 when Archduke Ferdinand of Austria issued an imperial mandate condemning the movement and threatening death to its followers that the attack on them became systematic.[16] Wherever they appeared, they were struck down. "They are persecuted in many parts with great tyranny," wrote a chronicler. "They are cast into bonds and tormented with burning, with sword, with fire and water, and with much imprisonment, so that in a few years in many places a multitude of them have been undone."[17]

In Salzburg, for example, a woman and a beautiful young girl of sixteen were drowned by the hangman in the horsepond when they refused to recant. In other towns the members of the sect were forced into one of their meeting houses which was then locked and set on fire so that all perished within. In five years in the Tyrol and neighbouring territories about 1,000 Anabaptists were done to death. They were everywhere treated not as devout men and women of peace—which most of them were—but as common criminals. Those who gave them shelter were themselves punished.[18]

Leonard Schiemer who was beheaded at Rottenburg in 1528 soon after the start of the Austrian persecutions wrote a hymn in prison which revealed the true depth of their misery. In its tone and language it echoed the plaint of the exiled Jews of the Old Testament and of the books of the Apocrypha, and that of the early Christians of the New Testament.

Thine holy city they destroyed,
Thine altar overthrew they,
Of us alone Thy little flock
But few are still remaining.
Throughout the land, in shameful flight
Disgraced, they have expelled us.
Scattered are we like flocks of sheep
Without a shepherd near us.[19]

Thousands fled the Continent for England where they settled mainly in the south, in Kent and Essex. They hoped for peace and security but they hoped in vain. Henry VIII persecuted them —the first fourteen were burned in 1525. Mary and Elizabeth continued to harass and maltreat them though by Elizabeth's reign most of them had either dispersed or were practising their beliefs under different names.

Even the most peace-loving men oppressed by such unrelieved suffering may come to believe in meeting violence with violence. Along with their bread of brotherhood, the Anabaptists swallowed whole the apocalyptic view of the End of the World, that they, the elect, were to engage in a final violent struggle with the godless in order to win the kingdom of Heaven.

In their circumstances they needed little persuasion to swing from a wholly peaceful movement to one of armed rebellion. As their sufferings multiplied so their hostility to the State increased. Like the Jews of old, like their historical contemporaries, the Marranos of Spain and Portugal, they hoped anxiously for the man who would lead them to the victory which they felt they so richly deserved.

The Anabaptist, Melchior Hoffmann, proclaimed Strasbourg as the New Jerusalem and 1533 as the year of the Coming of Christ and the inauguration of the reign of the saints. Excitement mounted. Throughout the Netherlands, Friesland, Brabant and the Rhineland, wherever there were Anabaptists, expectation grew that the promised messiah was about to save them.

The year 1533 came and passed without any change in their circumstances except, perhaps, for the worse. In addition to their own particular problems there had occurred a series of natural disasters. A violent inflammatory fever known as the "sweating sickness" had raged unchecked; bad harvests in 1529 and in the following two years had created inflation—the price of bread had almost tripled in a year.[20] The time was ripe for a new dispensation, but as it had not taken place in Strasbourg as predicted, where would it occur, where would the New Jerusalem arise?

The answer was the city of Münster, the capital of Westphalia, a city of about 15,000 inhabitants, a member of the Hanseatic League, and an important ecclesiastical centre.[21]

Münster had gone Lutheran some years before. Its moderate municipal council viewed with growing concern the activities of the Anabaptists who were pouring in from neighbouring districts in response to the call from one of their principal activists, Bernard Rothmann. Rothmann was the kind of man necessary to successful messianic movements and without which they seldom reach more than a handful of adherents. He was a born propagandist. An intellectual who had studied at the University of Cologne, he understood how best to express the longings of the hounded and harried members of his sect. He had a large following in Münster and he grew bold enough to attack both the Catholics and the moderates. His main support came from a man who was soon to play an equally important rôle in the Münster affair, a draper by the name of Bernard Knipperdolling.

Rothmann's and Knipperdolling's attempts to stamp out all remaining vestiges of Catholicism in Münster came to the notice of the Prince-Bishop who was nominally the city's ruler. Bishop Francis von Waldeck tried to shut Münster off by closing all roads leading to it and by declaring it to be in a state of blockade. This only served to increase the activity of the Anabaptists both within and outside the city. Rothmann prohibited all fast days and preached against the baptism of infants; von Waldeck responded by bringing a decree against the Anabaptists. Civil war between the latter, the Lutherans and the Catholics was about to break out. The continual influx of Anabaptists increased the confusion. They were now beginning to outnumber the inhabitants. Hermann von Kerssenbroek, a hostile witness of the rise and fall of the Münster Anabaptists, wrote of the swift progress of "disorder and infidelity" in the city; "the idle, rogues, spendthrifts, thieves and ruined persons swelled the crowd of Evangelists".[22]

In the first week of January 1534 two men entered Münster, proclaiming that God had sent a new prophet on earth to herald the end of the present world and the beginning of the Millennium. The prophet they spoke of was Jan Matthyson, the leader of the Netherlands Anabaptist movement. These men were his disciples. They told the Münsterites that Matthyson had declared their city to be the New Jerusalem where the saints would reign in unity and brotherly love. Neither law nor Church authority would hold them back, but they would rule by divine guidance only.

Matthyson, a master-baker from Haarlem, had rejected the pacifism of the early Anabaptists in favour of violent revolution. He had seen Münster as the place best suited to his plans since, thanks to the efforts of Rothmann and Knipperdolling, it had already gone a long way towards achieving the goal he had in mind.

In the middle of January another important delegate from

the Anabaptist world slipped into Münster; he stayed at the house of Bernard Knipperdolling, which was the centre of all the revolutionary activity. The man was Jan Bockelson, a former tailor, former bankrupt merchant. But for his looks, which were strikingly handsome with flowing fair hair and beard, Bockelson was undistinguished. Life and the world had rejected him. He was the bastard son of a Leyden merchant and his peasant mistress, a woman from Münster. He had tried his hand at various trades without success and had travelled without much purpose about Europe. For four years he worked in London. Then he met Jan Matthyson and Anabaptism and his life changed. For the first time he found a place in the world and a meaning to his existence. He devoured all the devotional writings of the Anabaptists, especially those of Thomas Müntzer, the hero of the militants.

Bockelson knew his way about Münster; he had been there before, most recently in 1533. He waited for the arrival of his leader and in the meantime prepared the Münsterites, Rothmann and Knipperdolling in particular, for the new order.

All the leading Anabaptists who took part in the creation of the New Jerusalem of Münster were lovers of extravagant spectacle. They knew, too, how important spectacle and display were in attracting and inspiring adherents to the cause. When Jan Matthyson arrived in Münster he was accompanied by his beautiful wife who was, to add scandal to spectacle, an ex-nun. Dressed in flowing robes of a prophet and holding two stone tablets, he appeared in the market place to announce that he had spoken directly with God Who had appointed him His servant. "The Lord has ordained me to impart His will to you," he told the amazed spectators who had gathered in their hundreds to hear him. They had never seen anything quite like this before. (Within the next eighteen months they were to see many more amazing sights, some wondrous, some horrifying.)

"Here is my helpmate, Jan Bockelson," he continued, pointing to the tall, handsome man standing at his side, also dressed in robes and flowing mantle and carrying a staff in his hand. "He will instruct you in the pure and holy service of God as is proper to a Chosen People."[23]

The audience applauded enthusiastically, accepting without question the new prophets whom they saluted as Enoch and

Elijah, both—the latter particularly—being by tradition associated with the coming of the messiah.*

The movement had sufficient support. What it now needed was funds. The Anabaptists were asked to give what they had, and since one of their principal beliefs was the sharing in common of their worldly goods, they gave unstintingly. The women played the most prominent part, putting all their jewels, gold and valuables into the common fund.

As in almost all messianic movements of note the rôle of the women was a critical factor in determining its size and fervour. Whatever social and economic disadvantages their men suffered women have always suffered the additional disadvantage of being subservient to men. There was nothing lower in the social scale than a peasant, journeyman or unemployed craftsman except the wife of a peasant, journeyman or unemployed craftsman. Religion gave women comfort; the Church provided them with an outlet for their emotions; but in addition to these, messianic movements gave them power. The messiah who did not first appeal to the womenfolk had little chance of achieving any hold over the menfolk.

Matthyson and Bockelson—both tall, the first dark-haired, the second fair—were extremely attractive to women. Their arrival in Münster set alight the enthusiasm of the Münster wives and daughters that so far had been simmering beneath the surface. Von Kerssenbrock described scenes that, even allowing for exaggeration inspired by his hatred of the Anabaptists, leave one with a vivid picture of a city gone mad with religious ecstacy.

> The madness of the pagan bacchantes cannot have surpassed that of these women. It is impossible to imagine a more terrible, crazy, indecent and ridiculous exhibition than they made. . . . Some had their hair disordered, others ran about almost naked, without the least sense of shame; others again flung themselves on the ground with arms extended in the shape of a cross; then rose, clapped their hands, knelt down and cried, grinding their teeth, foaming at the mouth, beating their breasts, weeping, laughing, howling, and uttering the most strange, inarticulate sounds.[24]

* Cf. *Malachi* 4:5. "Behold, I will send you Elijah, the prophet before the coming of the great and dreadful day of the Lord."

Every day someone reported a new sight, sign or portent of great significance. A blind Scots beggar, tall and gaunt, found his way into Münster, dressed in rags and high-heeled boots. He claimed he had seen a vision in which the heavens fell down. Running about, proclaiming the total annihilation of the world, he fell into a dungheap, and when he picked himself up, he ceased prophesying.[25]

The event that almost caused a riot of the Münster women took place one morning in the market-place. On the gable of one of the patrician houses in the square stood a proud gilt weathercock of an unusual shape. The women had gathered below in the square as was now their daily practice, waiting for something new to happen. The rays of the sun caught the weathercock and caused it to blaze with a bright light. The women saw the illumination and assumed that the King of Zion himself had arrived. They ran about in a frenzy, but before their hysteria got the better of them, someone found the cause of the excitement, climbed the roof and "removed this new sort of majesty". "A calm at once succeeded to the uproar; ashamed and full of confusion, the visionaries dispersed and returned to their homes. Unfortunately," added von Kerssenbroek, "the lesson did not restore them to their senses."[26]

He reported fantastic orgies, "too horrible to describe" which were supposed to have taken place under the aegis of Jan Matthyson himself. A procession was held at carnival-time which was turned into a direct attack on Catholicism. The maskers, dressed as monks, nuns, priests, led the way, singing ribald songs. On the floats lewd scenes were enacted, caricaturing different Catholic practices, such as the last rites.[27]

The Catholics of Münster watched what was happening with terror. To them it was the work of the devil and they knew their days were numbered. The moderate Lutherans were unsure what to believe. By resisting were they defying God or Satan? Matthyson, Bockelson, Rothmann and Knipperdolling had no doubts. They realized their strength was growing and while outside the city Bishop von Waldeck prepared for war against the Anabaptists, they prepared to consolidate their position.

On 23 February 1534 the Anabaptists won the election for the Great Council of Münster and were now the supreme political authority. This signalled an all-out attack on the Catholics whose churches and religious houses, with their priceless treasures and manuscripts, were stormed and sacked. On one very cold morning at the end of the month all Catholics who had refused re-baptism were driven from the city. What for centuries their co-religionists had been doing to Jews and more recently to Protestants was now happening to them. Von Kerssenbroek described how the women carried their naked babies in their arms, trying vainly to find rags with which to cover them. Barefooted children clung to their fathers' coats, crying piercingly against the cold. Old people bent with age tottered along, falling by the way if there was no one to help them; and even women in labour were forced from their beds to collapse in the snow.[28]

Rothmann, the propagandist in chief, circulated a letter to Anabaptists outside the city. In it he proudly declared

> that the Heavenly Father hath sent unto us certain prophets who proclaim the pure word of God with the most marvellous gift of tongue and in the spirit of everlasting salvation! He who seeketh his salvation let him forsake all worldly goods, and let him with wife and with children come unto us here to the New Jerusalem, to Zion, to the Temple of Solomon. Besides the treasure in Heaven it shall be requited to him tenfold in money and goods for that which he hath left behind him![29]

In response to the call, and in spite of Bishop von Waldeck's mercenaries posted outside the walls, Anabaptists managed to get into the city, but it was daily becoming more difficult. Münster was slowly being cut off from the rest of the world. The New Jerusalem, the New Zion was under siege.

Matthyson and Bockelson virtually ran the city. Their power was unchallenged. When a soldier spoke slightingly of these prophets who "had the devil in their bodies", they both attacked him and almost killed him.[30] At Easter Matthyson called for a huge feast during which he stood up suddenly and, in the words of Jesus before his arrest, said, "Oh, dear Father, not as I will, but as Thou wilt". To the surprise of all he went about, kissing his friends on the lips and shaking their hands. The next day, accompanied by twenty men, he made a sortie on the troops encamped outside the walls. He was quickly surrounded and though he and his men fought bravely, they were all killed. Matthyson's head was cut off, placed on a pike, and displayed to the citizens who stared at it in dismay from the city walls.

Now came Bockelson's chance and he seized it with both hands. "God shall raise up unto us another prophet who shall be greater and higher than was even Jan Matthyson," he announced.[31] After a vision in which God revealed to him that Münster had to be governed by God's Own Constitution modelled on the Old Testament, Bockelson appointed twelve elders, corresponding to the Twelve Tribes of Israel, to assist him in running the city. Rothmann was appointed Chief Orator, Knipperdolling Chief Executioner.

Matthyson, during his rule, had gone some way towards creating a spirit of unity so necessary if the Anabaptists were to win their struggle. He had, for instance, insisted that all meals be taken in common, and at each gate out of the city a house was taken over for this purpose. During the meals a youth would be chosen to read passages from the Old Testament, especially chapters from the Prophets. The more the community of saints heard of the struggles and triumphs of the people of Israel, the more they came to identify with them until their reality and the reality of the Bible merged. They were not *like* the Chosen People; they *were* the Chosen People. They were the saints to whom God would send His messiah.

Belfort Bax, an historian of the movement, summed up their state of mind as follows:

> They . . . were the Chosen People who had come out of Babylon, renouncing the world, the flesh, and the devil, prepared to meet the messiah when he should descend from the clouds upon the earth to establish the millennial kingdom of which the Apocalypse spoke. . . . [Their beliefs] were to them certainties as real and living as the world surrounding them.[32]

Bockelson knew and understood this. His assumption of power released all the latent energy that had been stored up in him during his years as a nonentity and failure. He revealed not only a keen insight into people and the way they thought, but also a capacity for organization. Blessed with a striking appearance and a sense of the theatrical, he set about turning Münster into the New Jerusalem that had been promised to the faithful followers by his predecessor, Matthyson.

New laws were brought in which were restrictive and permissive at the same time. Polygamy and divorce were permitted, but a woman had to marry whoever chose her even if the man had another wife. The punishment for refusing was severe and might even be death if she persisted in her refusal. Many of the new laws dealt with moral behaviour; acts such as blasphemy and impurity which included seduction and adultery were punishable by death.

In obedience to the new regulations the elders took new wives. Jan Bockelson took three at first, later he had no fewer than sixteen. His chief wife was the beautiful widow of the previous leader, Matthyson. Bockelson's wives were all given numbers and each night, after dining with them, he would indicate his choice for bedmate by placing a peg in the appropriate hole on a numbered board.[33] According to von Kerssenbroek, men and women were permitted to behave like "foul and furious beasts", yet the law required they ate in modesty at different tables.

An abortive attempt by Bishop von Waldeck to seize the city created the mood of uncertainty and fear which enabled Bockelson to impose his absolute rule. The city's senate had already resigned; the twelve elders were his own appointees; nothing stood in his way. Bockelson had a new prophet, Jan Dusentscheuer, run into the streets crying, "Jan Bockelson of Leyden, the saint and prophet of God, must be king of the whole earth. His authority will extend over emperors, kings and princes, and all the powers of the world, and none shall rise above him. He will occupy the throne of his father, David, and will carry the sceptre till the Lord reclaims it from him."[34]

The elders were requested to hand over their power to Bockelson, and the sword of justice of which they had custody was passed to him as a symbol of the transference of authority. In true Old Testament fashion, Bockelson was anointed with oil and made thereby king of the New Zion. "That which I do," he told the assembled populace, "I must forsooth do, in that God hath appointed me thereto." There were a few mumbles of protest. Bockelson turned in anger to the dissenters. "Even were you all to oppose me, I should nevertheless become king of the whole earth, and my royalty which begins now in this spot will last for ever. But I tell you, dear brethren and sisters, I had rather tend swine or follow the plough than be king."[35]

The people accepted his rule completely. They bedecked him

with rich gifts. The goldsmith, Dusentscheuer, made two crowns for him, a gold chain, a gold sheath for his bejewelled sword, and diamond encrusted rings for the messiah and his queen. The finest mansion in the city was turned into his palace; the house next door was prepared for his queens with a connecting door between the two. The Divara had her own court and bodyguard who were dressed in chestnut brown and green. Scarlet and blue were the colours of the King.

Bockelson had an intuitive understanding of the realities of power, especially the kind which, as in his case, derived almost entirely from the strength of his personality and was not bolstered by a constitution of any kind. His power was absolute and total, based on his assumed rôle of messiah, but at any moment his messiahship could be replaced by another. Bernard Knipperdolling did try on one occasion to oust him. After being seized by a fit of hysteria during which he danced about the King's magnificent throne which stood in the market-place, Knipperdolling told Bockelson that he should be sitting on the throne "since it was I who made you what you are".[36] Bockelson flung the man off the platform and had him arrested. Once in the cold dungeon Knipperdolling saw the error of his ways. He apologized to Bockelson, saying he had been possessed by the Devil, and was welcomed back into the community.

While Bockelson lived in great splendour, the rest of the population were required to observe strictness in their mode of behaviour and their dress. An edict against extravagance in clothes was announced by the prophet, Dusentscheuer, after he had had a revelation from God that a man was allowed only one coat, two pairs of hose, two doublets and three shirts; a woman only one skirt, one mantle, four chemises. No one could possess more than one bed and four sheets. Extra possessions were taken into custody and all the horses of Münster were kept in Bockelson's stables.[37]

The Münster messiah did not neglect his faithful supporters but gave them a sense of sharing directly in the splendours of the New Jerusalem. He provided daily processions to the market-place where he sat on his throne, he in his scarlet and blue, his throne bedecked in gold and purple silk. In the procession he rode on a white horse which was splendidly caparisoned in the royal colours. Before him went a band and the Grand-Marshal with a white wand; behind him went two pages, one carrying a

Bible, the other a naked sword. Behind them rode his own bodyguard on the finest horses in Münster and behind them followed Rothmann, Knipperdolling and the rest of the makers of the Münster rebellion, their demotion in status obvious for all to see.

Throughout that glorious summer of 1534 the people of Münster lived and feasted in a style to which most of them were wholly unaccustomed. They ate their way through about 1,200 oxen in addition to other meat, fish, cheese, butter, and bread.[38] They danced almost nightly in the square and if von Kerssenbroek is to be believed they fornicated nightly, too. He gives no details, however, preferring to "draw a veil over what took place, for we should scandalize our readers were we to relate in detail the outrageous scenes of immorality which took place in the town, and the villanies which these maniacs committed to satisfy their abominable lusts".[39]

Three days a week Bockelson dispensed justice in the square, most of the cases being, according to the chronicler, exceedingly indecent, relating, as they did, to divorce and other matrimonial issues. Women who refused to acknowledge their husbands' new wives, young girls who refused to be taken into concubinage were severely dealt with. In one case at least the accused was executed by decapitation.[40]

Great feasts were organized for the populace and at these Bockelson and his queen presided, going from place to place, greeting and blessing the people. The most magnificent banquet took place in the market-square—now known to the inhabitants as Mount Zion—on 13 September 1534. A great throng gathered—1,700 men capable of bearing arms, 400 old men and children, and 5,000 women.[41] The messiah wore a scarlet tunic over which was draped a silver mantle; on his head the crown and in his right hand the gold sceptre. His queen and all his fifteen other wives accompanied him, and they were surrounded by 32 knights in splendid dress. The tables were arranged along the sides of the square under the trees. From noon till late the people consumed a vast quantity of food: boiled beef and roots, ham and vegetables, roast meat; thin round cakes of fine wheat flour were served from baskets. The Divara went about with a chalice of wine, offering it to the celebrants as a sacrament.[42]

When the people had finished, the messiah and his wives sat down to an even more elaborate dinner. At its conclusion he had brought before him a captured soldier, one of the Bishop's men, and he executed him on the spot. Then he announced those who were to be his appointed apostles and who were to go forth out of Münster and summon the faithful to assist the New Zion in its battle against the evil beyond the gates.

So long as the messiah reigned nothing of the old Münster was allowed to remain. All had to be new because this was the new era which the messiah had ushered in. Now only the future mattered. Street and gate names were changed; Sundays and fast days were abolished; the names of weekdays were replaced by the first seven letters of the alphabet. Money was abolished but commemorative medallions were struck, showing Bockelson's head surrounded by the legend: "The Word Was Made Flesh".

In Münster the New Jerusalem had descended from the clouds. In the world outside nothing had altered. The Bishop had made yet another attempt to take the town in August 1534 and had lost 48 of his leading men for his pains. In October he wrote to other princes for aid in his war against the messiah, and in December the Diet of Coblenz decided that the continuation of the Anabaptist kingdom of Münster posed a threat to everyone. As a result, the Prince-Bishop's already substantial force was enlarged by fresh troops: 300 horse soldiers, 3,000 infantry, and most important, an experienced general to take command of the conduct of the siege.[43]

Within the walls the messiah had wasted no time in preparing his defences, "with the zeal, energy and readiness which would have done credit to a veteran general", von Kerssenbroek admitted. "Never will I lay down my arms which I have taken up for the defence of the Gospel," Bockelson told the people of Münster. "Never in cowardly fashion will I surrender my capital; on the contrary, I know how to defend it, even to the last drop of my blood, if the honour of God requires it."[44] He remained to the end true to his word.

The women contributed as much to the defence of the city as the men. They carried stones and ammunition. They learnt how to shoot the cross-bow and how to prepare the lime and boiling pitch to pour down on the beseiging army.

The over-abundance of the previous summer gave way to severe shortages of food by the autumn and by the winter famine had set in. The feasts were a memory to sustain the Münsterites during their long fast which began in 1535. To celebrate the New

Year an edict of twenty-eight Articles was published which showed these "maniacs" of Münster to be nothing of the kind. Drunkenness, adultery and fornication were forbidden; duels were suppressed. All violence among the elect was prohibited and spoils captured from the enemy were to go into a common fund. Because of the shortage of men, an unmarried woman could choose from the community any man to be her guardian and protector, and if a man absented himself from his wife for more than three days without the leave of his commanding officer, she could take a new husband for herself.[45]

The world rejected the Anabaptists and their New Zion. Luther published an attack on them and so did his close associate, Philip Melanchthon, the Protestant theologian. Persecution against them increased wherever they could be found. The apostles whom Bockelson had sent out to preach their message were hunted down and executed. His own first wife, a faithful Anabaptist who had remained in Leyden, was drowned. In Amsterdam, 600 Anabaptists tried to seize the town hall but it was recaptured. The Bockelson-appointed "bishop" of the city was put to death.

The general in charge of Bishop von Waldeck's troops sent the Münsterites an ultimatum, offering terms in return for the voluntary surrender of the city. He received no answer. At Easter 1535 Bockelson withdrew from public view. For days he remained isolated while about him the people suffered terribly. Again, allowing for deliberate exaggeration, von Kerssenbroek's description makes chilling reading.

> Terrible maladies, the consequences of famine, aggravated the position of the inhabitants of the town; their flesh decomposed, they rotted living, their skin became livid, their lips retreated; their eyes, fixed and round, seemed ready to start out of their orbits; they wandered about, haggard, hideous, like mummies, and died by hundreds in the streets. The king, to prevent infection, had the bodies cast into large common ditches, whence the starving withdrew them furtively to devour them. Night and day the houses and streets re-echoed with tears, cries and moans; men, women, old men and children sank into the darkest despair.[46]

Still the Anabaptists would not surrender. Bockelson emerged after six days to announce: "The Father has laid on my shoulders the iniquities of the Israelites. I have been bowed down under their burden, and was well-nigh crushed beneath their weight. Now, by the Grace of the Lord, health has been restored to me, and you have been released from your sins."[47]

He exhorted his faithful to trust in God and to be patient, and his message went directly to their hearts. Murmurs of discontent were stilled and his people re-dedicated themselves to the struggle. Dissident voices were instantly silenced. Knipperdolling was said to have killed his own mistress when she was caught, trying to escape from the city.

For those who wished to leave, permission was given and some 900 went out through the gates, carrying what few possessions they were allowed to take with them. The Bishop's men, however, did not let them pass and so they stayed in no-man's land outside the walls. There, watched by both those they had abandoned and those they looked to for help, they were left for more than a month. They had no food and were forced to eat grass, bark and sand until they died in terrible convulsions. The Bishop cried when he heard of their plight but did nothing to ease it. Of the 900 only 200 were eventually able to enter the Bishop's camp. Ringleaders of the original revolt who were identified were instantly put to death.

The siege of Münster which had lasted over a year might have gone on until every Münsterite had died of starvation. Almost to a man the people were united behind Bockelson. He was their saviour; there was now no other. The world might have abandoned Münster but they held to the belief that God had not. They were still His Chosen People.

Then, late in June 1535, four men escaped from the city and went directly to von Waldeck. One was Heinrich Gresbeck, a citizen and guildsman, and later one of the Anabaptists's most hostile critics; another was a freelance, Jan Eck. In return for a promise of a free pardon, they gave von Waldeck a complete and detailed description of the city walls, its defences and its weakest points. They even drew a plan for him.

Midsummer's Eve, 24 June, was hot and sultry. An atmosphere of foreboding was in the air. No one knew what was happening outside the walls; sentries reported no unusual movements; but the feeling that something was about to take place persisted.

Life continued; people went about their business such as it

was in those restricted and confined conditions. Bockelson conducted his daily court hearings which had lately been the scene of some vicious acts of summary justice against suspected traitors. According to von Kerssenbroek a starving child of ten was hanged for stealing turnips; a soldier was decapitated who refused to convert to Anabaptism; a woman, too, was beheaded for spitting at a preacher.

Meanwhile the real traitors were preparing to lead a specially chosen force of 400 men into Münster through entrances known only to them. When evening came and the people retired to their homes, the Bishop's advance troops entered in secret and took up their positions about the city. Fighting broke out when they were discovered and from street to street the troops were pushed back. When it seemed that their efforts were doomed, the Bishop's freelances smashed down the defences and breached the walls.

Battle raged for the whole of the 25th. The Anabaptists, starving and weakened by privation though they were, defended their New Jerusalem with great courage. The Bishop's mercenaries, who were entitled to take loot but had to spare the leaders, plundered and pillaged and cut down everyone whether they were leaders or not until the streets reeked with blood. Loot to the value of 100,000 gold florins was captured and handed to the Bishop who, by agreement with his troops, kept half.

The messiah and two of his deputies were caught. No one is sure what happened to Bernard Rothmann, the chief prophet of the revolution. Some say he was killed, others that he escaped, but he was never heard of again. Knipperdolling was hidden by a woman but when her house was searched she betrayed him in return for her safety. Bockelson was trapped in a tower by some soldiers who taunted him, saying (in the manner of Jesus's tormentors) that if he was the saviour, why did he not save himself. A third leader, Krechting, the Chancellor of the Anabaptist government, was also captured alive. The three were brought to von Waldeck, and Bockelson's sword, crown and spurs were formally presented to him as the victor.

After the city had surrendered, the Bishop ordered a *Te Deum* to be sung in all the churches. All Anabaptist women, including Bockelson's wives, were forced to leave the city. His queen and Knipperdolling's wife were both executed in July. Work on the restoration of the city began. In November the Diet of Worms decreed that everything should be re-established as it had been before the rebellion. All property and privileges were returned to the Catholic clergy and Catholic worship was restored, which is one reason why Münster remains today a Catholic island in a Protestant sea.[48]

Von Waldeck and other churchmen were eager to engage the former messiah in theological debate. They found themselves evenly matched. "Art thou king?" the Bishop asked Bockelson. "Art thou bishop?" Bockelson replied. "Who hath given thee right and power over Münster?" "The Cathedral Chapter," answered the Bishop, "and that appointment was confirmed by the Emperor and the Pope." "Ah," said the messiah with satisfaction, "I have been called by God and His Prophets."[49]

The leaders spent six months in custody during which time they were exhibited in chains on horseback in neighbouring towns. On 12 January 1536 they were brought to Münster for the final gruesome act of the drama. Their trial took place on the 19th, a mere formality confirming their already presumed guilt. The sentence of death was passed on them by the city judge. Two days later a platform was erected in the main square on which was placed a large stake and iron collars. On the 22nd the executions were carried out with cruel deliberation. The three men were burnt with red hot pincers then stabbed with hot daggers after their tongues had been torn out.

Bockelson was the first to suffer. While Bishop von Waldeck and his friends watched from a window immediately opposite the scaffold, the executioners heated the pincers. The messiah was fettered in a collar of iron and bound to the stake. Von Kerssenbroek was a witness to what then occurred.

"The executioners seized the glowing pincers and gripped him in all fleshy and other parts of his body in such wise that the flame shot out and such a stench of roasting meat arose that those on the market could not bear it."[50]

Bockelson endured the torture without crying out. Only at the end did he break down and ask for pardon. At a sign from the Bishop, his tongue was torn out and his heart pierced with the burning dagger.

Knipperdolling was next. He tried first to beat his brains out against the stake and then to strangle himself with his collar rather than suffer the fate of his leader; but the executioner tied his head fast to the stake with a cord through his teeth. He and Krechting were then tortured and executed.

The remains of the Münster messiah and his two elders were placed in iron cages and hung up on the tower of the Church of St Lambert where only three years before Bernard Rothmann, the publicist of the militant Anabaptists, had triumphantly preached their message to the world.

CHAPTER NINE

A PROFUSION OF MESSIAHS

THE FIGHTING ANABAPTISTS were virtually annihilated in the downfall of Münster. The great suppression of all Anabaptism which followed the defeat of Jan Bockelson forced thousands to flee from Germany and the Netherlands to England. There, in that "green and pleasant land" they began in secret to build yet another New Jerusalem.

No longer were they led by militants. Their new messiahs were men of peace who preached love, not war, like Henry Niklaes or Nicholas who founded what came to be known as the Family of Love. He wrote: "In the House of Love men do not curse or swear; they do not destroy nor kill any. They use no outward swords or spears. They seek to destroy no flesh of men; but it is a fight of the cross and patience to the subduing of sin."[1]

Nicholas who was usually addressed only by his initials—H.N.—was born in Münster in 1501 or 1502. As a child he displayed remarkable powers of religious understanding and insight far beyond his years. At eight he said that religion was of little purpose unless it produced in the believer a state of godliness and righteousness. From nine onwards he had visions of great beauty and power and he regarded himself as being "invaded" by the divine spirit. "I am," he said, "a begodded person."[2]

Unlike some of his predecessors, H.N. was not a failure in the world at large. He conducted a successful mercantile business and was happily married. After 1530 his movements in Europe are not known, perhaps because, having apparently associated himself with the rebellious Thomas Müntzer who was killed in 1525, he felt himself in danger of persecution.[3] He studied the writings of Martin Luther but did not agree with them. His direction was more towards the kind of direct and unified relationship with God that the Anabaptists sought. He had a number of ecstatic experiences as a result of which he felt himself in union with the Almighty. H.N., he maintained, no longer stood for his name, but for *homo novus,* the new man. Like Jesus he was born again. Through H.N. the Light of God would break into the new age of the world.

A man of gentleness and endowed with a spirit of grace H.N. was no better loved by the non-believers than any other Anabaptist with whom he was associated. The name "Anabaptist" itself had become a term of abuse. Of H.N. and his followers, the Family of Love, it was written: "They will have this blasphemer, H.N. to be the Son of God, Christ, which was to come in the end of the world to judge the world, and say that the day of judgment is already come, and that H.N. judgeth the world now by his Doctrine".[4] Their "blasphemous beliefs" included some that were singularly advanced for their time: Christ was not God; the Day of Judgment was not in the life to come but in this life; and the joys of Heaven were to be found here on earth.[5]

The Father of the Family of Love was himself a disciple of David Georg or Joris, a Dutch messiah described as being "of a grave Countenance, free in his Behaviour, having a very long yellowish beard, sky-colour'd and sparkling eyes". He was "mild and affable in the midst of his Gravity, and went very neat in his apparel". He attracted a large following "and heaped up vast riches",[6] an accusation frequently levelled against messiahs.

Georg claimed that he was Christ and the messiah and that he was born of the Holy Ghost. He alone was to be worshipped and all sins committed against God the Father were to be forgiven. The only sins which were unforgivable either in this or the next world were those committed against the Holy Ghost, that is, against David Georg.

Georg also claimed that he was immortal but, we are told by a later writer, "his Immortality ended by his Death on the 2nd day of August 1556". His writings were examined by the authorities in Basle where he died and found to be seditious. His body was dug up and he and all his books were "committed by the Common Hangman to the Flames".[7]

Georg's and H.N.'s beliefs were brought to England by a Dutch joiner named Vitells who arrived in Colchester in 1555. By employing men who led a vagrant life such as weavers, basket-makers and musicians, he managed to recruit an army of agents to spread the new gospel. Anabaptism in this way gradually was replaced by Familism and this in turn gave rise to a number of different sects, each one under its own messiah, much like the Brethren of the Free Spirit three centuries before.

By the start of Elizabeth's reign in 1558 England was becoming a veritable temple of cults and messiahs. The Family of the Mount lived in what would now be called communes. They denied all prayers and the resurrection of the body. They said that there was no Heaven or Hell; heaven was when they laughed and were merry and hell was when they were in sorrow and pain. The Sensualists or Essentialists held that there was no such a thing as sin; God did everything in love, be it good or ill. The Libertines believed that the true word of God was not the Bible but the spirit and life of each individual believer.[8]

Most Familists were strictly ruled by elders and their young disciples sometimes known as "Adams". The elders were subject to the father of the Family who was looked upon by all as the Christ. Those who were not of the sect were the Antichrist, the wicked spirit, the Kingdom of Hell, and the Devil himself.[9]

Elements of thirteenth-century Free Spirit anarchy, especially the disavowal of conventional sexual morality, was once again a prominent feature of the new gospel, the one played up most by their enemies. Ephraim Pagitt, the most famous heresiographer, or sect hunter, of his day who treated every deflection from Calvinism as heresy, wrote: "The Familists talk of love, and being in love, and nothing but love; but their love turneth into lust". He even managed to dig up a scandal about H.N.

> Hen. Nicholas, as I finde written, had in his house three women apparelled alike; the one he affirmed to be his wife, the other his sister, the other his cosin; which cosin of his falling sick, and doubtfull of her life, confessed to her neighbours that H.N. had often abused her body, and made her believe that she would never dye. Complaint thereof being made to the Governor, he came to the house to have apprehended him; but he fled.[10]

So dangerous in Pagitt's view were these people to the wellbeing of the nation that he felt it necessary to provide his readers with a guide how to "discover" them. "They are at present so close and cunning that they carry themselves, being directed thereunto by their Mr H.N., that ye shall hardly find them out. They will profess to agree in all things with the Church of

England, and also with the Church of Rome." His advice was to ask the suspected Familists to call H.N. blasphemer and his doctrines blasphemous. "This they will hardly doe, unless they be not yet fully his Disciples."[11]

In addition to the sect and their particular messiah-leaders there were others during Elizabeth's reign who set themselves up as messiahs and who were not connected with any organized groups. One of the first of these was John Moore who in 1561 was whipped and imprisoned for saying that he was Christ. His companion, William Jeffrey, received similar treatment for claiming to be Saint Peter. A shoemaker from Essex, John White, said he was John the Baptist, and a minister from the same county proclaimed himself King of Kings and Lord of Lords, saying that he would lead the saints to Jerusalem. In 1587 one Miles Fry said he was the child of the Queen by God the Father.[12]

The Familists as a whole were treated severely by the ecclesiastical authorities, but the individual messiahs were regarded more as "brainsick" or "frantic",[13] much as Maimonides had treated the "false" messiahs of his day. This tendency to look upon messianism as madness grew and, as we shall see, became in time predominant. However, when a messiah expressed views that were interpreted as endangering the monarchy, the full weight and majesty of the law was brought to bear upon him.

Such was the fate of the unfortunate trio, Hacket, Coppinger and Ardington. Hacket was a man of no education; an ex-serving man who had gone bankrupt. Claiming the gift of prophecy and miracle-working, he stated he was Jesus Christ, King of the Earth and Christendom who would bring justice in the form of plagues on England unless there was an immediate change of ways as proposed by him. He had the reputation for being a man of terrible temper and was said to have bitten off and eaten the nose of an enemy.[14]

Coppinger and Ardington (sometimes also called Arthington) also suffered from social disadvantages. Coppinger was a younger brother and therefore could not share in his father's estate, and Ardington was in debt.[15] They met Hacket and were persuaded that he was the supreme Lord of the world. He appointed them both his prophets; Coppinger was the prophet of mercy who sealed with his ring the foreheads of those who submitted themselves to their order and became one of the elect. Ardington was the prophet of vengeance who denounced their enemies and consigned them to eternal damnation.

More bluster and boasting than action characterized Hacket's activities, but he managed to collect a following of "lads and young persons of the meaner sort".[16] Then came the crisis which marks all messianic movements, large and small, the confrontation with the authorities. In his case, this took place in Cheapside in the City of London. The prophets had first run on ahead shouting, "Christ Jesus is come with his fan in his hand to judge the earth".[17] A few days later, on 16 July 1591 Hacket and his two prophets "began to put in practice their communication from Heaven, and amongst others, denounced their judgment against the Lord Chancellor and the Bishop of Canterbury whom they called traitors to God and the realm".[18] Much worse than this, Hacket said that the Privy Council should be reconstituted and that Queen Elizabeth should forfeit her crown.[19]

His words caused a riot and all three were dragged from their cart and arrested. They were brought before the Lord Mayor but they refused to back down. "I am that I am," Hackett stated. "That I have said, I have said."[20]

The memory of Jan Bockelson, who had been dead almost 60 years, lingered in the minds of those in authority and it was thought by some that the trio were planning another armed rebellion such as occurred in Münster. Others, the majority, thought that they were "mere fanatics", but it was noted that the prophets had attracted the favourable attention of a number of people close to the Queen, such as Robert Devereux, Earl of Essex, and the Countess of Warwick.

> Though the prophets be but in the rank of mad men, it is thought the State must be satisfied, especially on the prophet of vengeance, because he has said the Queen is not to reign any longer because she rejected the petitions of the faithful and neglected the cause of God and His Church, for which she must be punished, though her soul shall be saved.[21]

The chronicler noted that Elizabeth was "more troubled with the matter than it is worth"[22] and she converted her concern into action. Hacket was tried and sentenced to death for treason, not heresy; Coppinger was sentenced to imprisonment. He is perhaps one of the first men on record to have gone on a hunger strike in gaol and starved himself to death.[23] Only Ardington recanted for which he was treated with the honour due to a man who had seen the errors of his ways. He was pensioned off by the Earl of Cumberland and until his death led a blameless life, writing many pious works.

Hacket believed till the last moment that God would save him. On the scaffold he cried out, "Oh thou God of Heaven, come down and save me, or else I'll rent Thy Throne asunder". His threat went unheeded and he was hanged.

The reign of James I was characterized by an absence of "false" messiahs, possibly because those years were relatively stable. Certainly they were more stable than those of Charles I's strife-ridden reign which, of course, ended with his execution and the setting up by Oliver Cromwell of the Commonwealth. This period was tense with messianic expectation. Seldom, if ever, in English history was there such an all-pervading feeling of change about to take place. The old world was coming to an end and a new world, anticipated with fear as well as hope, was about to be inaugurated. Historians have noted that there are times when men believe that they have "used up" the world, that the world is disintegrating. "This sensible decay of the universe, the corruption of plants or creatures or of the heavens themselves, is confirmed by the unresolved conflicts within man's mind."[24]

By the beginning of Charles's succession in 1625 the sense of decay was gradually being modified by the growing expectation of renewal. Men were searching for new ways to look at their world; the old ways having failed them. "Old" included institutions, beliefs and values that had been accepted as unchangeable and permanent. Messiahs often emerge in response to this desire for and expectation of change. In a totally non-intellectual way they reflect the wish to set history on its head and to start again. However, there are those who have a vested interest in the past and its institutions and who show no patience with anyone threatening their power. In 1612 Edward Wightman claimed to be Elijah, the messenger, who would prepare the way for the coming of the Lord. All educated people who knew their Bible, knew that the coming of the Lord would be followed by "a swift witness against those that oppress the hireling in his wages, the widow, and the fatherless" and that "all the proud and all that do wickedly" would burn up like stubble.[25] Wightman was quickly arrested and he died at the stake—the last Englishman to be burnt for heresy.

Richard Lane, a tailor, was hauled before the Star Chamber in October 1631 for claiming to be both God and man. "I hear you are a high Familist," the Bishop of London said, "and hold it to be lawful to equivocate." Lane denied this and denied also that he said he was like Christ. "Through Jesus Christ I think I am perfect," he said. But the subtle distinction was wasted on the court. Sir Henry Martin, one of the judges, moved that Lane be sent to Bridewell, a notorious prison, adding as an afterthought that by the time Lane was released he would be "lesse perfect".[26]

In 1636 a pamphlet was published bearing the title: *A True Discourse of the Two Infamous Upstart Prophets, Richard Farnham, Weaver of White-Chappell, and John Bull, Weaver of Saint Butolph's Algate, now Prisoners in Newgate and Bridewell.* Farnham and Bull had denied the charge of being "false" messiahs. Instead they claimed to be the two witnesses spoken of in chapter eleven of the *Book of Revelation*: "And I will give power unto my two witnesses, and they shall prophesy a thousand two hundred and threescore days, clothed in sackcloth". Farnham said that the Lord had given him the power of opening and shutting the Heavens. The Heavens were now shut and the seed sown in England would never be reaped or mowed. A judgment of pestilence, famine and the sword was coming. He would see it fulfilled and be preserved. Bull said he would be slain at Jerusalem, would rise again and reign as a priest.

Both of them believed they could command the clouds and rain and that, though they were but simple tradesmen who had never been to university, they could speak all tongues and languages. In Jerusalem, when they arrived there, they would speak in Hebrew to the patriarchs. They considered themselves invincible and whoever attacked them would find their own hate turned against them and their enemies would be their own executioners.

Full of biblical fervour, the two prophets were clapped in goal where they remained. In a series of pathetic petitions to Archbishop Laud and others, they revealed the sad fate of those whose reality differed from that of the majority. "Why am I being detained for so long?" Farnham pleaded. "I have been kept for a year without being questioned. Have you forgotten me? If I am a false prophet and a blasphemer and a seducer as most people think I am, then let the High Commissioner bring me to trial."[27]

Three months later, the first petition having been ignored, Farnham begged again for his liberty. "If you will not bring me to trial, then free me; leave me in Lone Lane near Whittington's Cat, where I was arrested. Then I had a house to put my head in; now my children are dispersed—the parish has two of them, a poor widow the rest."[28]

John Bull who was sentenced to hard labour in Bridewell beating hemp claimed that the work was destroying his weak body. "Please bring me to trial and deal with me," he pleaded.[29] Their petitions echo unanswered over the centuries.

One of the harshest and most unjust fates to befall any of the messiahs of the period was that suffered by a woman, Mary Gadbury, who was naïve and foolish enough to love a self-deluded poseur, William Franklin.

Franklin was born at Overton near Andover, a market-town in Hampshire. He went to London as an apprentice rope-maker then set up in business for himself in the same trade. He married and had three children. For sixteen years he lived in the London suburb of Stepney where he was generally regarded as "a civil man, diligent in his Calling, honest in his dealings, careful to provide for his Family". In religion he was "esteemed by the godly as an eminent Saint".[30]

Franklin suffered a number of crises in a very short time. Illness took off some of his family and he was also "visited with the pestilence". A surgeon bled him in 1646. At about the age of 40 he had the revelations and vision and he began to speak "with new tongue". He would "babble out words which neither himself or others were able to understand". Eventually he came to believe that he was God and Christ. He started beating his wife, denied that they were in fact married and that the children were his.

It was at this time that he was introduced to Mary Gadbury by a woman friend. Mary was about 30, married but deserted by her husband who had run off with their servant seven years before. She lived with her daughter in Watling Street, London, selling pins, laces, and other "trifles for Gentlewomen".

Franklin had an immediate effect upon Mary. He spoke quietly to her and though she could not fully understand what he was saying, his words held her. Within a day of meeting him she began to have ecstatic fits which, according to a later confession of hers, "would set her whole body in a trembling, and shake the bed where in she lay, and continue upon her some times from two o'clock at night to seven in the morning". She heard a voice saying: "It is the Lord; it is the Lord; behold Babylon is fallen!" and she saw a bright light and stars inside the curtains of her bed.

When she met Franklin again at her house, she confronted him. "Has God revealed to you that his Son shall reign in the person of a man?" To which Franklin replied: "I am that man". She laughed. "You don't look much like the crucified Christ."

"That was my old body," Franklin said. "Now I have a new body."

"You also have a wife and family," she reminded him.

"I married my wife in my old body," he explained, "which was conceived in sin. My marriage and my children are of that body. Now they mean no more to me than any woman or child."

Mary, husbandless for seven years, who had lived a blameless life, selling her wares and taking care of her daughter, was suddenly released from her inhibitions by the power of Franklin's attraction. She gave up all to follow him when he told her that it had been revealed to him that she was the woman set apart for him by God. From then on she called herself the Spouse of Christ, the Bride, the Lamb's Wife, and other similar epithets culled from the Bible.

Together they travelled to Franklin's birthplace in Hampshire since he had a revelation to go into the "Hill County", into the "Land of Ham" with his Chosen Spouse. In Andover they stayed for a month at the inn, the Sign of the Star and, as it was later stated at their trial, "they kept company one with another, and as husband and wife they lay in the same bed together".

Franklin went off to find more followers while Mary remained at the Star. Her visions and fits during which she appeared as a woman in labour attracted the curious from all around. Many were convinced by what they saw and formed a small sect. When Franklin returned he was hailed as the Son of God, the Christ, the messiah.

Complaints were brought against them, not about their religious beliefs but about their living together as man and wife.

They and a few followers were arrested and brought before the Justices at Winchester in January 1649. Franklin confessed almost straight away to all that he was charged with. Mary was made of sterner stuff. She believed that Franklin was the Christ who had been crucified in Jerusalem. Were you there? the justices asked. Yes, she replied, but added before they could laugh her into silence, because Jerusalem was everywhere.

Franklin was warned that he might have to spend a long time in prison unless he recanted. He apologized to the court for calling himself Christ and blamed the Devil. Mary appeared before the justices looking so radiant that they thought she had secretly applied cosmetics. One of them held up a candle to her face to examine her more closely. "I'm glad the glory of God doth shine so bright in my face and that you are forced to admit it," she told them.

The two were found guilty of adultery and sent up to London to serve their sentences. There the court was determined to make Mary confess to her sins. She was sentenced to Bridewell for a week and "having now suffered a little hardship and tasted somewhat of the smart of the whip" she began to falter in her convictions. Tearfully, she made a confession that she had been "deceived by the temptations of the Evil One, the Devil, in a sinful way, accompanying Franklin, a married man, and ascribing to him what is proper to Christ".

She further admitted travelling with Franklin, "but as a spiritual not as a carnal wife. As a fellow-feeler of his misery," she added. The court was convulsed with laughter. "Fellow-feeler! Yea, we think you companied him as a fellow-feeler indeed," said one of her judges amid the general hilarity.

The case of William and Mary had become something of a *cause célèbre* and they were visited in gaol by "great multitudes". Many were prepared to speak out in their favour and to plead for them because it was generally felt that they had been wronged and unjustly treated. This outcry helped William, but did not save Mary. He was given a light sentence; he had to remain in gaol until he gave good security for his behaviour—which meant he could be released at any time. Mary, however, was committed to Bridewell for another year.

The judge told her on sentencing her, "Your offence is much the greater of the two because you committed it under the cloak of religion. Bridewell is too good for such a lewd woman as yourself".

Like Farnham and Bull, Mary Gadbury petitioned the authorities to be released. "I am utterly undone," she said in her petition. "Out of charitable goodness please let me go." Her plea was refused. She had to serve out her sentence to the full and came out of prison a ruined woman.

CHAPTER TEN

SHAKING, RANTING AND QUAKING

Charles I of England was executed in January 1649. In March of the same year the congregation of a small English church was interrupted in its service by six soldiers who marched through the open door. One held a lantern, another four candles. The lantern-holder asked the congregation not to go. He had a message to deliver from God. The vicar refused to let him into the pulpit but permitted him to deliver his message outside in the church-yard. The people stayed to listen.

"The sabbath is abolished," he declared, putting out one of the lighted candles.

"Tithes are abolished. They are Jewish and ceremonial and a great burden to the Saints of God—a discouragement of industry and tillage." He snuffed out another candle.

"Ministers of the Church are abolished. They are anti-Christian and now no longer of use because Christ himself descends into the hearts of his Saints." Another candle went out.

As the fourth and last candle was put out he said, "Magistrates are abolished. They are tyrants and oppressors of the liberty of the Saints."

Then he took out a little Bible and showed it to the spectators. "The Old and the New Testaments are abolished, too. They contain beggarly rudiments, milk for babes. Now that Christ is in Glory amongst us, he imparts to his Saints a fuller measure of his Spirit than this can afford. I am therefore commanded to burn it before your eyes."

The soldier set the book alight. The stunned audience watched it burn. To some it must have seemed like the end of the world; to others like the beginning of a new and freer world. The events in the church-yard caused enough sensation even in those sensational times to be recorded in the annals of the period.[1]

To us the fact that the men who had made the gesture were

soldiers might come as a surprise but not to the people at the time. Cromwell's army was, as one historian put it, "the conscience incarnate of Puritan England!"[2] Around their campfires they did not argue about the best beer or boast of their conquests with women as soldiers usually do. They talked religion. To relax they did not drink and carouse; they went to prayer-meetings. "Merrie" England was dead. This was a time of great seriousness when dancing and sports were considered the work of the Devil. What people most liked to do was debate theology.[3]

Once again the language of the Books of *Daniel* and *Revelation* became common currency; their metaphors adapted to suit present circumstances. The Thirty Years War between Protestant and Catholic which had divided Europe ended the year before Charles's execution. Protestantism had survived the struggle. Charles, the tyrant, who had been married to a devoted Catholic, was dead. Did these events not mean the end of Rome, the fourth kingdom predicted by Daniel? Did they not signify the coming of the fifth kingdom established by the God of Heaven "which shall never be destroyed but which break and consume all the other kingdoms"?[4]

The soldiers of Cromwell believed fervently that this was so. It was in this evangelical spirit that they had fought against the armies of the king and defeated them. The tumults and tribulations were but the preparation for the coming of Christ's monarchy, the fifth monarchy when, as the Lantern Soldiers had declared in the church-yard, the Sabbath, tithes, ministers and magistrates would be abolished; the Bible, too. All would be new.

The Fifth Monarchy Men, named for their belief in the imminence of Christ's Coming, were only one of a number of sects that emerged from those prayer-meetings in the military camps. When the battles were over, they entered politics and were loud in their praises of Cromwell. The rule of weak and sinful men was over, they believed; the government of saints could begin.

In such an atmosphere messiahs were bound to appear. This was ideal weather for their nurturing and sudden growth: heavy skies raining down portents of troubles still to come; overheated air thick with biblical symbolism; occasional refreshing breezes of hope for a new world, for a paradise called Jerusalem where men would live and work in peace and harmony under

Christ's rule, a place to which all the exiled from God would return.

To lead them there, to that Jerusalem, came Thomas Tany, a goldsmith who, in the same momentous year of 1649, had a revelation in which he heard God command him to change his name to Theaurau John. He did not know until God had spoken to him that he was "a Jew of the Tribe of Reuben" and that he had been sent to lead the Jews out of their captivity to the Holy City "built in Glory, in her owne Land, even on her own foundation, as the Lord hath shown me".[5]

To that end he pitched his tents in Eltham, outside London, for himself and his disciples, none of whom were Jews since they were not yet permitted to live openly and practice as such in England. On each tent was a figure depicting one of the Twelve Tribes of Israel. The expedition did not get further than Lambeth. Tany, or Theaurau John, now came to believe that he was also the King of France. He and his people dug themselves in, prepared to defend themselves against all opposition. *The Weekly Intelligencer* warned sightseers not to venture to St George's Field where their tents were now pitched. "Take heed of him, for if you crosse him, he will so lay about him and rebuke you with his Monumentall sword that you had more need to fear him as an enemy than to honour him as an instructor."[6]

Tany's expedition came to an end in late December 1654 when in a sudden fit of rage or despair he burnt everything—tents, pistols and Bible. With that, like a puff of smoke from his own bonfire, he disappeared into history.

John Robins and his wife, Joan, also planned to lead their people back to Jerusalem, fed on a diet of dry bread, raw vegetables and water. They hoped to collect 144,000 followers, the figure given in *Revelation* as the number of the "redeemed". Their small community lived in Moorfields, in the City of London, worshipping Robins as no less than God and Joan—who was pregnant at the time—as the Virgin Mary about to give birth to Christ. They also saw Robins as Melchisedec, the King of Salem, the priest of the most high God, who appeared in the *Book of Genesis*[7] and who later became transformed under Christianity into a precursor of Christ: "Without father, without mother, without descent, having neither beginning of days, nor end of life; but made like unto the Son of God".[8]

In May 1651, the Robins community was raided and Robins,

his wife and ten of the elect were sent to Clerkenwell prison. An Oxford student visited them and spoke to them, recording his interviews in a pamphlet in which Robins was referred to as the *Shaker God.*[9] "Shaking" and "speaking with tongues" were beginning to make their appearance in the repertoire of ecstatic religious experiences.

Robins seems to have been the victim of his own followers' enthusiasm, not unusual in the relationship between messiahs and their people. He denied being God. "I am but a mortal creature as you are," he told the visiting student, "only I have received many revelations from the Holy Ghost and am inspired by the blessed Spirit." But his people insisted he was king, priest and prophet, all the traditional attributes of the messiah. "You *are* God," said one woman standing nearby in the prison cell. "She is damned," cried Robins. The woman fell down on her knees, trembling and shaking all over, "to the great astonishment of the spectators". She was unable to stand until Robins commanded her to.

Mr Alexander, the Oxford man, then asked Robins: "How have you power to cast down, and raise up, unless it be by some satanical art and abominable witchcraft?" To which Robins replied: "All Arts come from the Devil, but my power proceeds from inspiration of the Holy Ghost".[10]

Robins and Tany have sometimes been called Ranters, a general term loosely applied to a number of sects that shared views not very different from those of the Familists of the sixteenth century and the Brethren of the Free Spirit of the late Middle Ages. The Ranters also held that there was no such thing as sin. It was the duty of each man and woman to act immorally—to swear, to smoke tobacco which in the seventeenth century was regarded as the wicked stimulant that marijuana is today, or to fornicate freely—for the very purpose of proving their freedom from social restrictions. Swearing, smoking and nudity were ways in which "the better to see Christ by".[11] In pursuance of this objective, one Ranter, Abiezer Coppe, was supposed to have sworn non-stop in a pulpit for an hour.[12]

Ranters were also anti-intellectual. What was written in books was of no importance compared to the spirit of God that dwelt in man. "It is not safe to go to the Bible to see what others have spoken of and writ of the mind of God as to see what God speaks within me and to follow the doctrine and leadings of it in me," wrote Jacob Bauthemley, a leading Ranter.[13]

Robins and Tany shared this negative attitude towards intellectual achievements. Robins said that he was able to speak Hebrew, Greek and Latin but through inspiration not book-learning. In an extraordinary tract called *His Aurora in Tranlagorum* Tany wrote: "Take notice, scholars, I am not book-learned, but I am heart-knowledged by divine inspiration". The tract was written in a mixture of English, untutored Latin and Hebrew, and a language known only to Tany but which resembled a transcription of speech "with tongues".

> Doctors I am the Doctor I am in your method thus a man is, but one man I grant that, but that man of many compounds, you will not deny me this.... O this English OF doth all the mischief in the whole tongue . . . almo Bonoso almare regel ophronorico ab se sola amantur abo boano so on abscissere nos peco oet nedet almahos annah alujah haheli lo . . . the english of these five languages cited, and all composure inunionsunion . . ."[14]

Ranters appeared all over England, in the North Midlands, Leicestershire, Derbyshire, the Peak District, Lancashire, Cornwall, Gloucestershire, Wiltshire, and the south-east.[15] In 1650 Cromwell's tolerance of religious sectarianism came to an abrupt halt when he brought in the Blasphemy Act which was designed to stamp out Ranters and others who denied sin and "the necessity of civil and moral righteousness among men". It now became a crime to maintain oneself to be God or equal to God, or to hold the belief that adultery, drunkenness, swearing, theft and other common crimes were not shameful, wicked and sinful.[16]

In spite of the Act, the Ranters continued to meet in taverns where they carried on as usual with their drinking and smoking and loud dissertations to the disgust and bewilderment of the habitués who were not used to behaviour of that kind from men and women of the respectable middle-class and under the guise of religion. This disgust was reflected in a play called *The Joviall Crew, or, The Devil turn'd Ranter*[17] which appeared at about the same time as the Blasphemy Act. For the plot the playwright, Samuel Sheppard, went back to the thirteenth century, to the story of the husband who suspected his wife of belonging to a secret, orgiastic religious sect and tricked her into giving herself away.*

In *The Joviall Crew* there were two wives involved in the plot and the secret celebrants were Ranters not Brethren of the Free Spirit. Sheppard was clearly no friend of the Ranters. Their activities were seen to have nothing to do with religion but a good deal to do with sex and sin. All the men were portrayed as drunken, noisy and quarrelsome, all the women as whores.

> About, about, ye Joviall rout,
> Dance antick like Hob-gobblins;
> Drink and roar, and swear and whore,
> But yet no brawls or squobblings.

Judging from the verses, the play when acted must have been quite as lewd as any meeting of genuine Ranters, if not more so.

> All lie down, as in a swown,
> To have a pleasing Vision.
> And then rise with bared thighs,
> Who'd fear such sweet incision?

The women were even more obscene in their thoughts and behaviour than the men, their only concern being to fornicate as often as possible with as many as possible. A trio of Ranter women sing:

> 1. Come some man or other,
> And make me a mother.
> 2. Let no man fear to board me.
> 3. Come as many as will,
> I give 'em their fill,
> And thank 'em for that they afford me.

The two young wives tell their husbands, whom they consider impotent, that they are going to church to hear a lecture. With "a great Bible of Geneva print" and a notebook to take notes, they go off in high spirits. They have heard of the Ranters, that "rare society" that enjoys drinking, love and "amorous

* See chapter six.

deportments", and they are pleased to be initiated into the sect. The initiation takes place, accompanied by more song and dance.

By Goat's desires, and Monkies heat,
Spanish flies and stirring meat
We adopt these happy pair,
Of our liberties to share.

Their plans, however, come unstuck when the whole meeting is taken into custody. The wives are led off to Finsbury gaol where their husbands, tricking them into believing that they, too, are Ranters, get them to reveal their true activities. They strip their wives and force them to join the others who are being soundly whipped by the Beadle. The one husband, so incensed by what his wife has done, tells the Beadle to lash her well, promising to pay him for his efforts. Decent society is thereby avenged.

Though a deliberate distortion of Ranter behaviour and attitudes, Sheppard's play did contain some half-truths, the most significant of which was the importance of women in the sect. The historian, Christopher Hill, confirms this. "Women had played a prominent rôle in the heretical sects of the Middle Ages, and this tradition came to the surface again in revolutionary England. Sects allowed women to participate in church government, sometimes even to preach."[18]

A clique of such women was largely responsible for the downfall of one of England's most important messiahs, James Naylor. Naylor himself was no Ranter. With George Fox he was a founder of the Quaker movement. Long before the Quakers became the eminently respectable and worthy Society of Friends, they and the Ranters were not entirely dissimilar in many of their beliefs. They both held to the central doctrine that man is guided infallibly by the Holy Spirit within him, or what the Quakers termed the Inner Light. As has been remarked: "The Quakers were but the Ranters turned from a horrid profaneness and blasphemy to a life of extreme austerity."[19]

James Naylor, like John Robins, was a victim of his followers' enthusiasm. Had it not been for their insistence on his godliness and divinity, he would probably have played an even greater part in the creation and development of the Quaker movement since he was, by all accounts, better educated than, and in the early days just as popular as, George Fox. As things turned out, he was brought down by the women who claimed to love him, horribly punished, allowed to die virtually alone, and then to be forgotten for all but his "crimes".

Naylor was of medium height and had the good, healthy complexion of a farmer and of the son of a farmer. He dressed in simple fashion, his hat hanging over his brows. He was close shaven and had a short beard. His expression was usually melancholy and he wore his hair shoulder-length and parted in the middle to resemble the conventional image of Jesus.

A gentle man by nature, Naylor had, nevertheless, a distinguished record in the army. He joined up in 1643 at the age of 25, serving for seven years in the Foot Regiment under Thomas Fairfax, later Lord Fairfax, the commander-in-chief of the New Model Army which defeated Charles at Naseby in 1645. He was promoted to quartermaster in the Regiment of Horse, and was described by the commander of that regiment as "a man of very unblameable life and conversation".[20]

The army eventually proved too much for his health. Sick with tuberculosis, he returned in 1651 to his home, his wife and his three daughters. He took up farming again; his health improved. He also became a regular churchgoer and in the winter of the same year he met George Fox who taught him about the doctrine of the Inner Light which became the central belief in his canon.

One day, while ploughing in his field, and meditating on "the things of God", he believed he heard God's voice. The voice commanded him to go West, just as he was, in his old suit, without any money and without bidding farewell to his family. He obeyed and left the Yorkshire farmstead to take up Fox's cause. He preached all over the county, rapidly building up a following of his own and a position in the movement second only to Fox. Wherever he went men, and especially women, moved by his eloquent sermons, his serious but graceful demeanour, his melancholy expression which told of suffering and the understanding of the suffering of others, flocked to him to be converted to Quakerism. They fell at his feet, foaming at the mouth, writhing in the agonies of an intense religious experience. Strangers stared in amazement at these people who trembled and shook when their preacher spoke to them of the divinity within them. They called them "the quaking folk", the Quakers.

The authorities had no more time for them than for any other sect. As Cromwell's rule continued so the intolerance of his government increased. When in 1653 Cromwell took upon himself the title of Lord Protector, sects like the Fifth Monarchy Men no longer supported him. The Moses who was to establish the new order had simply become a dictator; the government of the saints was now the government of one fallible human being. As loud as the sectarians had been in their support of Cromwell at the beginning were they now in their condemnation of him. Hannah Trapnel, a Fifth Monarchy prophetess, collected huge crowds to hear her attacks on the government and when she was arrested and sent to prison, the crowds followed. They watched and talked to her about the sins of the ruler while she fasted for twelve days.

The Quakers were high on the list of enemies of public order and they were constantly being arrested. On two occasions Naylor was brought before the magistrates and imprisoned for trifling offences, once when he refused to remove his hat in court and again when he addressed the magistrate with the familiar "thou". An old law from Elizabeth's reign against "wandering persons", originally passed to restrict the numbers of beggars, was now revived to strike at preachers like Naylor who took to wandering around the country.

The law did not stop Naylor. He continued to move about, finally reaching London where he came into his own, ascending to the pinnacle of his fame. In this sensuous age only pop stars so rapidly command the same adulation from the public that popular preachers received in that serious age. Within weeks Naylor was known; within months he was famous. His appearance as a simple countryman belied his quick wit and polished manners. Women of society took to him immediately and he to them. He attracted so many new converts to Quakerism that the two ministers previously appointed to serve the city were withdrawn and he continued unaided.

It was soon seen that Naylor was "fitted" to London and that "a great love was begotten in many towards him". He became for the London Quakers the final authority on all religious matters. "Doth James say so?" asked one London Quaker about a dispute that had arisen, "nay, then it is the truth!"[21]

Some of the women who flocked to hear James wherever he spoke were thought to be Ranters at heart. They began to stir up trouble within the Quaker ranks; causing dissension and creating unpleasant scenes. This was bad but what was worse was that they acted in the name of Naylor. They put it about that James was more holy, more divine than any other man, that his sermons more than those of any other preacher were the words of God. George Fox soon got to hear of this and he wrote to Naylor, warning him against the women and against allowing them to raise him up over his fellow-preachers. "Plucke in thy horns," Fox said. "You are becoming a shelter for the unclean spirits."[22]

Martha Simmonds, a married woman eight years younger than James, was the leader of this schism and when she was attacked in letters by other members, calling her and her friends "goats rough and hairey", she turned to James for help. Naylor spent three days at her home with husband and wife, hoping to find a place where he could be alone to "weep and cry before the Lord".[23] He felt that the Inner Light which so far had guided him was being withdrawn under the influence of these followers and of his own ambitions. Whether this was a serious attempt to reject the temptations or not, it failed miserably. He came out of the experience even more at the mercy of Martha and her friends. "I gave myself wholly to be led by others," he later wrote, trying to explain and justify his acts.[24]

For all their apparent worldliness, many messiahs are actually quite naïve. Caught up with their equally naïve followers in the fervour which they themselves generate, they cease to be able to distinguish between expressions of love and hysterical hyperbole. Whereas most of them give themselves over immediately and completely to their followers and, indeed, become their own most faithful follower, James Naylor at least tried hard to stand aside from the excessive enthusiasm for as long as possible. The only trouble was that his followers, and Martha in particular, would not let him do so.

He left London for Bristol and was found by his friends there in a distressed condition. Obviously something was very wrong and it was not long before they found out what. Martha arrived and went straight to see him. She fell down at his feet, bowing and prostrating herself, to the bystanders' intense embarrassment, Naylor's most of all. He was taken inside the house where he was staying and Martha had to be restrained from following him. When eventually she broke away and rushed into the house, the

Quakers had temporarily to forego their pacifist principles in order to throw her out.

George Fox was the only man strong enough to save James from his disciples and from himself. Naylor went to visit him in Launceston gaol in Cornwall which had become a kind of "shrine" to which Quakers from all over the country made their pilgrimage. The authorities stopped them for this very reason, and in the swoop on pilgriming Quakers, James was arrested and sent to Exeter gaol. He was not sorry because at last he could be alone to think and meditate on what was happening to him.

Martha, in the meantime, was not idle. Having been thrown out of Bristol, she went to Fox. She got through the cordon and faced Fox in his prison cell, "so loathsome that few come out of it alive". "Your heart is rotten," she told him. "You must yield up your command to James Naylor."[25] Indifferent to Fox's uncomplimentary reply, she went immediately to Exeter.

Obviously Martha was a woman of indomitable strength of purpose. That she loved James Naylor seems to be without doubt, but her love was that of a spider for its mate which it later consumes. She had wholly persuaded herself that James Naylor was more than a mere man. She had also persuaded her London friends that this was so. She had been collecting letters from the London clique, including some from her own husband, and she brought these with her when she went to visit James in Exeter. The letters were all couched in dangerously extravagant terms: "Thou King of Israel and Son of the Most High", was how Mr Simmonds addressed James. Another called him, "Son of Zion, whose Mother is a Virgin, and whose truth is immortal".[26]

Naylor should have torn up the letters when Martha showed them to him as proof of what everyone was thinking, but he did not. This was his weakness. He loved the worship bestowed upon him. No other conclusion is possible. Every Quaker believed in the indwelling of God in man. That God should have dwelt in him, James Naylor, in greater proportion than in any other man was not impossible. If others believed it, might it not be so?

Martha left him in no doubt. In the prison cell she fell once again at his feet. She kissed his muddy shoes while he placed his hands on her head and blessed her. Better he should have cursed her because at that moment his fate was sealed. In a nearby cell, another Quaker, a young woman by the name of

Dorcas Erbury, had fallen into a stupor from which she could not be wakened. Naylor was called to see her. He laid hands on her and she instantly recovered. Any doubt that may have existed in his disciples' minds was now dispelled. James Naylor was the Christ!

News travelled fast, and as soon as Fox was released, he went to see Naylor in a last bid to turn him from his delusions of grandeur. Unfortunately Fox was only human and, whereas he was prepared to forgive his old friend, he could not bring himself to raise James to the level on which he had previously stood. Perhaps personal ambition motivated him; perhaps he was horrified by what had happened to James. They met, but instead of receiving Naylor with the kiss of friendship, Fox offered him his boot to kiss as a sign of abasement. Naylor fell back. He felt himself spurned. He refused to grovel to Fox, he who had been called "Christ" by his followers. The meeting came to an abrupt end.

By order of Cromwell himself, James and his disciples were released from gaol on 20 October 1656. Exactly who planned the next and most disastrous step in Naylor's career is not known though it bears the hallmark of Martha Simmonds's unhinged enthusiasm. The month of October had been unusually wet; the roads leading to Bristol were deep in mud. One cold morning, from that centre of English mysticism, Glastonbury, which has seen many a strange gathering, one of the strangest set out for Bristol.

In the middle of the small procession was a man on horseback. His head was bowed; his hands folded in front of him. His wide-brimmed Quaker's hat sat low on his forehead, almost covering his eyes. Two women walked on either side of the horse, leading it through the thick mud, their feet sinking into the deep ooze with each slow step. Before them went a young man, bare-headed in spite of the rain. Following up behind came two more men on horseback with a third woman riding pillion. They were all chanting quietly, making strange humming noises. All, that is, but the man on horseback, James Naylor. He seemed to share none of the jubilation of those with him. Trance-like he had withdrawn deep into himself, allowing himself to be led towards the Radcliffe Gate of Bristol City.

A crowd began to collect as they approached their destination. They watched, were serious; a few only jeered. They heard the humming noise from the procession grow louder and louder until, as the Gate came into view, it broke out into a triumphant shout:

"Holy, holy, holy, Lord God of Israel!"

The women, one of whom was Martha Simmonds, tore off their cloaks. They threw them down in front of the horse so that it could walk over them into the city. The crowd, by now large and excited, following the procession to a humble Quaker inn, the White Hart. There Naylor was helped down and led into the parlour to a large fire. He and his companions dried themselves off and sat quietly, waiting. Naylor still said nothing.

The magistrates had been informed and a messenger came, summonsing the group to the Guildhall. Naylor had by now recovered. The challenge of meeting the magistrates revived him. The examination was neither long nor harsh and the whole incident might have been put down to a temporary fit of madness but for one thing: Naylor's followers. They refused to be moved on the question of his divinity.

Dorcas Erbury, whom Naylor had "raised" in Exeter gaol and who was one of the three women in the procession, was cross-examined:

Magistrate: And is he the only begotten Son of God?
Dorcas: He is.
Magistrate: Do you know no other Jesus, the only begotten Son of God, but him?
Dorcas: He hath declar'd him to be the Son, and I know no other saviour but him.
Magistrate: Do you believe in James Naylor?
Dorcas: Yea, I do believe in him who thou callest so.
Magistrate: What name do you give him?
Dorcas: The Son of God.[27]

The magistrates wrote immediately to Parliament. They told of the blasphemous parody of Christ's entry into Jerusalem which had been enacted in the city, and of the followers of Naylor who believed he was a second messiah. They requested Parliament's advice how to deal with the matter which, because of the publicity given to it, was now becoming a matter of public importance. Parliament replied: Send him to us.

The fuss made about Naylor might have been motivated by

factors other than religious horror at what he had done.[28] Messiahs, as we have seen, were a-plenty and most of them, even Mary Gadbury, were treated with much greater leniency than Naylor. But they differed from Naylor in this one respect: they were individuals with only few adherents. Naylor, however, was still regarded as a Quaker and Quakerism was gaining adherents at a rate rapid enough to worry the authorities.

While the country buzzed with talk about the extraordinary event that had taken place in Bristol, 55 Members of Parliament were chosen to consider Naylor's case. He appeared before them in London and answered their questions with such wisdom, meekness and clarity that all but some who were violently opposed to him "were strangely astonished and satisfied with his answers".[29] His guilt was presumed before his trial but the question still remained how to proceed with it. Thomas Carlyle in his biography of Cromwell described what he called the "James Naylor Parliament" when his case was debated as follows: "Shall we hang him, shall we whip him . . . shall we roast or boil or stew him? Shall we put the question whether this question shall be put? debate whether this shall be debated?—in Heaven's name, what shall we do with him, the terrific Phenomenon of Naylor?"[30]

Beneath the great timber roof of Westminster Hall, the scene of the trials of Sir Thomas More and Charles I, James Naylor finally confronted his judges in November 1656. The stuporific trance in which he had lived through much of the past events was now altogether replaced by his intense intellectual energy. He was determined to yield nothing as the record shows:[31]

"Art thou the Son of God?" they asked him.

"I am the Son of God but I have many brethren."

"Art thou the prophet of the Most High?"

"Thou hast said, I am a prophet."

"Was thy birth mortal or immortal?"

"Not according to the natural birth, but according to the spiritual birth, born of the immortal seed."

"Who was thy mother? Was she a virgin?"

"Nay, according to the natural birth."

"Who is thy mother according to thy spiritual birth?"

"No carnal creature."

"How dost thou provide for a livelihood?"

"As do the lilies without care, being maintained by my Father."

"Whom dost thou callest thy Father?"

"He whom thou callest God."

"What business hadst thou at Bristol?"

"I was guided and directed by God."

Quoting from a letter addressed to him, they asked: "Art thou the unspotted Lamb of God, that taketh away the sins of the world?"

"Were I not a lamb," came back the answer, "wolves would not seek to devour me."

"Art thou not guilty of horrid blasphemy, by thy own words?"

"Who made thee judge over them?"

They did not answer; instead they asked him what was meant when his entourage had cried out, Holy, holy, holy.

"Let them answer for themselves," Naylor said. "They are of age."

Unfortunately for James, they did. With none of his debating skill and certainly none of the subtlety of his religious understanding they spoke out for him, condemning him with every word. Martha Simmonds said: "He is a perfect man; he is the Prince of Peace. I ought to worship him on my knees. He is the Son of Righteousness. James Naylor," she declared, "will be Jesus when the new life is born unto him."[32]

Dorcas Erbury repeated for the judges what she had told the magistrates in Bristol. "He is the holy Lord of Israel. I know no other Saviour. He raised me. He laid his hand on my head, after I had been dead two days, and said, Dorcas, arise, and I arose, and live as thou seest."[33]

Naylor was found guilty of horrid blasphemy, of being a grand imposter and a seducer of the people. Now the question of his punishment had to be decided upon and once again the debate was lengthy and impassioned. Many called for his death, but not all were against him; a few had even taken an interest in the Quaker doctrine of the Inner Light. "If you hang every man that says Christ is in you the hope of Glory," said one, "you will hang a good many."[34]

By a narrow margin of fourteen votes, Naylor was allowed to live. Some said he should be sent into exile in the Isle of Scilly or the plantations in the West Indies, but the majority felt that a more painful punishment was called for since he had cheated death. The Speaker pronounced his sentence. He was to be whipped by the hangman through the streets from Westminster to Old Exchange where he was to be pilloried for two hours, wearing a paper inscribed with his crimes. His tongue was to be bored through with a hot iron and his forehead branded with the letter "B" for blasphemer. Not satisfied with that, the court further decreed that Naylor was to be sent to Bristol, to ride through the streets seated backward on a horse and once more to be whipped publicly. He was then to be returned to London to serve a term of imprisonment with hard labour in Bridewell until Parliament decided to release him. His imprisonment was to be made as unpleasant as possible: a bare cold cell, solitary confinement, and nothing with which to write.

In sentencing him, the Speaker said, "In your sentence, judgment is mixed with mercy. We desire not your destruction but your reformation." Which moved a Quaker to write an open letter, saying "whether such Mercy be not Cruelty, let all Men judge that have Reason".[35]

Men did judge and a good many found in favour of Naylor. Petitions were quickly got up and presented to Parliament but they were all ignored. Naylor's women were sent back to their own counties to serve their sentences of imprisonment with hard labour while Naylor was prepared for the show.

Naked to the waist with a white cap stuck on his head, he was tied to a cart in such a way that the horses could tread on him. Through the cold November streets he was led, besmattered with mud, to the Old Exchange, the hangman applying the whip with deadly accuracy. "Not a space bigger than the breadth of a man's nail was free from stripes," a witness recorded.[36]

A week intervened before the next part of the sentence was to be carried out so that the "horrid blasphemer", the "grand impostor and seducer of the people" could all the better contemplate what he had done and what was still to come. Petitions continued to arrive at Parliament; five of the country's leading churchmen, including Cromwell's own chaplain, came to the prison to make Naylor repent.

"Why did you let those women worship you?" they asked.

To the last Naylor refused to betray Martha Simmonds or her companions. He replied:

"If they beheld the power of Christ wherever it is, and bow to it, I have nothing by which I may resist that or gainsay it."

Nine days later Naylor's tongue was burnt through with a hole the size of a pipestem and his forehead was branded with the "B". One friend remained faithfully at his side all through his punishment and he licked the martyr's forehead, sweating and swollen with the heat of the branding-iron, as the silent crowd looked on. He went with him to Bristol where the further sentence of whipping was carried out, only here, because of the high feelings running in Naylor's favour, the whip was applied lightly.

In Bridewell, Naylor's wife, whom he had abandoned six years before and yet who petitioned for his release, came to visit him. She was horrified by what she saw. The dank cold cell, the silence of all but his warders, his solitariness were destroying his health, already considerably weakened by his terrible punishment. Yet he refused to recant. Only to the Quakers was he prepared to admit his errors and to ask their forgiveness which was now freely given.

Naylor was released in 1659 after Richard Cromwell's abdication, and he went to Bristol to make a voluntary confession. He and George Fox were reconciled and Naylor was permitted to preach once again. The London crowds still went to see him, but he was ill and he knew he had not much longer to live. In October 1660 he left London on foot for the last time to see his wife and children. He managed to travel only about 60 miles when he collapsed. He was found and taken to the house of a Quaker where he died shortly afterwards. He was buried on 21 October 1660. Martha Simmonds who had served penal servitude with hard labour followed her beloved James to the grave five years later.

Naylor's last recorded words admirably summed up not only his own life and mission but that of many a messiah: "I have fellowship therein with them who live in Dens and desolate places in the earth . . ."[37]

CHAPTER ELEVEN

SABBATAI ZEVI

THE NEWS REACHING Smyrna from Poland early in 1648 was very serious. Bogdan Chmielnicki, the Hetman or Chief of the Ukraine Cossacks, had launched successful attacks on the Polish army. Chmielnicki was a wealthy landowner's son who, it was said, lost his only love and his estate to his rival and in disappointment joined the rebels in their uprising against the Polish landlords.[1] The Cossacks were renowned for their ferociousness and their new Hetman who had organized the disparate groups so effectively was notoriously cruel even for a Cossack. Many in the Ukraine shivered while they waited the outcome of his war against the landowners who were supported by the Polish army, but those with most cause to worry were the Jews.

Until the seventeenth century the Jews of Poland had lived in comparative security. They were allowed by the landlords a certain degree of autonomy in return for which they were employed in some of the landlords' least pleasant tasks such as overseeing the peasants, administering estates in their owners' absence, and collecting taxes from the peasants for everything from births and baptisms to burials. The Polish landlords who imposed the taxes were usually out of reach as far as the oppressed and angry peasants were concerned, but not the Jews. The Jews could be attacked with ease and impunity, and when Chmielnicki's Cossacks began their offensive on the Polish army, the signal was given for one of the most terrible massacres of Jews in their long and bloody history. The estates of the Pans, or overlords, were attacked and destroyed and the Jews with them. Not satisfied with this, the rebels moved into the towns and villages and tore the small communities to shreds.

Those Jews who could not escape, join the Polish army, or convert to Catholicism were killed or sold into slavery. The lucky ones died quickly, by sword or beneath the hooves of the horses as they lay spread out in the streets on the Holy Scrolls plundered from the synagogues. The others died horribly; some were skinned alive and their flesh thrown to dogs. Some had their hands and their feet chopped off and were left to bleed to death. Some were buried alive. Children were slaughtered in their mother's laps. Pregnant women were sliced open and their babies torn from them and thrown in their faces. Cats were then sown into the bellies and the victims' hands were lopped off so that they could not tear at their wounds and release the animals. The Scrolls of the Law were used to make boots and shoes and the sacred books paved the streets. Women and girls were raped before their husbands and fathers. Many drowned themselves to escape being forced into marriage.[2]

One young girl found a desperate way to escape from her Cossack husband. She told him that she had magic powers that made her immune to any weapon. If her new husband did not believe her, he could strike her with his sword and see for himself. The Cossack struck and she died.[3] On 10 June 1648 the town of Nemirow was attacked. The Jews hid in the fortress for protection. A message came that the army was Polish, sent to save them. They opened the gates and the Cossacks rushed in with the townspeople close behind, wielding their swords, spears, scythes and clubs. The slaughter was terrible.[4]

Tens of thousands perished in the Chmielnicki pogroms; contemporary chronicles numbered the dead in excess of 100,000. Three hundred communities were completely wiped out.[5] To mark the catastrophe, the rabbis ordered a three-year period of mourning for all Jewish communities. For a year Jews were not permitted to wear elaborate clothes or ornaments, and no music was to be played at their weddings.[6]

Those who were fortunate enough to escape scattered all over Europe. Many fled to the Turkish empire, especially to the prosperous cities of Smyrna (Ismir) and Salonika. They brought with them, among the rags and tatters of their previous life, a treasure that not all the Cossacks in the world could steal from them, the Kabbalah. They found in the Turkish communities a love for the Kabbalah as deep as their own.

Kabbalah spoke to the homeless. Kabbalah spoke to those seeking redemption, personal, national and universal. Kabbalah spoke of exile which was spiritual death, of repentance and spiritual rebirth. Kabbalah spoke of the glorious union with God that would follow repentance when the exiles of the world would be gathered together and restored to their original home. Kabbalah spoke of "tikkun", of mending, of repairing the world's blemishes. It spoke of rebirth and of the time when man would cease to be alone, cut off from God and from his fellow-man. Kabbalah looked forward to the messiah whose coming would mark the end of the process of rebirth and the beginning of the new world.

The word "Kabbalah" means in Hebrew "the receiving of tradition", and referred to the teachings which the first Kabbalists had "received", either by personal revelation or through the traditional sources of the Bible and the commentaries thereon. It was in Spain that it had first come into prominence in Jewish thinking. Before that it had been the work of a small and obscure group of rabbis living in the Provence district of southern France. From there it had moved to northern Spain where in the thirteenth century it established itself. When these Spanish communities were driven out of existence in 1492, the Kabbalah travelled with the exiles to its new home in Safed, a small Palestinian city in the mountainous Galilee. There in the hands of devoted rabbis the great themes of Exile and Return first enunciated by the prophets after the fall of the first Temple in Jerusalem were once again brought to the fore. Kabbalistic speculation became a way of interpreting the relationship between Israel and God, between God and man, a way of explaining how Israel and mankind came to be exiled from God. It promised a reconciliation with God with every individual participating in the process. It promised rebirth and hope. It promised the messiah.[7]

"At the moment of the appearance of the messiah, Son of David, many signs and wonders will be made manifest and many miracles will take place," said Rabbi ben Jochai to his pupils as recorded in the *Zohar*, or *Book of Splendour*. A column of fire would appear to the whole world and the messiah would declare war on the world. Many nations would submit to him but many would do battle against him. Finally the Righteous would place a crown on his head and a belt around his waist made up of the letters of the Holy Name. A voice would be heard from the Garden of Eden, calling upon the saints in Heaven to witness the marriage of the messiah and his heavenly bride. The holy saints led by Moses, with Abraham on his right hand, Isaac on his left and Jacob in front of him, would dance for joy at the head of the Righteous in the Garden of Eden.[8]

Because of the universal appeal of its messianic message of hope, the Kabbalah spread out from Safed to Italy, the Orient, Germany and Poland. It was also taken up with great enthusiasm by Christians and as far back as 1601 an English clergyman could wrongly associate Kabbalism with Familism.[9] Christians hoped that by reinterpreting the *Zohar* as a promise of the coming of Christ (as they had done the Old Testament) they would convert the Jews to Christianity, but they were captured by the beauty of its visions and the complexities of its mysticism, and the converters were themselves converted. The strongly pro-Jewish mood that was so apparent in England in the seventeenth century and resulted in the unofficial readmission of Jews to the country can be attributed in part to the influence of the Kabbalah.

By the mid-seventeenth century the Kabbalah had entirely permeated Jewish thinking though it was by no means accepted by all. Indeed some rabbis regarded it as a kind of lunacy. "Many of the masses of the people pounce upon the study of the Kabbalah," wrote a Polish commentator. "Even ordinary burghers who cannot distinguish between their right hand and their left, who walk in darkness and who cannot explain a simple Talmudic argument or a section of the Bible rush to study Kabbalah."[10]

Since the Chmielnicki massacres in Poland the Kabbalah was read with even greater avidity. The "birth pangs" of the messiah were there to be seen in the frightened eyes of the new exiles who had witnessed such horrible sights in the streets of Polish towns and villages. Surely the time was nearly ripe for the messiah to come. The Kabbalah had said that all mankind was in exile since the very beginning of creation and that the task of restoring the world to its proper place in relationship with God was given to the Jewish people whose fate symbolized the fate of the universe at large. The Polish exiles, steeped in these beliefs, and their new comrades in the Turkish communities could now see themselves in the forefront of a great and awe-inspiring task which the Kabbalah had set for them. They could hasten the coming of the messiah whose appearance would mark the end of "tikkun", the process of universal "healing" or restoration.

In 1648, the year of the Chmielnicki pogroms, Sabbatai Zevi was a young man of 22 whose upbringing and personality inclined him to take all this excited talk of the coming of the messiah with great seriousness. His father, Mordechai Zevi, was a wealthy Smyrna merchant who had started off as a humble poultryman but who, in the economic boom which had developed in Smyrna in the first half of the seventeenth century, founded a very successful agency for Dutch and English traders. Mordechai had spoilt his youngest son and given him the best Jewish education possible. Rabbis, learned in the Talmud and the Kabbalah, had come to the house to teach the young boy who had shown signs of remarkable swiftness of comprehension.

Despite his father's indulgence, Sabbatai Zevi leaned more towards his mother whom he adored. He was a quiet boy and he shunned the wild play of other children in order to dwell on the mysteries of the religious books. As he grew older, he came to believe that his destiny was different from that of everyone else, that in some way he had been marked out by God to perform great deeds.

As the Kabbalists of Safed had taught, each man was capable of helping in the bringing about of the messianic age provided he lived a pure and sinless life. This meant prayer and fasts and ritual ablutions to purify body and soul. Sabbatai followed the precepts of his holy teachers in his own peculiar way. He lived a life of strict ascetism. He fasted frequently and for six years, between 1642 and 1648, he virtually cut himself off from the rest of the world. A marriage had been arranged for him but this was never consummated and it ended in divorce. A second marriage went the same way for the same reason.

Sabbatai was given to having fits of great elation followed by periods of deep depression with long normal periods in between. Today he would have been said to have suffered from manic-depressive psychosis, but in the seventeenth century he was regarded by many as half-mad, half-fool. His withdrawal from society, his failure as a husband, his long fasts and all-night prayer sessions were looked upon as the actions of a man whose mind had been turned by too much study. This belief grew when in 1648, at the time of the Polish tragedy, he suddenly did something which all orthodox Jews regarded as the height of insanity. Having heard of the terrible massacres, he went about telling his friends that he was the messiah sent to lead his people back to the Holy Land. Worse than this, he stood up in the synagogue to announce in his powerful voice the Ineffable Name of God, the sacred word all Jews were prohibited to speak.

The community was horrified but some were impressed by his

strange behaviour. It was said that in the hubbub following his pronouncement of the Holy Name, someone in the congregation whispered, "Messiah?"

Sabbatai, though not particularly striking-looking, was of pleasant appearance and when he was behaving normally was a man of great charm. His musical voice delighted his listeners. It was not long after this incident that he began to collect a small following who did not laugh at his strange acts but treated them rather as signs of special significance. They called them his moments of "illumination", or of "fall" when God's face was turned from him. In time to come their explanation was incorporated into the theology of the movement.

To the Jews of Smyrna, however, Sabbatai's behaviour was blasphemous and intolerable and they eventually banished him in 1651. He travelled through Greece, stopping for a time in Salonika, "the Jerusalem of the Balkans" as it was called because more Jews lived there than either Greeks or Turks.[11] On the Jewish sabbath the whole city came to a halt. Many of these Jews were the descendants of the Marranos from Spain and Portugal who had looked to David Reubeni and Solomon Molcho as the messiah and who were still deeply marked by the apostasy and exile of their ancestors. When Sabbatai came among them and spoke to them, they listened and sensed that his message of universal restoration taken from the Kabbalah was specifically meant for them. During one of his fits he walked about holding a basket with a fish in it, and to those who asked he explained that the fish represented the Zodiacal sign of Pisces, under which the Jews would be released from bondage. On another occasion he arranged a sumptuous feast to which he invited the rabbis of Salonika. While they were eating and drinking, he stood up and took a Scroll of the Law into his arms, bearing it to a marriage canopy that had been erected beforehand. This ritual "marriage" of Sabbatai, the messiah, to his bride, the Torah, mentioned in the Kabbalah, shocked the rabbis and he was expelled from the city.

Sabbatai, in his normal periods, was terrified by the acts committed during his manic state. As a future member of his sect wrote in 1665, "he is pursued by a sense of depression which leaves him no quiet moment".[12] He sought for assistance to rid himself of the "demons" which were plaguing him. In Constantinople he went to a Practical Kabbalist to learn of ways to cure himself, but in vain. His behaviour got him into trouble again and he was ordered from Constantinople after publicly declaring all the Ten Commandments to be abolished and pronouncing a prayer to "Him, who allows the forbidden".[13]

He returned to his own city of Smyrna and remained there until 1662. Then he decided to settle in Jerusalem. By this time he had collected a devoted following who travelled with him wherever he went. He never worked, but his brothers supported him in comfort and he gave alms freely to all who asked. His generosity as well as his charm brought him more disciples. He is described by one during this period of his life as "tall as a cedar of Lebanon, his fresh, brown-complexioned face framed by a black beard radiated beauty, and with his princely garments and proud bearing he was a magnificent figure to behold".[14]

One day while walking in the streets of Jerusalem, he was seen by a young man named Nathan, or to give him his full name, Abraham Nathan ben Elisha Hayyim Ashkenazi. He was the son of a rabbinical scholar and was himself a brilliant student of the Bible, happily and comfortably married to the daughter of a wealthy merchant in Gaza. Whether young Nathan actually met Sabbatai and spoke to him is not known for certain, but he saw him, and this was to have enormous importance for both of them within the next few years.

On the occasion of both his divorces, Sabbatai had said that neither of his wives had been sent to him by God and that he was still awaiting the right woman to be his chosen bride. Unbeknown to him, she was about to come into his life. So many stories have been told of the marriage of Sabbatai to Sarah that it is impossible to separate fact from fiction; even the facts that are known tend to read like fiction. Sarah was a Polish girl, a victim of the Chmielnicki catastrophe. According to the story she gave of herself, she had been caught and put into a convent at the age of six and had later escaped to join her brother in Amsterdam. Either before or after joining him, she learnt that she was not a Catholic but a Jew and she converted back to her original religion. She left her brother to travel around Europe, by all accounts leading a life of sexual abandon. This did not prevent her from declaring to one and all that she was to be the destined bride of the messiah.

Sexuality and messianism are related both in theory and practice. In Judaism and in Christianity the connection between God and the world, between God and Israel, between the messiah and his people, between Christ and his Church, have frequently been expressed in sexual terms. The *Song of Solomon*, a favourite of Sabbatai and his disciples, has been variously interpreted as an extended metaphor for all these spiritual relationships, yet few love poems are as heavily charged with eroticism.

> A garden inclosed is my sister, my spouse. Let my beloved come into his garden, and eat his pleasant fruits. I am come into my garden, my sister, my spouse. I have put off my coat. My beloved put in his hand by the hole of the door, and my bowels moved for him. I rose up to open to my beloved, I opened to my beloved; but my beloved had withdrawn himself, and was gone. I charge you, O daughters of Jerusalem, if you find my beloved, that ye tell him, that I am sick of love.[15]

Sabbatai and separately Sarah, too, may well have been influenced by these Biblical passages, and they contrived to meet. It is not known who made the first approach, but legend has it that the messiah-to-be heard of the beautiful Polish courtesan and sent a delegation of twelve men and two women to Leghorn in Italy where she was staying to ask her to come to him in Cairo where he was temporarily lodged. The delegation went with an offering of precious stones and exquisite garments and a letter from Sabbatai which consisted mainly of quotations from, appropriately enough, the *Song of Solomon*. "How fair and how pleasant art thou, my beloved Sarah, daughter of Isai, the Pole! Make haste, my beloved, and be thou like to a gazelle, or to a young hart . . ."[16]

Sarah, apparently, needed little persuading. She joined Sabbatai and married him in Cairo at the end of March 1664.

Sabbatai was still sorely troubled by his "fits" and he searched for a way to heal himself though it is also possible that he regarded these states of severe alienation from reality as symbolic of the Jews' plight in exile, of mankind's perpetual separation from God. Throughout his travels he had been in close touch with the Kabbalists in the communities he had visited. He knew that Jews all over were becoming increasingly desperate in their desire for the messiah promised to them by the Kabbalah. To see himself as something special had always been part of his personality. To see himself as Exile and Redemption personified would not require much effort of his agile mind.

He heard of a miraculous young man in Gaza who through the Kabbalah had found the way to restore the soul to a state of peace. He went to seek him out. The same young man had recently had a vision in which he saw Sabbatai and the messiah. This young visionary was none other than Nathan ben Elisha Hayyim Ashkenazi, and his vision may have been inspired by the memory of his sight of Sabbatai in the streets of the Jewish quarter of Jerusalem two years previously.

When the two met in April 1665 Sabbatai was nearly 40 and Nathan only 22, yet it was the latter who dominated the former. Sabbatai told Nathan of his attacks; Nathan did not attempt to cure him, but took these as confirmation that Sabbatai was the messiah. Sabbatai had believed in this himself for many years, but he needed more convincing. The two men walked the streets of the Holy City, deep in discussion of the Kabbalah and its messianic message. Nathan even "found" a text supposedly written centuries before, prophesying that Sabbatai would come as the redeemer of Israel. One night Nathan fell into a trance and announced to all present that his new friend and master was the messiah!

This overwhelming faith in Sabbatai had its desired effect; the master accepted his disciple's view and became wholly convinced in himself as the messiah. He returned to Gaza to announce his mission and the town was thrown into a state of confusion and excitement. Soon the whole of Palestine was buzzing with the news: the messiah had come! But when Sabbatai went to Jerusalem to address himself to the rabbinate there, he found hostility and disbelief. Seven times he rode around the city on horseback, but his messianic act earned him only another banishment and he left once again for Smyrna, only this time he was coming as the long-awaited Son of David, the holy messiah.

The world, it would seem, was expecting him. Apart from the Polish exiles whose terrible experiences had been transformed through the Kabbalah into the messianic "birth pangs", other peoples and nations were gripped by a messianic expectation. In England, James Naylor's ride into Bristol had taken place only a decade before. More recently the Puritan sects were predicting on the basis of *Revelation*'s mystic number "666" that 1666 was to be the start of the Millennium. Things Jewish had become of great fascination to Christians everywhere, especially to those of a mystical bent. The Kabbalah, the Ten Lost Tribes which were constantly being found by travellers in different parts of the world, the belief that until the Jews were returned to the Holy Land there would be no Millennium, all these were spoken about, debated at length in churches and in religious tracts published throughout Europe. It did not take long, therefore, for what had started as a purely Jewish movement confined to a handful of disciples to become the subject of intense interest in the Christian as well as the rest of the Jewish world.

Sabbatai's journey to Smyrna resembled that of a large ship through the ocean. Wherever he went he left in his wake ever-widening waves of excitement. That this should have happened is also to be explained by Nathan's intense propaganda activities. The prophet, as he was now designated, was—like Bernard Rothmann of Münster—the right kind of man to turn a small sect into a world-wide cult. He was a man of great energy, intelligence and learning which he devoted to the service of his master. He has aptly been described as "at once the John the Baptist and the Paul of the new messiah".[17]

Without a theology no religious movement can hope to survive and expand. This Nathan realized and he set about, by re-interpreting the Kabbalah, to create a theology centred on the messianic mission of Sabbatai Zevi. Scribes were kept busy writing letters and proclamations at Nathan's dictation which were sent to Jewish communities throughout Europe and avidly read not only by the Jews but by Christians, too.

> The only, and first-born Son of God, Sabbatai Zevi, the Messiah and Saviour of Israel, to all the Sons of Israel, peace. Since that you are made worthy to see that great Day of Deliverance and Salvation unto Israel, and Accomplishment of the Word of God, Promised by his Prophets, and our forefathers, and by his beloved Son of Israel: let your bitter sorrows be turned into Joy and your Fasts into festivals, for you shall weep no more, sons of Israel, for God having given you this unspeakable Comfort rejoice with Drums, Organs, and Music, giving thanks to Him for performing His Promise from all Ages.[18]

Nathan wrote prophecies of how Sabbatai would take the royal crown from off the head of the Sultan of Turkey and place it on his own. After a period of withdrawal, he would return to marry the daughter of Moses and ride into Jerusalem on a dragon whose bridle rein would be a snake with seven heads. Gog and Magog would attack him with their armies but with the breath of his nostril he would rout them and by his word alone utterly destroy them. In Jerusalem God would send down a temple of gold and precious stones from heaven in which Sabbatai would offer up a sacrifice as the High Priest. "And in that day shall the dead throughout the world rise from their graves."[19]

The deliberate extravagance and exuberance of the letters had their desired effect. They were the sparks to set alight a messianic flame that quickly spread around the world. In Smyrna where Sabbatai rode about in glory there were riots. Thousands of Jews followed him and the foreign merchants whose ships were lying idle in the dock for their cargoes to be loaded gazed on in amazement. When they reached their home ports of London or Amsterdam or Leghorn or Hamburg, they told of what they had seen and thereby helped to fan the flames.

They told of how Zevi, dressed like royalty, went to the synagogues in large processions and how he attacked the rabbis and their old ways, advocating a new set of rules, new prayers and new rituals. They told of how he had said to the Jews: eat the forbidden foods, pronounce with joy in your hearts the forbidden Name of God; of how at midnight he would rise up and go to the seaside to perform ritual ablutions; and of how the crowds gathered in their hundreds to listen to his beautiful voice: men of great wealth as well as poor men, merchants, scholars, fishermen and artisans.

When the news of Sabbatai reached the Jews outside Smyrna the excitement it caused is probably unparalleled in Jewish history. In Hamburg, for instance, they rushed to their synagogues and listened while the letters from Nathan were read aloud. The young men dressed themselves in their best clothes and put on green silk ribbons—Sabbatai's colours. People sold their houses and their lands and sat, waiting for the moment when they were to be redeemed. Commercial centres which owed their vitality to the Jews came to a standstill because the Jews ceased to trade in anticipation of the Day of the Lord.

In Poland a chronicler described how the communities "raved" about a messiah who would take them on a cloud to Jerusalem and how they fasted for days at a time, preventing even their children from eating. "They looked haughtily down on the Christians and held their messiah as a threat over their heads, saying, 'Only wait; soon we shall be your masters!' "[20]

Amsterdam was in a state of wild excitement. Crowds collected in the streets and began dancing, indifferent to the Christian bystanders mocking them. In England, true to style, bets were laid for and against Sabbatai being the messiah. Samuel Pepys reported in his diary:

> I am told for certain what I have heard once or twice already, of a Jew in town that in the name of the rest do offer to give any man £10 to be paid £100 if a certain person now at Smyrna be within these two years owned by all the Princes of the East, and particularly the Grand Signor, as the King of the world, in the same manner we do the King of England here, and that this man is the true Messiah. One named a friend of his that had received ten pieces in gold upon this score, and says that the Jew hath disposed of £1100 in this great action; but what the consequences of it will be, God knows![21]

In some business communities Jewish creditors cancelled all debts owing to them, and created confusion by releasing all mortgages. In others, England for instance, they refused to pay their own debts. Nathan heard of this and immediately addressed an epistle to them:

> To you of the Nation of Jews, who expect the appearance of the Messiah, and the Salvation of Israel, Peace without End. Whereas we are informed that you are indebted to several of the English Nation: It seemeth right unto us to enorder you to make satisfaction to these your just debts: which if you refuse to do, and not obey us herein: know you, that you are not to enter with us into our Joys and Dominions.[22]

Christians saw in Sabbatai Zevi the hope of converting the Jews to Christianity and so hasten the Second Coming of the real messiah, Jesus Christ.

> He is a civil man in his Manners and Discourse; of a Comely

> Countenance, Cloath'd in the Habit of a Jew, [wrote one Christian to a friend in London]. He daily frequents the Jewish Synagogues, Disputing with the Rabbins concerning the most weighty Mysteries and Matters of Faith, especially Concerning Jesus Christ; that He was the true Messiah whom God had promised to the Israelites. He understands the Languages of all Nations: Whatsoever he Speaks and Teaches, he confirms by Miracles. The hungry he feeds with variety of Meats, and the thirsty he satisfies with Drink. Water he turns into Wine; he gives sight to the Blind, He makes the Dumb to speak, Cures the Sick, and many other Wonders! Perhaps God by this Man is willing to Convert the Jews and other Infidels.[23]

The comparison with Jesus Christ was not accidental. Since the advent of Christianity in the Holy Land 1,700 years before, the Jewish communities had not been so affected by controversy and division. As enthusiastic as some were in Sabbatai's favour others were in their derision of him. With fine alliteration, one rabbi described the new movement as "the filth of the false faith of Sabbatai Zevi".[24] Rabbis of repute in the main centres of learning were inundated with pleas, whether or not people should accept Sabbatai as the messiah. In one such correspondence between the Venice community and the community in Constantinople, the latter replied in a letter cleverly disguised for security reasons as a business communication about the quality of a consignment of goatskins.

"So we looked into the matter and examined what Rabbi Israel [Sabbatai] had bought, for his goods are displayed here under our very eyes. We have come to the conclusion that they are very valuable; they are being purchased in every country, and whoever speaks ill of them will have to answer for it before the court."[25]

To these Constantinople rabbis there was "no doubt any longer about the matter", Sabbatai was "devoted to God", but to other rabbis he represented Satan himself. To the Smyrna Jews who were in a state of frenzy over him a college of rabbis wrote, warning them to turn from their obstinate worship of him. "Restore the Crown to the ancient custom and use of your forefathers, and the Law, and from thence do not move under pain of Excommunication and other penalties."[26]

Their caution had little effect. People were prepared to risk excommunication for the freedom Sabbatai offered them from the restrictions of rabbinical law, much as Jesus had done. He declared fast-days to be feast-days. The ninth day of Ab, traditionally kept as a fast in commemoration of the destruction of the Temple, was also supposed to be Sabbatai's birthday. On his behalf, Nathan declared that it was to be a day of great joy and that Jews were to celebrate it "with choice meats and pleasing drinks, with many Candles and Lamps, with Music and Songs".[27] Rules for the Divine Service were radically altered and indulgences were awarded to those who prayed at the tomb of Sabbatai's mother. In true messianic tradition he appointed his apostles and gave them titles: King David, King Solomon, King of King of Kings for his own brother; King of the Kings of Judah for another.

Sabbatai introduced into Judaism a form of spiritual anarchy not very different from that advocated by the Brethren of the Free Spirit and their many Christian heirs and descendants. "Praised be He who permits the forbidden," Sabbatai declared early on in his mission and the nihilistic ideal implied by this was extended as his movement expanded. Nudity, fornication and incest were now practised by the most devoted of his followers as a way of showing their freedom from the conventional notions of sin. Sabbataians came to accept the view that mankind, like Adam in exile from Paradise, had need of clothing; but at the time of redemption when mankind was restored to Paradise, clothing was unnecessary. Men and women could discard their clothes and, once more, stand together as they had in their original existence.[28]

He offered liberation to men of a kind they had never before known; he offered women even greater freedom. Jewish women were by tradition excluded from taking a leading part in ritual and worship; in synagogues they had to remain in separate sections, away from the centre of worship—the Scrolls of Law. In some houses of prayer their sections were divided off by screens so that they could barely be seen or see what their men were doing. Sabbatai ended all this. Women were of equal importance to his movement. His two divorced wives were welcomed to his court in direct contradiction of the rabbinical law forbidding a man to consort with his ex-wife. Sarah, the beautiful whore, had been raised to an eminence which nearly equalled that of

Sabbatai himself. Her lurid past was well known; yet the messiah loved her. Was this not justification enough for all women to follow her example into promiscuity and sexual licence?

Women flocked to join and were the most enthusiastic of his followers, ensuring the movement's success. They and their men indulged themselves in an orgy of sexuality. They also joined in the most exruciating acts of penance that was a remarkable feature of Sabbataianism in its early days. People starved themselves almost to death; they buried themselves in their gardens "covering their naked Bodies with Earth, their Heads only excepted, remaining in their beds of dirt until their bodies were stiffened with cold and moisture".[29] Where snow was available, they rolled around naked in it. They also had melted wax dropped on their naked shoulders, and whipped their skin to shreds.

The reason for this self-mortification is not hard to find. A good many, perhaps well over half, of Sabbatai's people were either Marranos themselves, that is, Jews recently forced into Catholicism by the Polish Cossacks or others, or they were the descendants of the Spanish and Portuguese Marranos from the time of the great exile. In either case they bore the terrible scars of guilt for their apostasy. The sympathy which Jewish communities first showed to the secret Jews of the Iberian Peninsula was with the passage of time diminishing, thereby increasing both their isolation and their guilt. Sabbatai offered them a release by the very nature of his attack on orthodoxy. They could once more share with others the sense of being *outside* the mainstream of Jewish life. At the same time, by indulging in acts of ritual penance, they could assuage the guilt they felt so acutely.

Events were beginning to move that were to make the Marranos even more involved in the movement. The messiah himself was approaching the climax of his mission that would turn him into one like themselves, though in 1665 no hint of this fate was yet to be discerned. Sabbatai was then at the height of his fame. The divisions for and against him were turning in some places into violence, so intense were the feelings he inspired. In Venice the Constantinople letter disguised as a business communication caused an immediate reaction. Those for Sabbatai silenced their opponents by threatening them with physical assault. When one tried to speak up against him, he was struck down. The day was the sabbath, the most holy day in the Jewish calendar. The act was therefore adding the greatest insult to injury. Yet when Sabbatai heard of it, his secretary wrote to the culprits, praising them. "There is no better way of keeping holy the Sabbath Day than the one these people have chosen." The letter was signed, "The man who is the divine Messiah, mighty as a lion, strong as a bear, the Lord's appointed".[30]

Sabbatai's opponents, however, were to have their revenge. In December 1665 he left Smyrna by boat for Constantinople. The Grand Vizier was warned of his impending arrival. Sabbatai's enemies told him he was not the messiah as he claimed but a charlatan, dangerous to public order because he openly declared his intention of removing the crown from the head of the Sultan. The Turkish authorities had also heard news of the disturbances his appearance and the mere mention of his name had caused. After 40 days of terrible storms, Sabbatai and his disciples found themselves under arrest before they were even allowed to land. Sabbatai was brought to shore in chains.

His opponents were chagrined to find that Sabbatai was not immediately put to death; instead he was treated with the utmost respect. This was partly because he gave a display of great holiness, bathing, praying and fasting, that appealed to the Turks; partly because large sums were paid by wealthy members of the sect to ensure his safety.

In April 1666 he was installed in the castle of Abydos in Gallipoli where the cold bare cells were transformed into an ornate Citadel of Power (Migdal Oz)* where visitors from all over the world were permitted to come and pay court to Sabbatai and his divine Queen, Sarah. During this period Sabbatai was at the very peak of his charm and magnetism. Visitors came away awestruck by the brilliance of the man. He was surely, as the prayers written in his name boldly declared: "the Messiah of the God of Jacob, the Heavenly Lion, the King of Justice, the King of Kings".[31] All were impressed except one visitor, a certain Kabbalist from Poland called Nehemiah ha-Kohen who came to see Sabbatai to argue out his messianic claims. The Kabbalist arrived in September and the two men debated together for three days. Though he was poor and unknown, Nehemiah refused to be dazzled by the pomp surrounding Sabbatai and to be silenced by Sabbatai's insistent monologue. Are you the suffering messiah? asked the Kabbalist. Do you call this suffering? he said,

* The title is derived from *Proverbs* 18:10, "The name of the Lord is a strong tower: the righteous runneth into it and is safe".

pointing to the luxury around them. If you are the messiah, son of David, who was the messiah, son of Joseph who by Talmudic tradition was supposed to precede him?

Sabbatai answered him as best he could but the persistent Kabbalist was not satisfied. Sabbatai, he decided, was an impostor and had to be exposed and destroyed.

Nehemiah was not especially stable by nature. It was thought at the time that he was prompted by jealousy for Sabbatai since he believed himself to be the messianic precursor, Messiah ben Joseph. Had Sabbatai acknowledged him as such all would have been well, but the Kabbalist was spurned. In revenge he betrayed Sabbatai to the Turks, telling them that Zevi planned to overthrow the Sultan. Sabbatai was taken from Gallipoli to Adrianople and in September 1666 was brought before the 23-year-old Sultan, Mehmed IV.

Reports say that in the presence of the Sultan Sabbatai was utterly passive, possibly indicating that he was passing through the depressive state of one of his manic-depressive cycles. When he was given the choice—death or apostasy—Sabbatai flung off the cap worn by Jews and picked up a turban. The Sultan, a religious man, welcomed the new convert and named him Aziz Mehmed Effendi; Sarah followed her husband into Islam and she was called Fatima Radini.

"Now have done with me," he wrote to his brothers who had been among his most fervent disciples, "for the Almighty hath made me an Ishmaelite. He spake and it was so. He commanded and it came to pass."[32]

Given a pension and granted the title of "keeper of the palace gates", Sabbatai—or Mehmed Effendi—lived in comfort till 1672. Now he was, like so many of his followers, a true Marrano. In secret he conformed to the precepts of his own version of Judaism; in public he performed the duties of a Muslim. His mental state did not improve with age and in one of his manic moods he divorced Sarah but remarried her when he was normal again. He continued to advocate and practise various forms of sexual licence, attracting animosity from Jew and Muslim alike. In August 1672 he was arrested once more, but this time he had nothing left to give the Muslim authorities; his soul they had already taken. They banished him to a small and remote village in Albania called Dulcigno.

In spite of what he had done, many of his followers refused

to give him up. Nathan, the prophet, declared: "My loyalty is unshaken".[33] To Sabbatai's brother Nathan wrote explaining Sabbatai's apostasy as one of the "strange acts" to which he, as a holy man, as the messiah, was prone. This was not a matter of amazement or even comment because "we have surely often enough seen the strange things our wise men have done".[34]

To the movement as a whole Nathan addressed one of his famous epistles, encouraging them not to waver. "Let not your hearts faint or fear but rather fortify yourselves in your Faith, because all his actions are miraculous and secret which human understanding cannot comprehend and who can penetrate into the depth of them."[35]

Though Nathan and Sabbatai hardly met during the two peak years of Sabbatai's career, they were never out of touch with each other. This closeness remained right till Sabbatai's death. Nathan continued to love and honour his master and to travel about, preaching his faith in him.

Sarah died in 1674 and Sabbatai married his fourth and last wife, Esther, the daughter of a rabbi. Right till the end, he had his "fits" during which he claimed that he was the messiah, only now there was no one to hear him. A few months before his 50th birthday he wrote to some friends, asking them for a prayer book for the forthcoming Jewish New Year and Day of Atonement. The book was sent but he never used it. On the Day of Atonement, 17 September 1676, Sabbatai Zevi died.

CHAPTER TWELVE

IN THE FEMALE LINE

MOST MESSIAHS HAVE been men. The messianic ideal was of a man more honoured and honourable than the rest of *man*kind. *Woman*kind was not considered at all though, as we have seen, she provided the most faithful and devoted following.

There have been messianic partnerships where the woman has occupied a place almost as important as the man—William Franklin and Mary Gadbury, for example, and John and Joan Robins. As far back as the thirteenth century chroniclers mention a Jesus and Mary. The man had five wounds made in his body to resemble the five wounds of Jesus on the cross. They had considerable success until the magistrates arrested them. "Gentile (gentle) Methods were us'd to bring them to an open Confession, or Recantation. But their madness and Obstinacy were too great to be brought under; so that at last they were adjudged to be inured and shut up betwixt Two Walls, (to the End their contagion might spread no further) where they miserably ended their Days."[1]

At the beginning of this century the House of David was run jointly by King Benjamin and Queen Mary Purnell, two Kentuckians, in Benton Harbour, Michigan. They and their community of about 70 preached and practised community of goods and strict chastity. Claiming to be free from death, the joint messiahs set up a profitable publishing business and accumulated a small fortune. In 1923 a family of believers brought an action against the "king" for misappropriating the community's funds to the sum of £40,000 and charged him also with assaulting two young girls, driving one mad. When the police came to arrest Benjamin Purnell he had disappeared. Large rewards were offered for his capture but for five years nothing was heard of him. Then two disillusioned members of the House of David tipped the police off that Benjamin had been living in luxury in an underground room in the central building of the community village. Armed with axes and searchlights, the police broke into the grounds in the middle of the night and arrested Purnell. He was sent to prison.[2]

Messiahs in the female line have not been numerous though they are by no means unknown. They have tended to consider themselves prophetesses rather than messiahs for the reason mentioned above, that the messiah is traditionally a male rôle. Nonetheless their function as charismatic leaders of messianic sects has been the same, and they have attracted followers, both male and female, quite as devoted and loyal as any male messiah.

In America in the last years of the eighteenth century, Jemima Wilkinson, a twenty-year-old Quaker girl, "died", was mourned, and prepared for burial. As her funeral was leaving the house, she "came to life" again. From then on she believed that she had been specially chosen by God to raise up a Church which would enjoy the joys of the First Resurrection due before her second death. She established a community that practised strict celibacy and waited for the Coming of the Lord in 1786. A tall, active woman, Jemima established friendly relationships with the Indian tribes surrounding her community in the wilds of eastern America and became known as The Universal Friend. She would go about her daily work dressed in a kilt and a broad Quaker's hat, ruling her people like an autocrat. They grew rich and they loved her; when she needed funds, she merely said, "The Lord hath need of it" and the money was forthcoming.[3]

On one occasion she led her people down to the edge of the water, saying that, like Christ, she would walk across it. However, before setting out to perform the miracle, she asked them if they believed she could do it. With one voice they affirmed their faith in her. Jemima turned back from the edge. If they believed she had the power, then that was sufficient and she had no need to prove it. And with that she led them back.[4]

Jemima foresaw her death and warned her followers that they were not to bury her because she would revive once again. She died in 1820 and remembering her strict orders, they hid her body in a secret place, anxiously watching for her to awake from her "sleep". She never awoke. There was no Second Revival and, disillusioned and saddened, her followers slowly dispersed.[5]

Anticipating Jemima by but a few years, and of much greater importance, was one of America's first women sectarians to establish a large and successful community—the Shakers.[6] Ann

Lee, or Lees as she was born, arrived in America in 1774. Her birthplace was England, her father a blacksmith and a part-time tailor. Like most messiahs, Anne Lee did not come into full possession of her theology alone and unaided but extended and developed existing theological beliefs. In her case she was influenced by a society of dissenters whom she joined when she was 22 and who practised ideas similar to the Quakers. They would begin their meetings like the Quakers, sitting in silent meditation, but then, unlike the Quakers, when the spirit moved them, they would begin to sing, shout and stamp about, mouthing meaningless phrases and words, that is, "speaking with tongues".

Ann reluctantly entered into marriage with a blacksmith from Manchester and they had four children, all of whom died. She considered this a divine judgment on her for the carnal sin of marriage. She underwent a spiritual rebirth and, newly inspired by a mission, she took over the leadership of her sect which grew in strength and attracted increasing notoriety. Charges of blasphemy were brought against her and the first of her "martyrdoms", which became part and parcel of Shaker tradition, began. She was cross-examined by magistrates and she claimed to answer their questions in twelve languages—in 72 according to another tradition. She was said to have suffered terrible deprivation for four days without food and water in a darkened cell so tiny she could not stand. She later said that only because one of her disciples managed to inject the stem of a pipe through the keyhole and pour into it milk and wine for her to drink, did she survive the ordeal.

In the cell a vision of Christ appeared to her and told her to preach the gospel of the sinless life. In common with many other mystics, Ann believed that Christ dwelt within her and that when she spoke it was not her voice but his that was heard. "I am Ann the Word," she said. "I am married to the Lord Jesus Christ. He is my head and my husband, and I have no other!"[7] Of course she did, but the poor blacksmith to whom she was married could not compete with the Son of God, so he became one of her disciples and ceased to play any important rôle in her life.

On 10 May 1774 Mother Ann, as she was now called, the Redeemer of the race of man, left with a few followers for America, arriving in New York three months later. Her start in the New World was unpropitious. Without friend or money, she and the chosen few had to take menial jobs in order to survive. But Mother Ann was a woman of enormous energy. She was shorter than average and thick-set. She had a fair English complexion and keen, penetrating eyes. She was entirely without false airs; a simple, plain woman. To her followers, however, she was "beautiful"!

"Her countenance appeared bright and shining, like an angel of glory, and she seemed to be overshadowed with the glory of God," recalled one of her disciples. "As I sat by the side of her, one of her hands, while in motion, frequently touched my arm; and at every touch of her hand, I instantly felt the power of God run through my whole body."[8] Another remembered how, by her quiet singing and gentle movements, she could hold an audience entranced.[9]

She needed every ounce of her vitality to keep her sect going in their harsh new surroundings; and she did. Together they set up a community in Niskeyuna, eight miles north-west of Albany, the capital city of New York State. The region was desolate but her people were charged with enthusiasm and love of their Mother for whom they would have laid down their lives. Combining their skills as blacksmiths, carpenters, weavers and shoemakers, they created a community which soon became well known in the area.

Religious extremism was not unknown to that inhospitable part of America. New York and neighbouring Massachusetts were swept by numerous waves of messianism. In less than 75 years after Mother Ann set up home there, the millenarian, William Miller, sparked off yet another outburst of fanatical enthusiasm when thousands of people waited in readiness for the Millennium which Miller predicted would arrive in 1843.*

Wherever there are these manifestations, there is usually also the backlash of intolerance and persecution by those who do not accept the reality of the enthusiasts. Mother Ann had her full share of both. She preached celibacy, hatred of sin and lust; she was accused by her enemies of witchcraft, blasphemy and conducting orgies. On one occasion she was brought before the Justices of the Peace in Richmond. She and some of her elders were fined twenty dollars as disturbers of the peace and told to leave the State.

During a stay in Massachusetts they upset the locals by their

* See chapter four.

odd behaviour and they again met with mob violence. Mother Ann's closest associates, Father James and Father Williams, were severely beaten. Father James was caught and tied to a tree. His assailants cut some sticks from the bushes and began beating him. Scourging him "till his back was all in a gore of blood, and the flesh bruised to a jelly".[10] When Father Williams' turn came, Father James leapt on him to protect him and so did one of the women, who was beaten so badly that she bore the scars till the end of her life. "After the mob left the ground, the Elders, and those few Believers who were with them, retired a few rods, and all kneeled down; and Elder James had a new song of praise put into his mouth, which he sung on the spot as he was kneeling."[11]

Mother Ann became known as a woman with supernatural powers and people for miles around came to her for comfort and cures. She was supposed to have healed wounds, sores, rashes, mouth cancer, lameness, and broken limbs merely by the strength of her faith. For her, sin was the basis of all evil and her followers were required to lead lives of extraordinary rectitude, as can be gathered from the rules of the Shaker community. These millennial laws kept brethren and sisters almost completely segregated except on formal occasions. They could not sleep together, nor even pass each other on the stairs. They were not allowed to talk to each other in the halls, nor to shake hands with each other. Brothers were not even permitted to be in the same room with sisters when the women were making up the beds.[12]

The rigours of her life took their toll and Mother Ann died in September 1784. Father Williams had died a few days before her and Father James, who was only 37, died three years later. But the community survived and grew in strength.

Mother Ann did not believe in her own immortality but many of her followers did. Sister Jemima Blanchard, a Shaker, remembered that when she heard of Mother Ann's death,

> I felt so distressed and sorrow-stricken that I thought it was impossible for me to live. I returned in secret and lay prostrate upon the floor, expecting to breathe out my soul in sorrow—for the more I tried to refrain the deeper my sorrow became. This continued without cessation, until I saw the appearance of Mother Ann, about the size of a child of three years old.

> This beautiful messenger held something in each hand that appeared like a wing which she waved inward, and advancing toward me said, "Hush, Hush!" This took away my sorrow, so that I was able to attend to my duty.[13]

In August 1837 three young Shaker girls fell into a trance and described a journey in which they saw angels. Soon others were having similar mystical experiences, claiming to receive messages from "our Heavenly Parents", Jesus and Mother Ann. This period of intense revivalism which lasted ten years became known as Mother Ann's Second Appearing.

Mother Ann exemplifies what can be achieved by a group of people devoted to one person in whose name and through whose leadership they triumph over the enmity and scorn of the rest of the world. At the height of their strength the United Society of Believers, as they called themselves, numbered 6,000 members in eighteen different communities. Their relationship with their neighbours steadily improved as the latter saw that they were not devils and that their strange dancing, their "groaning, jumping, laughing, talking and stuttering, shooing and hissing" in their worship of God did not threaten the peace. "They were good men and good women," summed up an old survivor of the sect, and they came to be respected as such.

Margaret Peter, however, was the exact antithesis of Mother Ann. She exemplified messianism gone mad. Whereas Mother Ann desired to build, Margaret Peter wanted to destroy. Both were successful; but whereas Mother Ann's story is one of courage and tenacity, Peter's is one of violence and horror. Today there may be no more than a handful of Shakers living in the United States, but they are remembered by history with affection. In contrast, the house in which Margaret Peter held her messianic rites was, by order of the Zurich judges, razed to the ground. A plough was drawn over the foundation and no dwelling was allowed to be erected in that place ever again.[14]

The house was in Wildisbuch, eight miles from Schaffhausen on the Swiss-German border, and it belonged to John Peter, a widower with a son and five daughters. The youngest was Margaret, who was born in 1794. Her mother died when she was still an infant and she was brought up as the favourite, spoilt and petted. She was also very precocious and from the age of six began reading the Bible not only to herself, but also to her family.

She would lecture them on the Old and New Testaments and would pray ardently in front of them, cautioning them to lead sinless and God-fearing lives. In other families this behaviour might have earned her a cuff around the ear, but in the Peter's family she was treated with special consideration. The fact that she had been born on Christmas Day was regarded as further proof of her uniqueness. One of her sisters said of her years later, "I am satisfied that God worked in mighty power, and in space through Margaret, up to the hour of her death". By the time she had entered adolescence she was the absolute ruler of the household. Her will, said her pastor, was obeyed as the will of God.

In her early twenties, Margaret began a career as a roving preacher, stirring up a spirit of revivalism wherever she preached. Her travels took her as far as Zurich, then she came back to her father's house and spent her time in seclusion, locked in a room with the windows shut, reading her Bible, meditating, praying and writing letters to a cobbler she had met on her travels, one Jacob Morf, who had left wife and family to follow her.

The Peter household had grown. In addition to the father, the son, Caspar, and the daughters, two of whom were married, there was young Heinrich who helped in the fields and stable, and a young girl called Ursula. She had suffered in an unhappy love affair and had come to Margaret to seek spiritual guidance, remaining on to work as an unpaid maid. Margaret Jäggli, a strange and unstable woman, had also come to Margaret to be cured of epilepsy; she, too, stayed on and worked in the house as a maid. Jacob Ganz, a tailor turned preacher, was usually in attendance and so, too, were the brothers-in-law. Without exception, they all looked to Margaret Peter as their spiritual guide and leader.

Easter 1823 approached and Margaret came out of seclusion, convinced that Satan had made his abode in a nest under the roof of the house and that it was in her power to remove him. She wrote to Jacob Morf, the ex-cobbler, inviting him to come and witness Armageddon when Satan would be expelled. Morf arrived on 8 March, stayed a few days, then returned to his home.

The house now gave itself up to a week of religious ecstacy. On the Monday they prepared to fight the final battle against evil. On Tuesday, while some went about their normal work, others gathered in prayer with Margaret. "My struggle with Satan is severe," she told them. "He strives to retain the souls which I will wrest from his hold." In the evening she led a procession up the stairs to one of the rooms. "Lo!" she cried. "I see Satan and his first born floating in the air."

Wednesday was given up to wresting the spirits from Jäggli and Elizabeth, Margaret's favourite sister. On Thursday she announced that the hour had come when they would battle against the Antichrist. They went up to the room in which she had seen the vision of Satan and she bade them fetch axes, clubs and whatever implements they could find to fight the last fight. While the others went about searching for weapons, John Moser, her brother-in-law, saw the room "fill with a dazzling glory, such as no tongue could describe," and he wept for joy. By late afternoon the weapons were gathered together. Margaret was sitting on the bed, wringing her hands and exhorting them all to pray. "Help, Help! all of you that Christ may not be overcome in me. Strike, strike—everywhere on all sides—the floor, the walls. Smite and lose your lives if need be."

The small congregation were quickly stirred to uncontrollable fury against the unseen forces. They battered and smashed the walls, the floor and all the furniture with such frenzy that soon the place was in a shambles. They had also succeeded in knocking out part of one wall so that their madness was visible to the stunned spectators who had gathered down below in the road, drawn to the house by the commotion.

A complaint was lodged against them. They were brought before the magistrates who sent a report to Zurich. A reply came that Margaret and Elizabeth should be immediately confined in an asylum. Unfortunately for both of them, the reply arrived too late. On the Saturday the group were back at the house—twelve of them in all. They assembled in a room upstairs, aware that something awesome was about to take place. Margaret turned on her brother, Caspar, and declared that the devil was within him. She struck out at him with a wedge and he stood still, making no attempt to resist her blows until he was covered in blood. He was led downstairs by the old man who was charged with keeping strangers away from the house.

To those remaining Margaret announced her messianic mission. "I shall offer myself up as the final sacrifice," she said, "so that Satan may be defeated." Elizabeth, who was normally a quiet, dull young woman, threw herself on the bed, begging to give herself up as a sacrifice. She had already been badly beaten in the previous furore, but now she took a mallet and struck herself fiercely over the head. "It has been revealed to me," Margaret shouted, "that Elizabeth shall sacrifice herself." With that, she took up an iron hammer and hit her sister on the head. The rest set upon Elizabeth, beating her almost to death. She lay on the bed, writhing in her blood and moaning, "I am ready to die".

Margaret grabbed Ursula and told her to finish Elizabeth off. Ursula refused. "She is too dear to me." Margaret insisted that Ursula did as she was told. "I will raise my sister again," she promised, "and after three days I, too, will rise again. So strike!" Terrified, Ursula did nothing, but John Moser snatched the hammer out of Margaret's hand and hit Elizabeth again and again on her head, chest and shoulders. Susanna, another sister, struck at her with a crowbar; Heinrich hit her with a piece of flooring. Finally Ursula, with Margaret at her side, screaming, "Die for Christ, Elizabeth!", beat in the woman's skull with a wedge.

The ghastly rites were not yet over. Margaret now declared to the exhausted group that she had to be sacrificed as Christ had been. "You must crucify me," she told them. John and Ursula refused. "It is better I shall die than thousands of souls should perish," she exclaimed. Then she hit herself in the left temple with the hammer. She held the weapon out to John, ordering him to use it on her. He hesitated. "Strike," she commanded. He struck, but not hard.

"Now you, Ursula," she said, turning to the maid. "Crucify me."

"I cannot," the maid replied.

"You will be responsible for all the souls that will be lost unless you fulfil what I have appointed you to do," she said. She ordered her sister, Susanna, to fetch some nails while the rest made a cross for her out of loose flooring boards.

Heinrich, who had left the room after Elizabeth's death, was working quietly in the vines, making stakes. Susanna came down to him and asked for nails. He gave her some, apparently not knowing for what purpose they were to be used. Margaret Jäggli had also returned to her domestic duties; she was preparing a meal for the family. Upstairs Margaret Peter was lying stretched out on the bed next to her dead sister. She was neatly arranged on a cross. The final ritual was about to take place.

Ursula and John took the nails from Susanna and hammered them into Margaret's elbows. In spite of their frenzy the sight of blood made them hesitate. "Go on," Margaret urged, and to reassure them added, "I will rise in three days." They drove nails through both her breasts. She made no sound as they went in, but some of the others were at last beginning to react to the horror before them. One, John Moser's brother, Conrad, was in a faint; another was sick; a third wept.

"I feel no pain," Margaret assured them. "Now finish the task and drive a nail through my heart." Ursula tried with a knife but it bent against the ribs. "Beat in my skull," Margaret cried. Conrad could stand it no more. He picked up a hammer and, with Ursula helping him, smashed in the woman's head. Then, much subdued, they all filed downstairs to eat the dinner Jäggli had made for them. It was noon.

While they were finishing, a policeman arrived to request the presence of the two girls before the magistrates in accordance with the Zurich order. He did not know, of course, that they were both dead upstairs. Old man Peter promised him that they would attend on the day appointed.

The next day, Heinrich galloped off to Margaret's friend, Jacob Morf, to invite him to witness the miracle of resurrection. Morf returned with him and went into the room where Margaret and Elizabeth were lying on the blood-soaked bed. When he saw them with their heads staved in, the one nailed to the rough planks, he fainted away. As soon as he recovered, he rushed off home and went straight to his pastor.

The others paid no attention. They still had work to do. On Sunday night, when Jacob had gone, they went to the room and with pincers removed the nails from Margaret's body, the better to facilitate her resurrection. Monday and Tuesday were spent in fervent prayer while they awaited the miracle. Nothing happened. On Tuesday the old man went to his pastor formally to report the deaths of Margaret and Elizabeth, giving the times as 10.00 a.m. and 12.00 a.m. respectively on the Saturday. In the meantime, Morf's pastor reported to the authorities what his parishioner had told him, and the whole Peter household was placed under arrest.

The trial took place in Zurich in December 1823. All those

involved were sentenced to varying terms of imprisonment, Ursula to the longest—sixteen years. Before the house was finally levelled to the ground by order of the court, hundreds of religious enthusiasts and morbid sightseers had come to pay their last respects at the shrine of "holy" Margaret.

Martyrdom, so fervently sought and so horribly achieved by Margaret Peter, evaded Joanna Southcott until her 65th year. When it came, it was the martyrdom of ridicule that she suffered, not death, though that followed, too, releasing her from her unhappy fate. This plain daughter of a poor Devon farmer made a remarkable career for herself as the prophetess-in-chief of a countrywide religious sect. She was born in the village of Gittisham, between Honiton and Ottery St Mary in east Devon in April 1750.[15] Until the age of 42 she lived a quiet life in service with various families. Like Ann Lee she did not care for marriage. "Though all her lovers tried in vain," she once wrote in the doggerel with which she expressed most of her prophecies, "her hand nor heart could ne'er obtain."[16]

In 1792 Joanna had nightly dreams of the Apocalypse and heard the voice of God say to her: "The Lord is awakened out of sleep. He will terribly shake the earth."[17] She advised her employer to lay in stocks of food because prices would soar and when, in reply, her employer asked if she was a prophetess, Joanna answered firmly, "I am". From those small beginnings grew the Southcottian sect into one of considerable size with chapels all around Britain. Joanna saw herself and was regarded by her followers as the woman of *Revelation*, "clothed with the sun", travailing in birth for the Christ she was to deliver.[18]

Her hunger for martyrdom led Joanna to some strange excesses. She burdened bishops, judges and politicians with letters demanding that they test her prophetic gift and charge her with deceiving the public if she was found wanting. When they did not reply or take up her challenge, she arranged her own public trials. The first was held in 1804, three years after the publication of her first book of prophecy, the second in 1814 soon before her last act of martyrdom.

> I have borne the mockery and abuse of men, [she wrote in the advertisement for the second trial]. I defy all the Bishops in England, the Members of Parliament, and all the judges in the land, with all the judgment they can form together, to be

> able to prove these (her prophecies) were ever brought round by the wisdom and knowledge of the devil, or by the wisdom and knowledge of an Impostor.[19]

Perhaps the worst fate that can befall the would-be messiah is public indifference—worse even than death. The latter, at least, is confirmation that the rôle chosen has been the right one. The former, the silence of the multitude, leaves the messiah with the nagging feeling that the choice is a delusion. Joanna, it would seem, suffered from this uncertainty all through the years of her great success as a prophetess when thousands—in one year alone 14,000—rushed to receive her seal, a small piece of paper sealed with a seal which she had found one day when sweeping the floor of her last employer.*

At her public trials only the converted turned up. The prosecution and her judges, therefore, were all convinced believers in the powers of Joanna. A Southcottian lawyer examined the witnesses who gave evidence of her truthfulness and the accuracy of her prophecies. Her judges declared that all her communications emanated "wholly and entirely from the Spirit of the living Lord".[20]

Joanna was not satisfied with their judgment. She wanted more proof to still the nagging doubts. In a curious document entitled *Joanna's Dispute with Satan*[21] she projected her own uncertainties on to the devil and had *him* accuse her of delusion and deceit. "There is not one whit of the Spirit of God in thee," he says to her. "Satan is angry; the jest is carried too far. God is a liar. Thy writings are not true." Joanna answers weakly, "All these things may come true; there is nothing impossible with God".

The "jest" had to be played out to its absurd end. Either she was "the woman clothed with the sun" who would bring forth "a man child to rule all nations with a rod of iron", or everything had been delusion and lies. So long as no one in religious authority would pronounce one way or the other on her claims, so long as she remained the final arbiter of her pronouncements, Joanna needed definite—objective—proof of her mission. Finally,

* The seal had inscribed on it the initials I.C. with a star above and below the inscription. Joanna regarded the finding of this as being of special significance and interpreted I.C. as standing for the name, Jesus Christ.

in 1813, she took the irrevocable step towards the final proof—and her martyrdom. In the *Third Book of Wonders* she records the Spirit telling her: "This year, in the 65th year of thy age, thou shalt have a Son by the power of the Most High".[22]

If any of her followers showed consternation or alarm at the announcement, there is no record of it. Rather, they received the prophecy with wonder and amazement and began making elaborate preparations for Joanna's accouchement. She had for some years been living in the home of a wealthy widow, Mrs Townley, and her companion, who acted as Joanna's secretary. The house was now inundated with gifts: laced caps, embroidered bibs, robes, a mohair mantle worth £150, splendid spoons and cups, and a superb satinwood crib which cost over £200 to make. The expected god-child was called the Shiloh. The name derived from a misinterpretation of *Genesis* 49:10. This records Jacob's prophesy: "The sceptre shall not depart from Judah, nor a lawgiver from between his feet, *until Shiloh come;* and unto him shall the gathering of the people be." Shiloh, however, was a place, not a person.

A small detail like this did not disturb the Southcottians. In their chapels they sang:

Shiloh to our faith is given,
On this bright auspicious morn
Shiloh, choicest gift of heaven,
For a faithless world is born.
Hail Joanna! favoured mortal,
Chosen maid of Heav'n's love
Thou canst ope the blessed portal,
Of the joyful seats above.[23]

The public was shocked, angered, amused and contemptuous. The main Southcottian chapel in London was besieged by mobs. In some villages Joanna was burnt in effigy. Lampoons abounded, showing Joanna in obscene poses and suggesting that if this old woman *was* with child, one of her faithful male disciples was the father. That she might not be a virgin angered Joanna more than anything else said against her. She went into print to contradict the rumour. "And this I can take a solemn oath to," she wrote. "I never had knowledge of a man in my life. So that if the words of the Spirit are fulfilled in me this year to have a son, it is by the power of the Lord and not of man, and this sign is set to prove the truth of the Gospel or to prove that the Gospel is not true."[24] Thus, in one throw, she was casting the dice not only for the truth of her own beliefs but also for the whole Christian faith.

Joanna, like so many of her predecessors, was given to alternate fits of elation and depression. Her most outlandish prophecies tended to be made while in the former state; her self-doubts experienced in the latter. Whether in one of her manic moods she first showed symptoms of pregnancy and then made her prophecy about the Shiloh, or made the prophecy and then showed the symptoms was never known. What was clear, however, was that nine months prior to Christmas 1814, she began to show signs of pregnancy. She invited the Prince Regent, two archbishops, the dukes of Gloucester and Kent to send their own physicians to confirm that she was with child. The invitation was ignored and so she called in her own doctors.

The first to see her in April 1814 was a Dr Mathias.[25] He was interviewed by Mrs Townley who asked him: Would he believe that Joanna could have child by divine agency if he saw the child at her breast? "Seeing is believing," the doctor replied, and his services were summarily dispensed with. The next physician to call was the eminent Dr Reece, a member of the Royal College of Surgeons and author of a standard medical guide, who was to rue the day he stepped into the Townley household.

He saw Joanna on 7 August. He, too, was asked the question put to Dr Mathias but in Joanna's presence. When he answered cautiously that she might be pregnant, she went into a rage. "This will not satisfy the public," she shouted. He offered to examine her *per vaginam* but she refused, permitting him only to inspect her through her nightclothes. This he did and after what he called "a thorough examination", he pronounced her pregnant. "The appearance of the mammary glands I considered the leading point in her favour. I saw no reason for supposing the smallest deception."

Reece was not the only doctor to confirm her pregnancy. At least six others backed him up, but it was Reece who became the target for public vilification. He was denounced in the press, libelled and made out to be both dupe and rogue who took large fees from the Southcottians in order to substantiate their leader's claims. To defend himself he published a pamphlet setting out the events as clearly and precisely as possible. From this we know what happened in those last months of 1814.[27]

He found Joanna to be a woman of mild temperament and simplicity of manners with a "motherly kindness that distinguished her behaviour". Whereas Dr Mathias stated that Joanna was living "much of her time in bed—in downy indolence", eating often and praying never, Reece said that her apartment "was paltry and mean, and she did not appear to be loaded with the delicacies of life, or to press upon her followers for more than the bare necessities of existence".

In spite of being rejected once, Mathias was called again to see her in August. After examining her, he said she was suffering from "biliary obstructions" and that her excess weight was due to lack of exercise. She replied that if she was not pregnant then something was wrong that would kill her. The doctor, clearly not a man of much sensitivity, agreed with her and gave her some medicine. He was not to see her alive again.

To preserve the proprieties, a husband was found for the virgin "mother". Many had offered their hand, from merchants to bankrupts, but she chose one of her friends and disciples and married him in a quiet ceremony on 12 November. Reece was brought in a week later. He found her exhausted, "low and dejected and unable to speak her mind". She was obviously passing through one of her depressive states and suffering from self-doubts. She told Reece that if she died, her body was to be kept warm for four days and then opened up. "You will find something alive in me," she said, "which will prove to my friends that I am not an impostor." A kind if gullible man, Reece offered to try to save the child but Joanna declined. She then burst into tears.

Recovering her composure, she asked her friends to gather around her. Since the announcement of the Shiloh, Joanna had never been left alone by her faithful. Now they came close to her four-poster bed. What they heard, however, was not what they expected. Her words are worth repeating in full because they reflect one of the main aspects of the relationship between the messianic leader and his or her followers, that of mutual support.

My friends, some of you have known me nearly twenty-five years, and all of you not less than twenty. When you have heard me speak my prophecies, you have sometimes heard me say that I *doubted* my inspiration. But at the same time you would never let me despair. When I have been alone, it has often appeared delusion, but when the communications (of the Spirit) were made to me, I did not in the least doubt. Feeling as I now do feel, that my dissolution is drawing near, and that a day or two may terminate my life, it all appears delusion. [She then wept bitterly.] It is very extraordinary that after spending all my life in investigating the Bible, it should please the Lord to inflict this heavy burden on me.[28]

A messiah inspires his followers with a fervent belief in him; this belief becomes their sole support so that even when the messiah lapses or weakens, the followers persist in their belief, thereby reviving his own belief in himself. This is exactly what happened that day in Joanna's bedroom. The followers heard her say that "all appears delusion", but refused to accept her own judgment. Mr Howe, one of her followers, spoke up in answer. "Mother," he said, "your feelings are human. We know that you are a favoured woman of God, and that you will produce the Child; and, whatever you may say to the contrary will not diminish our faith."

The reassurance immediately revived her and tears changed into smiles. Once again Joanna became her own most ardent supporter. But she was a dying woman. In December Reece saw her again and found her condition much worse. However, she continued to maintain her belief in this child and told Reece she had felt him move. The doctor now had *his* doubts. Joanna was very emaciated; the hysteria that might have produced the semblance of pregnancy had disappeared, leaving her "sallow, cadaverous and dying". To one of her followers she said, "What does the Lord maen by this—I am certainly dying." But he replied, smiling, "No, no, you will not die, or if you should, you will return again".

Joanna died at four o'clock on Monday 27 December. Following her instructions, her followers kept her body warm for four days with hot-water bottles, then invited Reece, Mathias and other doctors who had visited her to conduct a post-mortem. Had it not been pathetically absurd, the scene would have been horribly morbid. Perhaps it was both.

On the bed lay the body of Joanna. Around it stood no fewer

than fifteen medical men. Behind them were her most faithful disciples, many of them smoking heavily to hide the stench which became almost unbearable when the dissecting knife was applied to the livid, putrefying flesh. The uterus was examined and dissected. The faithful leaned forward on tiptoe to see the Shiloh appear who would lead Israel back to Palestine and rebuild Jerusalem. As Mathias reported with medical precision: "Neither the promised Shiloh nor any other foetus was found within it; and it was apparently free from disease; the ovaria were in a healthy state."[29]

The fact that no organic disease could be found saved the faith of the disciples. And when Reece in surprise uttered the words, "Damn me if the child is not *gone*!" they took this to mean that Shiloh had been there in the womb as Joanna had said. It had not died, but it had "gone", that is, it had been "caught up unto God and to his throne", as the *Book of Revelation* had prophesied of the man-child born of the "woman clothed with the sun". Mrs Townley, Joanna's faithful friend for many years, at first did not know what to believe, but soon after she could write: "Joanna will appear much like a ghost, and will remain in that state, till the Spirit of the Lord enters her."[30] Then the Shiloh, too, would return in God's good time to claim his throne.

Throughout the months preceding Joanna's death the faithful had been harassed by mobs bent on violence. Fearing now for their safety and for that of their beloved Mother's body, they quickly arranged for a secret burial in St John's Wood cemetery. They continued to be mocked and laughed at for their beliefs, but they would not be put down. The Southcottian sect led by a series of minor messiahs claiming to be the Shiloh lasted in various guises for the rest of the nineteenth century and well into this century both in Britain and America. The famous box in which Joanna was supposed to have kept all her prophecies and which was to have been opened up in times of national crisis remained a perennial newspaper story till quite recently.

It may perhaps be said that Joanna and her followers had the last word:

> Oh yes, although no Shiloh has appear'd,
> And fancied triumph glads your laughing minds,
> Soon shall your jest and mirth no more be heard:

Despair, you scribbling liars of *The Times.*
What if Joanna's wrath on scoffers hurl'd,
Implores the Powers above to change her doom,
Serenely quits a persecuting world,
And sinks content to a lamented tomb.
Shall these things for a single moment make
A *true believer* venture to complain?
No, tho' mysterious, like her prophecies
All shall at last be clear to vulgar eyes;
All doubt in time be gloriously solv'd.[31]

CHAPTER THIRTEEN

REBELS AND BILLIARD PLAYERS

HAD RICHARD BROTHERS published his book of prophecies, *A Revealed Knowledge*[1] in any decade of the eighteenth century other than the last it would probably have been totally ignored. Instead the book was a best-seller, going into numerous editions in Britain, France, Ireland and America, and attracting the attention of a wide public which included some very important people—artists, Members of Parliament and wealthy merchants.

The eighteenth century was, as the historian G. M. Trevelyan has said, one whose "special function" was "to diffuse common sense and reasonableness in life and thought".[2] There was little of either common sense or of reasonableness in *A Revealed Knowledge*, "Wrote under the Direction of the Lord God, And publish'd by his Sacred Command; It being the first sign of warning for the benefit of all Nations".

The last decade, however, was ready for one like Richard Brothers.[3] It was a time of war, of revolution, when the accepted order of the world was being overturned, of industrial and economic upheaval with new and marvellous machinery offering untold riches to some and threatening unimagined suffering to others: a time of uncertainty. People wanted answers to questions they were yet unable to formulate, especially frightened people like small tradesmen who could not cope with the new ways of making money and skilled artisans who could not respond to the new ways of making goods.

It was to such people that Richard Brothers spoke. They listened and rallied to his call—the oldest call in Western religion—the return to Jerusalem. Instead of anxiety and uncertainty, rising prices and lowering standards, he offered them visions of hope:

I cast my eyes over the surface of the land; it was scorched

> dark brown, and frightful to look at: I could see no Grass in the Meadows, and the Bushes in the hedges were all burnt brown; *so great and mighty was the heat*. I could see no Beasts in the field, and the Fouls [*sic*] of heaven were all flown away. After this I was in a vision, and saw a large SWORD unsheathed in Heaven: soon after I saw a large CUP full of red wine, and much froth on top, lifted up and held out to all nations.[4]

To the prophet's home in Paddington Street, London, the crowds came, plain, ordinary folk as well as the very wealthy. French aristocrats in exile from the Revolution wanted to know whether they would recover their estates in France. Rich ladies sought answers to matrimonial problems or affairs of the heart. Businessmen asked whether the time was ripe to sell or to buy. Brothers received them all and they were impressed and inspired by his mild manner, his tall figure and handsome face.

Brothers enjoyed this reverence, short-lived though it was. It was a great change from what he had been used to. Twice before he had been locked up for debt, on one occasion in notorious Newgate where, but for a kind woman, Miss Isabella Wake, who brought him every Monday morning a three-penny loaf of bread, he might well have starved to death.

Before falling on bad times Brothers had been a sailor. Born in Newfoundland in 1757, he had gone to sea at the age of fourteen and had fought with bravery under Admiral Rodney against the French in 1781. In 1783 he was promoted to the rank of lieutenant; but after the Peace of Versailles, he was discharged at half-pay of £54 per annum, not (even in those days) much recompense for a man who had fought bravely for his country.

Brothers then joined the merchant navy and married. Cutting short his honeymoon to join his ship or lose his job, he returned home later to find his wife in another man's arms. He went up to London and apart from spending his time in Nonconformist chapels, possibly with the Quakers, and hiding himself in his room, he appeared to do nothing. This was his period of "incubation", one which most messiahs seem to experience before their spiritual rebirth and the receiving of their "call". He mulled over his own life and the state of the world and found both wanting. As to the latter, he thought that war and everything to do with it was evil. No man should draw his sword against another, he said, and he broke his own sword in two as a sign of his pacifism.

His sole income was his pension, but to draw this, he had to swear an oath of allegiance to King George. The oath was supposedly voluntary, but no claimant could obtain the pension without first swearing it. Brothers refused to take the oath and wrote to the Admiralty Board informing them of this. As a result, they amended the offending "voluntary" clause to avoid asking future claimants to perjure themselves. Brothers still refused to swear allegiance to the King "as his Sovereign Lord", so he fell deep in debt.

He had been writing furiously to the royal family and the government, warning them of war and terrible destruction. War between Austria, Prussia and France was about to break out, he prophesied. He presented himself in May 1792 at the House of Commons to tell the government, but he was sent on his way. Whitehall was about to be destroyed. The "number of the beast" 666 of *Revelation* corresponded—more or less—to the number of members sitting in the Houses of Parliament. Parliament was doomed. So, too, was the great city of London.

> The Lord God knowing that I loved him with all my heart was now pleased to give me another proof of his unalterable regard, and convince me by it, that, although he could not in justice to his recorded judgments spare London, yet, for my sake he would shew mercy to some: and take care to remove the persons I desired should be saved to a sufficient distance beyond the limits to be destroyed and sunk.[5]

William Pitt, the Prime Minister, William Wilberforce, the leader of the anti-slave trade movement, Brinsley Sheridan, the playwright and politician, Charles Fox, the parliamentarian, the King and his family—none of these illustrious personages "saved" by Brothers took the slightest notice of him and his threats, or thanked him for his intervention with the Almighty on their behalf. In disgust, Brothers decided to give up prophesying. After his release from Newgate prison, his debt having been paid by the Admiralty from his accumulated pension, he left London. He had not travelled far when he received his "call". God ordered him to cut from a hedge a hazel twig. This was the sign. He obeyed and turned back.

In his Paddington Street lodgings he shut himself up and

devoted himself to writing *A Revealed Knowledge*. The fame its publication in 1794 brought him, brought also the unwelcomed attention of those in authority who had so far ignored him. This was a period when anyone who showed any sympathy for France, the enemy, or the Revolution was regarded in England as a "Jacobin", a threat to peace and order. The government had launched a campaign to wipe out political dissent and Richard Brothers was caught up in it. He had prophesied that in July 1795 he would go to Constantinople; that by August the English government would fall; that on 19 November he would be revealed as the Prince of the Hebrews, and George III would yield up his throne to him. The Jews would follow him, Brothers, the Nephew of the Almighty, the direct descendant of James, brother of Jesus, and would return to the Holy Land with all their property on ships provided by France, Spain and England. The Redemption would be consummated in 1798 by their rebuilding of Jerusalem.[6]

Prophecies about the Jews and their return to Palestine worried Pitt and parliament not at all; but talk of the King giving up his throne to Brothers sounded too much like Jacobinism for their comfort. On Wednesday, 4 March 1795, the same day as *The Times* attacked him as being "revolutionarily exalted",[7] two King's Messengers knocked at his door with a warrant. A crowd was always to be found hanging about his house and they cheered and booed loudly as Brothers was pushed into a waiting carriage.

The panicky state of the nation at the time can be gauged from the fact that, in order to charge him with some misdemeanour, the government had to dig up an old Elizabethan statute against "unlawfully, maliciously, and wickedly writing, printing and publishing fantastical prophecies with the intent to cause dissension and other disturbances within the realm".[8] Brothers was brought before the privy council. His performance, like that of other messiahs before their accusers, brought him only credit. Pitt and his ministers who attended the hearing were put to shame by the mannerly and gentle conduct of the Nephew of the Almighty. The Lord Chancellor, having heard him answer all the harsh questions put to him, came to his decision: "I see nothing in the words of Mr Brothers but what is sensible and proper. He may withdraw".[9]

Brothers was not without friends in high places and the verdict was warmly received. One of his closest disciples and his principle champion in parliament was Nathaniel Brassey Halhed. A small, wizened man, Halhed's insignificant looks belied the fact that he was one of the most brilliant linguists in the country, "a pioneer of modern philology",[10] and the man credited with inventing the term "Aryanism", that is, the language group from which the majority of European and some Indian languages are derived. Halhed had tried to lay before his fellow-members on the table of the House of Commons the prophecies of Richard Brothers without success. He wrote a *Testimony of the Authenticity* of Brothers's prophecies,[11] stating his absolute conviction in the claim that Brothers was the Nephew of the Almighty by his relationship to Jesus through James and that he was, consequently, divinely inspired. "For as Moses ascended from the ark of bullrushes, so did Mr Brothers rise from a ship, having been bred to the navy."[12] He also calculated that the Millennium was due to commence in November 1795.*[13]

Richard Brothers, alas, was not to share in it. The government had not yet done with him. No sooner had he been released by the privy council than a lunacy enquiry was instituted against him. The "trial" was a travesty of justice. Some years later, Brothers described what took place:

> I was carried to an inn, where I saw a number of men respectable enough sitting around a large table.... No friend was permitted to appear for me, no witness in my favour, nor counsel to assist me; all was darkness and gloom like the Spanish Inquisition determined on death; they never even told me who they were, for what cause assembled, or by what authority. They had provided a counsel against me like cowards determined before hand on my condemnation and confinement for life.[14]

Neither Halhed nor any of Brothers's friends could help him. He was found insane and committed to an asylum where he remained for the next eleven years.

> With such inveterate malice I have been treated [he complained with justification] and such pains have been taken to

* See chapter four.

make people believe I am insane, that, since my confinement here all liberty has been denied me of sending for an independent physician, for fear he should see the fraud of my confinement, and have honesty and courage enough to make it known.[15]

Most of his friends and support fell away. Only one man remained faithful, a young Edinburgh lawyer named John Finlayson who sold up his practice after reading Brothers's works and came to London to be near him. He became a successful estate agent, dividing his time between his business and Brothers, who insisted he learnt draftsmanship in order to carry out a new project he was developing—the planning of the new city of Jerusalem.

Brothers had greatly interested himself in the Jews, as did so many Christians and especially Christian messiahs, but more as symbols for their messianic dreams than as real people. He spoke of the "visible" and the "invisible" Jews, the latter being the descendants of the Ten Lost Tribes who, he said, were now living in disguise as Englishmen. It was for them and not for the real Jews that he prophesied the return to the Holy Land; it was for them that he planned the New Jerusalem.

Richard Brothers may have been adjudged mad by his own society, but his prophecies about the restoration of the Holy Land have for us today a ring of truth that is no less than uncanny. His readers, he said, could rely on it "as a positive truth, that many of their descendants, sons and daughters, will be respectable inhabitants of this city".[16] This, doubtless, has come true. He said Jerusalem was desolate and barren with poor villages, as indeed it was in his day, and advised that the Hebrews be assisted with corn and cattle "for stock and food, until they are regularly settled to supply themselves".[17] He also advised the building of harbours in the Mediterranean and at Eliat. All difficulties would be conquered, he said, "by a wise people, fortified with courage and perseverance; for it is our own country, and the only one we can live free in. To be great from a small beginning, we must all become farmers and merchants; and every one of our senators, I hope, will attach one of the two honourable distinctions to his high rank."[18] A more accurate blueprint for early Zionism could scarcely be found, and certainly not in the first year of the nineteenth century.

The "visible" Jews, however, did not thank him for his concern. They were, on the contrary, insulted by his claims. Wrote one: "In no part of the sacred writ do we find that the messiah is to be brought up to the profession of a mariner, much less a lieutenant of a man of war". More important, Brothers was not even circumcized. "Jews who are strict observers of this rite will sooner remain in bondage for ever, than consent to be led home by an uncircumcized Philistine."[19]

The "invisible" Jews, on the other hand, were intrigued by Brothers's idea that the English people were the descendants of the Ten Lost Tribes of Israel. In time they expanded the notion and developed it into a substantial body of beliefs which formed the basis of the organization called the British Israelites that still numbers many thousands of members both in Britain and America.

Brothers languished in the asylum for eleven years. Then at last, after the death of his inveterate enemy, William Pitt, in 1806, he was released. He went to live with his last-remaining disciple, Finlayson, through whose ceaseless efforts his release was obtained. By now he was a pale, thin, weak old man, embittered by the treatment he had received and by the obscurity into which he had fallen. He died on 25 January 1824, leaving Finlayson to carry on publicizing his prophecies. The latter finally exhausted his resources and his strength in the task and died penniless in 1854.

The fate of most messiahs is either to be locked up or to be killed. Some are simply killed; some are locked up and then killed, and some are locked up and, having been punished for their "crimes" against society, forgotten, like Richard Brothers. How society reacts depends on the extent to which it is prepared to tolerate the messiah's deviation from the accepted views of reality and his challenge to the accepted values of society. Inherent in every messiah's message is a criticism of his society; he promises his followers a new reality, a New Jerusalem, but this implies a condemnation of the old. Because of this, society invariably over-reacts and accords the messiah treatment out of proportion to his challenge. In this way society turns messiah into martyr.

Sir William Percy Honeywood Courtenay, as he called himself, is still remembered with great affection by people living in the vicinity of Canterbury in east Kent. His standard—a white banner bordered in blue with a red lion in the centre—has been preserved for over 130 years, an unmarked grave is pointed to as his resting-place, and there are some who proudly claim to be his illegitimate descendants.

Courtenay arrived in Canterbury in 1832.[20] His appearance was so extraordinary that he could not fail to attract attention as he strode the streets, entering The Rose, where he was to stay. He was over six feet tall with the shoulders of a wrestler; his complexion was dark; his long hair and thick flowing beard black; his eyes were penetrating; his features those of an aristocrat. He wore a suit of crimson velvet trimmed with gold, a cap and a mantle of the same colour. His silk stockings were also of crimson and his slippers of Turkish design.

Only a foreigner could look so strange and so it came as no surprise to the citizens of Canterbury to learn that his name was Count Moses Rothschild. He certainly spent and gave money away in the manner expected of a Rothschild. Within a few days of his arrival he was the most famous man in the city. People flocked to the inn to see him. He spent much of his day walking about and crowds followed him wherever he went. Like the good servants they were, the waiters and chambermaids at The Rose did not let on that the "wealthy" count borrowed money from them for his extravagances and did not pay it back.

Without explanations or prior warnings, Moses Rothschild suddenly emerged one morning from The Rose as Sir William Percy Honeywood Courtenay, Knight of Malta, Rightful Heir to the earldom of Devon, and of the Kentish estates of Sir Edward Hales, King of the Gypsies, and King of Jerusalem. The metamorphosis was accepted apparently without question. Indeed, in his new guise, Courtenay actually began to attract the interest of some of Canterbury's leading citizens. Those who bothered to check up on his claim to be the heir to the earldom of Devon and the Hales estates would have learnt that the real Earl of Devon, Viscount Courtenay, was living abroad after some scandal and that the Hales estates did exist unclaimed as there were no direct descendants.

Details such as these did not concern the local tories, who came to Courtenay to ask him to stand as their candidate in the General Election, the first after the Reform Act of 1832 which extended the franchise. His election appeal was to all: the rich, the poor, the religious, the radicals and the conservatives. "Follow

Courtenay," read his manifesto, "and you will see the good old days back again; the old days of the good old England, with roast beef, plum pudding, and nut brown ale for all."[21]

He lost, but this did not in any way diminish his popularity; in fact, it increased, and he was soon an honoured guest at every important dinner party. Women particularly were drawn to him; mothers wanted their daughters to marry him, and when he walked down the street it was not unusual to see a well-dressed lady lift up the hem of his coat to kiss it.

Early in March 1833 he brought out the first issue of a newspaper called *The Lion* of which he was the sole editor and publisher. Again, as in his electioneering, he appealed to the widest possible readership. The banner of *The Lion* No. 5 (there were only eight issues) reads: "Justice for the Poor! Justice for the Rich! Heaven protect the widow, fatherless, and distressed".[22] His politics, such as they were, tended towards popular radicalism. He attacked taxes and tithes of all kinds, aristocrats and the clergy: "The Root of all evil is in the Church—Lucre! Lucre!! Lucre!!!"[23] but not the monarchy: "To support the Throne as the birthright of the Princess Victoria, should be the object of all loyal subjects".[24] His religious views, too, were all-embracing and undefined: "To exalt the Cross as our national banner is the only road to England's liberty".[25]

Like Richard Brothers, Courtenay identified himself with the Jews whose demands for emancipation were then being hotly debated.

> We must know that it was from the Jews we received the truth and light of life; that their persecutions have all been for our advantage and gain; then, surely let Christians love Abraham's race; for Christ also was a Jew. No people have ever suffered so much as the children of Israel; and all this for being faithful to the laws of our beloved Moses, and for the good of mankind.[26]

Had Courtenay continued as he had begun, attracting attention and followers to his ill-defined but popular sentiments, he might have lived a long and comfortable life and died a prosperous minor prophet, as his most recent biographer has suggested.[27] But he was reaching for more than mere fame. He had begun his voyage into messiahship which, as we have seen, leads to inevitable confrontation with the authorities and ends eventually with pain, torment and possibly death.

Some men unknown to Sir William had been charged with smuggling in February 1833. Courtenay put himself forward as the defending counsel for one of them. Why? There is no one obvious answer. He gained nothing from it, not money because the man was poor, and not fame because he was already famous. It was something more: the need to stand out above all, to appear as the *saviour* of all.

The proceedings were a fiasco. Courtenay's man was found guilty. Courtenay then offered to give evidence on his behalf and under affirmation he gave information that was easily and quickly shown to be untrue. The interest that had been shown in him at the start of the trial now turned to contempt and anger. His clothes and manner were ridiculed, but worse than this, he was charged with perjury, found guilty, and sentenced to seven years' transportation—a punishment far in excess of his crime.

When given permission to speak in mitigation, he harangued the court. "I did not do it to be well thought of," he cried. "I hate popularity! What if this were the justice of the whole country! I would lay down my life for you. I would take all my prosecutors and jurors to my heart, for they know not what they do." At this point he clasped his hands and looked upwards. "Kent! your God will see me done justice to. If I have been convicted on mistake . . ." But here the judge intervened to say, "No mistake at all, nothing can be clearer". Patient to the end, the judge allowed Courtenay to continue until, exhausted, he sat down. "Have you done?" the judge asked. In a low voice, very different from his previous loud declamations, Courtenay answered "Yes, my Lord". When he left the court, reading his Bible, a reporter said he revealed "a mild firmness of mind and unrepining acquiescence in his fate, worthy of a better cause".[28]

The transportation never took place. Courtenay was declared insane by the court, perhaps as a result of the ensuing public outcry at the severity of the sentence. He was sent to an asylum where he stayed from October 1833 to October 1837, released finally under his father's protection. The citizens of Canterbury had not heard the end of Sir William.

His father, needless to say, was not a Courtenay. He was plain William Tom, an innkeeper from Bodmin in Cornwall, and his illustrious son had been born John Nichols Tom on 10 November

1799. Before his change of character, John Tom had been a solicitor's clerk and then a clerk in a firm of wine merchants where he had done so well that on the retirement of the partners for whom he worked, he took over the business. He was also a good cricketer and one of the best wrestlers in the county, justly proud of its long wrestling tradition. He was married and in every way conformed to his society. What, then, happened to make him alter so radically?

Before embarking on their careers as messiah, many appear to have suffered personal catastrophes which have profoundly affected their self-identity and their relationship with the world. As I shall discuss further in chapter fifteen, psychologists have identified sudden trauma as one of the possible causes of severe identity-crisis and consequent schizophrenia. Courtenay certainly had his fill of tragedy which came suddenly and inexplicably to turn his world upside-down. His mother, to whom he was devoted, suffered a breakdown in 1827—six years before his arrival in Canterbury—and was removed to an asylum where she died. His business suffered and in the following year, 1828, the shop premises were destroyed by fire. In 1829 he experienced periods of melancholy and for the next three years he was in and out of different jobs. In May 1832, the year of his change, he took a boat for Liverpool with a cargo of malt and never returned. No one knows for sure what happened to him between May and September of that year, but when he came to Canterbury in September his transformation into a new identity—that of Moses Rothschild in the first instance—was already well advanced. It needed only one more step from Rothschild to Courtenay to complete it.

Courtenay was released from the asylum in 1837 into a countryside seething with discontent. The New Poor Law of 1834 "made the rural labourer a pauper", according to Trevelyan, "and discouraged his thrift and self-respect. . . . Wealth was increasing so fast in town and country that the contrasts between the life of the rich and the life of the poor were more dramatic and more widely observable than of old. . . . It was these contrasts that made the Radicalism of the new era."[29]

Courtenay immediately identified himself with the downtrodden against the rich and powerful. He lived on a farm named Bossenden with the Culver family and spent his time going about talking to the farm-labourers, sympathizing with their complaints and enchanting their wives. Sarah Culver, the 40-year-old spinster of the family, fell deeply in love with him and became his most devoted follower. Once more Courtenay tasted the power of leadership and this in turn enhanced his magnetism. William Wills, a local smallholder, announced that Courtenay was divine—the first person to do so—and soon the word went about that he was the reincarnation of Jesus Christ.

Courtenay, too, became a devoted believer in his messianic mission and he now took to addressing large gatherings of people, prophesying to them in the words of St James: "Go to now, ye rich men, weep and howl for your miseries that shall come upon you. Ye have lived in pleasure on the earth, and been wanton. Behold the husbandman waiteth the precious fruit of the earth. Be ye also patient, for the coming of the Lord draweth nigh".[30] When their attention strayed, he would shoot his pistols into the air to show how he would make the stars fall.

A disciple said of him: "Courtenay had a tongue which an unlearned person could not get over. A man that I knew could not sleep all night for thinking of him and told his wife that he must go with Sir William, for if he did not a shower of fire would come down from heaven and burn him and his children to ashes".[31]

By the end of spring 1838 a full-scale religious revival had erupted in the vicinity of Canterbury, centred around "the peasants' saviour". Crowds followed him about, kissing his simple farm-labourer's smock which he had now taken to wear in keeping with his new rôle. Women brought their children to him for his blessings. The poor, the maimed, the halt and the blind came to be cured. In secret and only to the chosen few he showed what passed for the marks of nails on the palms of his hands and on his feet.

From revivalism to revolution is, in certain circumstances, but a short step. The dissidents whom Courtenay claimed to represent wanted more than mere words. It was not enough to denounce the rich as corrupted, to condemn their gold and their silver as "cankered" in bold Biblical phrases. Their main wealth lay in the land and this had to be wrested from them and given to the poor.

Courtenay, sensitive as are most messiahs to the feelings and desires of his followers, underwent his final transformation. His name remained the same but now he was the bold and daring leader of a peasant army, a nineteenth-century Wat Tyler. His army numbered only about 60 men and their armour consisted mainly of farm implements and one or two firearms, but it was quite enough to worry the authorities in Canterbury who sent three constables to arrest Courtenay for disturbing the peace.

In the lives of many messiahs, and especially Sir William Courtenay, one cannot avoid the suggestion that there is a strong element of play-acting. Like children who run away from difficult problems, from stress and anxiety with which they have failed to cope, into the world of the imagination, messiahs (and their followers) "dress up" as it were in the clothes of imagined beings, and seeing themselves in their glorious garments convince themselves that they are what they seem. Unfortunately, a time comes when the acting has to stop.

The constables met Sir William at the door of the farmhouse where he and his men were encamped. He was carrying his two pistols and a sword in his belt. When he knew what they had come for, he shot one of the men. The other two ran off while he furiously stabbed the wounded man three times with his sword and then discharged the loaded pistol at his body. "I have killed his body," he cried out to his horrified disciples, "but I have saved his soul."[32]

The murder sealed Sir William's fate. The 37 men who finally went with him to nearby Bossenden Wood must have been aware of this, but they feared him, were devoted to him, and had gone too far along in their self-created drama to back down. "We would have fought 2,000 men if we'd had to," one said later. "He told us we could not be shot."[33]

Two companies of soldiers from Canterbury were sent to meet the peasant army. Courtenay promised his men that his divine powers would protect them, much as another peasant messiah, Thomas Müntzer, had promised his followers three centuries before that he would catch the army's cannonballs in his sleeve. Both were believed—to their cost.

Lieutenant Bennett was a keen young soldier. He had seen Courtenay fire on his major when the two armies first caught sight of each other. He now called upon Courtenay to surrender; the rebel took no notice. Angered, Bennett ran forward. His commander ordered him back, but too late. Courtenay raised his pistol and fired. The ball entered Bennett's body on the right side and passed out through the left, killing him instantly. Courtenay's followers, brandishing their staves and cudgels, attacked the army. The soldiers were ordered to fire. Courtenay was cut down in a hail of bullets and so were eight of his followers, a ninth died later. Only two soldiers including Bennett were killed.

The bodies were taken away and laid out in the parlour of an inn where, according to the reporter from *The Globe*, "Courtenay appeared as a giant amongst men of moderate size". The rumour went about that he would rise again and the inn was besieged with men and women, especially the latter, hoping for a miracle. "A more convincing proof of the fanaticism that prevails," wrote the same reporter, "can be afforded by the fact that a woman was apprehended yesterday who was discovered washing the face of Courtenay, and endeavouring to pour some water between his lips."[34] The woman was poor Sarah Culver, the spinster who had worshipped him.

Courtenay's death ended the short-lived rebellion. Ten of his disciples were sentenced to imprisonment and transportation, and the excitement quickly died down. But the peasant's saviour was remembered with love and reverence by those "ignorant and deluded persons" whose cause he had taken up. There was much silent weeping in the poor cottages on the estates of east Kent. Some time after his death, a placard appeared mysteriously on a tree in Bossenden Wood on which was scrawled: "Our real true Messiah, King of the Jews".[35]

"In Canterbury," Sir William had once boasted, "the name of Courtenay will never be forgotten while memory holds her seat." Time has proved him right.[36]

Historians argue over the reason for Courtenay's success with the peasants. Some contend that the rebellion was a true proletarian uprising, motivated by genuine social and economic grievances, and that the messiah was merely a leader to which the dissidents could rally. The implication of the argument is that if Sir William had not led the army of peasants, it would have been led by someone else. Others contend that the main motive was religious fanaticism resulting from ignorance and boredom.[37] The evidence of a barrister commissioned in the same year as the rebellion to conduct a study on the neighbourhood by the Central Society of Education seems to verify this view. The barrister reported "an absence of all lively and innocent amusements. For them [the peasants] there appeared to be no recreation of either an active or a quiet character, unless they resorted to the beershop".[38]

Boredom is one of many circumstances which give rise to messianic movements. Some movements are associated with very real deprivations—of food, of shelter, and primarily of safety and security—but emptiness of the spirit, the lack of excitement and of propulsion—a sense of going forward to something—play a large part in attracting followings. The messiahs offer diversion, direction and certain, if intangible, goals. That is one reason why they appeal to all classes in society, not only to the poor and the physically deprived.

Henry Prince's nineteenth-century sect, the Abode of Love, or Agapemone, was more than a faint echo of Henry Niklaes's Family of Love of the sixteenth century. They both appealed to people who were neither very rich nor very poor, who had a roof over their heads, a fire in the hearth, and food in the pantry. The women of both sects were sheltered from society, or at least the less savoury aspects of society, as much as possible. Not for them was there any danger that their fathers or husbands would force them out to work or sell them into prostitution.

Yet these women who followed their messiahs were obviously looking for more than protection and support of their families. By acting as they did, they cut themselves off from that support. Their narrow, insular lives offered them no scope, no challenge, no hope of *change*. They had their comfort and security; they had their church and their acquaintances; but still they felt themselves unfulfilled, cut off, lonely, adrift, their souls in exile. They, if no one else, understood instinctively what Brother Prince meant when he said, "The human body dwells in an enemy's country, amidst enemies, all of whom are in league with that enemy within him—death".[39] They, too, sought a spiritual re-awakening, spiritual release from the bonds of family, duty and society that bound them. They wanted to be free, and Brother Prince offered them freedom—of a kind.[40]

The five Nottidge sisters lived with their mother and father near the village of Stoke in Suffolk. Josias Nottidge, their father, had made money in London and had retired to the country with the family. The daughters had not married; the youngest was 40 when Henry Prince came to Stoke in the late 1840s to preach at the church there. They came to listen. Very soon they were under his spell. He was a quiet-spoken man, slender and neat in appearance, with a pallid face, and a soft, endearing smile. Before he had become a minister, he had qualified as an apothecary, but after a very serious illness, he had a "calling" and in 1837 went to a Church of England theological college at Lampeter in Wales where he distinguished himself by stirring up a spirit of revivalism.

In his first curacy in Charlinch, Somerset, his fiery sermons against sin, his prayer-meetings, sometimes lasting for days, and the passionate adherence he evoked in his parishioners got him into trouble with the Bishop; he was politely but firmly removed.

From Charlinch he went to Stoke and met the Nottidge family. Josias laughed at his daughters' reverence for him and their mother refused to have him in the house, but they clung to him against the persecution of the world. Prince had already experienced his spiritual rebirth when, as he later wrote, "I passed right through the middle of life, and came out on the other side of God".[41] Now he could offer the Nottidge women and all who followed him a lead towards their own spiritual re-awakening. As he moved nearer his own epiphany, so his followers moved with him into a fellowship with God. "I am utterly absorbed and swallowed up in God," Prince wrote.[42] So, too, would they be.

From Stoke he went to Brighton and from Brighton to Weymouth. At each stop he gathered more followers and took a further step towards declaring himself a messiah. At Brighton he announced that the promised Comforter was come; at Weymouth in the plush assembly-room of the Royal Hotel, he told his audience of squires and old ladies that only those who received the Holy One in his own person would be saved. Soon his disciples were beginning each prayer meeting with the auspicious words: "Lo! He cometh!"[43]

Prince's first and most faithful disciple was the Reverend Samuel Starky, a man well-connected to some of the leading families of Somerset. He now began with others to collect funds so that Prince would have a church of his own. Followers sold up land, farms, houses, the tools of their trades in order to make a contribution. Starky himself gave £1,000, his sister to whom Prince was married, his first wife having died, transferred to him her annuity of £80; another man and four of his sisters gave £10,000. The Nottidge sisters, three of whom had followed Prince to Weymouth, were left £6,000 each by their father who had since died. They made a gift of this money to swell the fund. The church could now be built.

The place chosen was the village of Spaxton, close to Charlinch where Prince had his first curacy. Here they built a church and other buildings and laid out spacious and beautiful gardens. Here came more followers to live with them in spiritual harmony. Here they celebrated the Agapae, the love-feasts, in the manner of the early Christians, who by doing so were commemorating the Last Supper. They ate, drank, sang, and "rejoiced as one family in the Lord".[44]

The Nottidge sisters and three male converts had, at Prince's command, been given away in marriage to each other. Others followed suit, but their marriages were in spirit only. The brethren and sisters lived celibate lives. All worshipped Henry Prince who was called "the Beloved" after the *Song of Solomon*, his favourite book of the Old Testament since his student days in Wales. He regarded himself as Christ's Beloved. He taught that there had been four Dispensations, four ages characterized by God's covenant with man: the first was with Adam, the second with Noah, the third with Abraham and the fourth with Jesus. Henry Prince was the Fifth Dispensation. "In me you behold the Love of God," he told his people. "Look on me. I am one in the flesh with Christ. I died to God and was renewed in the Spirit to do His work. By me, and in me, God has redeemed all flesh from death, and brought the bodies of breathing men into the resurrection state."[45]

Quietly the Agapemonites conducted their lives behind the walls of their Spaxton community. They paid their bills promptly and gave no one any cause for complaint. "Violence was not heard in the land, nor wasting or destruction within its borders. How harmless was the earth *then*! how beautiful!" Thus, Prince's description of Paradise,[46] but the idyll was rudely interrupted by Agnes, one of the Nottidge women. She was less reverential towards "the Beloved" than the others; she tried to influence her husband, one of Prince's earliest converts, away from him, and to make matters worse, her marriage was somewhat less than spiritual: she fell pregnant. Her husband remained but Agnes was driven out of the Agapemone and only after a vigorously contested court action was she permitted to keep the son of the marriage.

While Agnes was being expelled, Louise, the youngest of the sisters, was trying to gain entrance to the Agapemone against the objections of her family. They actually resorted to violence, dragging her kicking and screaming out of the House of Love, and placing her in an asylum for the insane. It was only through the intervention of the Commissioners in Lunacy at the behest of one of the Agapemonites that her case was examined and she was released. She went straight back to the House of Love and remained there happily for the rest of her life.

Except for the court cases, the public paid scant attention to Brother Prince and his disciples; but this situation was to change. At the Great Exhibition in 1851 "the Beloved" attended in splendour, driving a fine carriage and distributing leaflets about himself in many languages to the visitors. Then, soon after the Great Exhibition came the Great Manifestation. This nearly finished the community.

Prince announced to his people that the time had come "to complete the great work of reconciling the fallen creature to the Holy One". Said he, "It was God's purpose to extend His love from heaven to earth, from spirit to flesh, from soul to body. Jesus Christ was going to carry out his purpose of grace and love towards the flesh, to save it, not by telling or explaining to flesh what his mind was towards it, but by *living it out*, through his own spirit."[47]

A virgin had to be found who would undergo with Prince a form of marriage and public consummation so that God would know "the creature" and "the creature" God. Prince would choose his bride from among the women of the Agapemone by placing a kiss on her face. In fact, he had already made his choice. She was the daughter of a widow who had followed him from Weymouth and who had since died. The girl, Sister Zoe Paterson, fitted the rôle of the Bride of the Lamb perfectly; she was young, fair and a virgin. She was not asked whether she wanted to enter into the "marriage" or not. As Prince later wrote of the event—deifying himself in the third person: "He consulted not anyone's pleasure in doing this. He had no respect to any other will than His Own. He did not even consult or in any way make known His intention to the flesh He took until He actually did take it in the presence of others."

On the day appointed, the brethren and sisters walked in solemn procession to the great hall of their main building. They sang anthems and waited anxiously for what was about to take place—the most important, the holiest event, of their lives.

Brother Prince swept into the hall. "The Holy Spirit has come as the bridegroom to his bride," he announced. "Light and clay are to join in marriage."[49]

He walked up to the girl, took her hand, and kissed her. Their union, he told her, was the mark of God's love for the flesh. Not that she had any say in the matter. "He took it in love," Prince wrote. "Not because it loved Him, for it did not; but because it pleased Him to set His love upon it. He took it with power and authority, as flesh that belonged to God, and it was at His absolute disposal; so that in taking of it He left it no choice of its own."[50]

"It was a very tender and solemn time," recalled one of the women years later. "The most tender and solemn time we have known."[51] Unfortunately, the Great Manifestation of God's love for them did not occur as they had hoped. Miss Paterson continued to live with Prince "to make it one with Him, even as a man is one flesh with his wife",[52] but contrary to the expectation of Prince and all his disciples, they did not cease to be flesh because of what had happened. They had hoped to be immediately released from all bodily existence into a life of pure spirit, but flesh won over spirit. Miss Paterson fell pregnant.

In the testing time which followed a number of members left the House of Love disillusioned. They told newspaper reporters what had happened and the place was besieged by angry and sensation-seeking crowds. The remaining disciples withdrew even further into their own world and reduced contact with the outside world to a minimum. A child was born to Miss Paterson, a girl, whom Prince and his followers called "Satan's offspring", because as Prince explained to them, he had, in fact, won the battle against the devil in the flesh—the child had been Satan's parting gift. The Evil One was gone from their House, which was now the redeemed and sanctified earth. The child remained, isolated and cast aside, as a constant reminder of their victory and Satan's defeat.

Fortunately for historians of the Agapemone, Henry Prince and his people were visited many years after the event by a distinguished writer and journalist, William Hepworth Dixon, who was editor of the *Athenaeum*. Dixon had no axe to grind. He wanted to see for himself what the Agapemone was really like; so much sensational nonsense had been written about it as an orgiastic sect of debauched Bacchanals who kept vicious bloodhounds behind huge walls to frighten away the curious. He asked if he could come and talk with them and they agreed. From him we have an intimate picture of a messiah and his disciples "at home", drawn with affection and an almost total lack of either reverence or hostility—a rare thing indeed in messianic historiography.[53]

There were no high walls and no bloodhounds. Instead Dixon found 60 middle-aged men and women living quietly in their spacious commune under the absolute rule of "the Beloved". "Each Saint appears to keep watch and ward upon his fellow. Prince may dwell apart, and hold himself accountable to none. But the rest of his people lie under bonds, and only act and speak in each other's presence." They invited him into their hall, the one where the Great Manifestation had taken place. They left him with a plate of biscuits and two decanters, one of dry sherry and one of sweet port, both of excellent quality.

He was much impressed by the church. "I had come to Spaxton from a country house; and nothing in the room appeared to me much unlike what I had left behind, except the men and women who peopled it with life." The only thing that struck him as incongruous was the presence of a billiard table among the heavy church furniture of oak and brass. Above his head, the sacred symbol of the Lamb and Dove was "flanked and supported by a rack of billiard cues".

Prince entered the room and sat in a semi-circle of his elect. Reverends Starky and Thomas, the two "Anointed Ones", as they were called, were in attendance. At Prince's side nestled two beautiful women; one was the "flesh" of the Great Manifestation, Sister Zoe Paterson. Dixon was told that the men and women lived apart and knew "no craving after devil's love", thus, there were no children. But, asked Dixon, did he not see a girl playing about on the grounds by herself? She was Satan's offspring, they answered, Satan's doing in the flesh, the broken link in their line of life, a child of shame, a living witness of the last great triumph of the devil in the heart of man.

During this tirade, Dixon turned to look at the girl's mother, Sister Zoe, expecting her to react to the cruel reference made about her and Brother Prince's child. But she sat silent, never altering "the sweet serenity of her countenance".

"Do you expect to die?" he asked the Agapemonites.

"No, never," replied one. "We have no such thought. We are

the Resurrection. Though I should see the valley choking with ten thousand corpses, the sight would not convince me that I should one day have to die."

"What about disciples—saints—who have died?"

"They have erred," came the immediate response.

After the Great Manifestation and the uproar it caused outside the walls of the Abode of Love, nothing much happened to stir the calm of the little Paradise they had made for themselves. Dixon wanted to know what they did to occupy themselves. Did they try to communicate their ideas to others, to recruit new members? "If men will not hear us," Starky replied, "what are we to do?"

"Do you teach?" Dixon asked.

"No," they said.

"Preach?"

"No."

"Read?"

"Not much."

"Farm?"

"No."

"Feed the poor?"

"No."

"Then how do you pass the time?" he asked.

"We do not live in time," they said. "We know nothing of it."

The men and women of Agapemone, Dixon concluded, had once been smitten with the passion for saving souls. They had been possessed of the power to inspire and the softness to persuade. But after a few attempts to change mankind, to steer it away from its sinfulness, they ran away and shut themselves up in a garden, "to muse and dream, eat from rich tables, pretending that the passions are dead". And in the place where once they had witnessed the attempt by Brother Prince, their messiah, to end forever fleshly desire and temptation and thus bring about immortality by uniting him, Christ's Beloved, with flesh, they now drank good dry sherry and played billiards.

Prince died in 1899, an old man of 88. His successor was John Smyth-Piggott, formerly a Church of England minister and a major in the Salvation Army, who took to preaching Agapemonite doctrines to the comfortable middle-class congregants of Clapton, east London.[54] He had great success and a church was built for him by his parishioners. After Brother Prince's death

Smyth-Piggott began to talk of the late messiah as John the Baptist who prepared the way for a Second Coming. And on one Sunday in September 1902 he ascended the steps to the altar of his church to announce that he was the Lord Jesus Christ who had died and rose again into heaven. "Behold," he declared, "I am alive for evermore."[55]

The news was received by his congregation with hysterical joy. They rushed to kiss his hands and to touch his clothes; but a news reporter in the church, realizing that he had a scoop on his hands, went straight to his office and had the so-called Second Coming boldly trumpeted in the following day's editions. This brought mobs of 5,000 and more to the doors of the church and to Smyth-Piggott's handsome rectory nearby, demanding to see miracles and the wounds of the nails. Police had to be called to protect him. This did not prevent him from declaring on the next Sunday from the same steps that he was not pastor of the church but "Him who has come again, the Son of Man himself come in My own Body, come to bless My people; come to receive them Myself; come to give everlasting life to all flesh."[56]

The announcement of his messiahship was his last public act. So harassed was he by the crowds that he closed the Clapton church and ran to hide at the Agapemone. There he remained for the rest of his life. Like Brother Prince, he, too, took a spiritual Bride of the Lamb in addition to his ageing wife, and she, too, went the way of all flesh and conceived. Only her child, Glory, a son, was treated with reverence and was anointed with holy oil, so unlike the unhappy "offspring of Satan" of the previous messiah.

After Glory came Power, another boy, and Life, a girl. Their father was still ostensibly a minister of the Church of England which was more concerned to deal with his apparent immorality than his heresy. It ignored his declamation that he was the Son of God, but unfrocked him for living in sin. Thereafter, the messiah and his devoted disciples hid themselves away at the Abode of Love, making no contact with the outside world.

Stories and rumours continued to circulate about the orgies that were supposed to take place there, but as there were no facts for these to feed on, they eventually died away. Smyth-Piggott lived with his followers in peace until his death in 1927, like Brother Prince and his followers, playing billiards in their church and waiting for the world to be damned.

CHAPTER FOURTEEN

FULL CIRCLE

ALL MEN HOPE; what the prophets of the Old Testament did was to provide their own people and—through Christianity—much of the world with a vocabulary of symbols and metaphors by which to express their future hope. Time was seen as a straight line—a progression from the present with its fears, anxieties, uncertainties, its oppression and injustice to a future when men would be at peace with God, themselves and their fellow-men. The present and the future were separated, divided by the Day of the Lord, the day of universal judgment. Things would alter for the best, but not before they became a good deal worse.

The messiah stood at the threshold of past and future, waiting for the destruction of the old, and ready to usher in and rule with justice and mercy over the new. The prophets promised Israel destruction and exile for its sins. "For Israel hath forgotten his Maker, and I will send a fire upon his cities, and it shall devour the palaces thereof."[1] But they also promised a Return. "And I will restore to you the years that the locust hath eaten, and ye shall eat in plenty, and be satisfied, and praise the name of the Lord your God that hath dealt wondrously with you."[2] Between both times: "the sun shall be turned into darkness, and the moon into blood, before the great and terrible day of the Lord come".[3] Then: "Behold, before the days come, that I will raise unto David a righteous Branch, and a King shall reign and prosper, and shall execute judgment and justice in the earth".[4] Thereafter:

> in the last days it shall come to pass that the mountain of the house of the Lord shall be exalted above the hills; and people shall flow unto it. And he shall judge among the people, and rebuke strong nations afar off; and they shall beat their swords into plowshares, and their spears into pruning-hooks: nation

shall not lift up a sword against nation, neither shall they learn war any more.[5]

In the last century or so movements were started in Africa, Asia, South America, the islands of the Pacific, all of which were influenced to a greater or lesser degree by this messianic ideal. Whatever part of the world has been touched, no matter how lightly, by the Judeao-Christian tradition, men have translated their desire for freedom into the vocabulary provided for them by the Old and New Testaments. Their aim, like that of the Jews at the time of the Babylonian exile, has been primarily to free themselves from the foreign invader and to return to their own, uncontaminated way of life. Their leaders have risen to perform these deeds in the manner of the hoped-for Jewish messiah of the House of David.

Though they have adopted many of the messianic themes, they have not merely copied them. They have used the vocabulary creatively, adding to it their own metaphors from their own histories and religions, thereby imparting to messianism a new vitality.

In their own land the Jews experienced the shock of their culture and religion being usurped by that of the oppressor. In exile they were always a minority, an island within a sea of Islam or Christianity. On the messiah rested their hope of deliverance from exile and a return to their native land where they could live as their forefathers had lived. Similarly, those who in the last 150 years have been overwhelmed by invaders from Europe have found their culture and religions usurped by those of the foreigner. Though still in their native lands, they have found themselves exiled from their own ways and have longed for a return to them. On their messiahs have rested their hope for deliverance from oppression and a return to what was best in their past.

Isaac Shembe who died in 1935 wrote a hymn in which he told his people:

> Today you are the laughing-stock
> Of all the Nations.
> So wake up Africa
> Seek thy Saviour.[6]

In the Congo Simon Kimbangu learnt about the Old and New Testaments from the British Baptist Mission.[7] In the early 1920s, while working as a servant in a white household, he had visions of God. He became a prophet and quickly developed a reputation as a healer and miracle-man, capable of raising the dead. He taught that there was only one God, that idolatry was sinful, that a man should marry only one woman, and that the white man would eventually be defeated and driven from his country. His people called him the God of the Black Man. He assured them that the time was coming when Africa would rise from the dead and the Golden Age would begin. The whites opposed him and imprisoned him. He escaped, then gave himself up, and died in prison in Elizabethville in 1950. Like Jesus he had been martyred, and like the Christians his people continued to believe in the living Kimbangu.

Andre, or Jesus, Matswa died in 1942.[8] In life his people called him messiah, in death the black Christ. When making the sign of the cross, his followers still do so in the name of the Father, of Simon Kimbangu, and of Andre Matswa. They believe that when Kimbangu and Matswa return, the two men chosen by God will, like the messiah of old, drive out the persecutors and usher in an African Millennium.

The Israelites of Queenstown in South Africa believed that they were Jehovah's Chosen People whose task it was to throw off the foreign invaders. Their messiah, 'bishop, prophet and guardian", was Enoch Mgijima[9] who rejected the New Testament as a fraud perpetrated on the Africans by the white missionaries. He preached from the Old Testament, and his people celebrated the sabbath and other Jewish holy days.

When the government ordered the sect to disband and their village to be razed, Enoch worked his disciples up into a rage of vengeance. Armed with no more than sticks and spears, but believing in the power of the messiah, they confronted the troops. The result was massacre: more than 100 of the 500 villagers were killed.

The American Watch Tower movement founded by Pastor Charles Taze Russell of Pennsylvania had a considerable influence on some of the African messianic movements led by men trained by Watch Tower missionaries. Russell had claimed that Christ returned to the earth in 1874 but he was invisible to most men. The Day of the Lord when judgment on the sinful would be meted out began, according to Russell, in the same year and would cease about 1915.[10] African messiahs took the Day of Wrath to be a judgment on the whites for their sins against the blacks, and the Millennium that would follow would come only when the whites left their country.

John Masowe was one such messiah who turned the white man's view of the Apocalypse—as delineated by Russell—against the white man.[11] He was from the Shona tribe of Rhodesia, and so powerful was his command on his people that he managed to unite within his sect Shona and other tribes hostile to them. In the tradition of the messianic leader, John Masowe "died" and was reborn at the age of seventeen. His physical grave was actually being dug for him when he recovered. He went up into the mountains and returned, clad in white, as God's Messenger, and calling himself Johannes Masowe, John the Baptist from the Wilderness.

He told his followers that they would never die but that the judgment of the Lord would be visited upon the white government and its churches. His followers called him "the Saviour Jesus", and he acknowledged being the Son of God. He came to South Africa from Rhodesia in the 1940s and wandered about in the area of Korsten where his people became known as the Basket Weavers. To the outside world, however, the identity of the messiah was kept a very close secret; his name was disguised by various aliases; the church itself was registered in the South African Companies Register as a furniture factory! Where this messiah is today and whether he is still alive only his closest disciples know.

George Khambule,[12] another South African messiah, called himself Nazar from the Old Testament Nazarites who abstained from strong drink and from cutting their hair. His other chosen names were "A and O", for Alpha and Omega, the beginning and the ending and also "the Judge". A powerful Zulu, Khambule surrounded himself with two apostles, a general of the Lord, and a general's clack of the Lord, the latter two being young women with whom he had entered into a spiritual marriage though still legally married to his first wife. He attracted a large following who saw in him a possible reincarnation of the great Zulu chiefs of the past. But opposition from other, real, chiefs and from the South African government forced him to keep moving between Natal and the Transvaal. Since the 1930s when he had his first major impact, his sect has dwindled almost out of existence.

Hatred of the whites and of the destruction they wrought on their ancient tradition has also inspired messianic movements among the Red Indians of North America. Their leaders, like the Africans, have mixed Biblical messianism with their own religious beliefs and from this produced a heady potion with which to stave off the despair caused by their dejected and inferior position in American society.

Handsome Lake was strongly influenced by the Quakers who had settled in the vicinity of New York where he was born in 1775.[13] A spendthrift youth followed by a grave illness led to visionary experiences during which he received his "call" to "save" his people from their love for the white man's liquor which was rapidly demoralizing them. He went out to teach sobriety, fidelity in marriage, and adherence to the old ways. Tenskwatawa was a Shawnee who had a vision in which he was told to preach the liberation of the Indian peoples from the whites. His people saw him as the incarnation of a legendary Algonquin chief until his defeat in 1812 which brought disgrace to him and his movement.

The judgment of the Almighty, the cataclysmic defeat of the usurper followed by a return to the "true" way were apocalyptic themes incorporate by Indian prophets into their own traditions. One of these prophets, Smohalla, began preaching in about 1850 to the tribesmen of the Nez Perces, or Pierced Noses, who lived in the north-west.[14] His gospel was one of passive resistance to white civilization. Though he did not claim himself to be the man, Smohalla prophesied that one day an Indian would come who would drive the white man out of their country and raise the dead. He reminded his tribesmen that the earth was their mother. By becoming farmers and raising cattle as the white man taught them to do they were injuring their sacred mother.

Described as a "large-headed, hump-shouldered, odd little wizard of an Indian", Smohalla was, like so many messianic leaders, an inspired speaker. Even white men who did not understand his language were moved by his oration. Gifted also with a sense of the theatrical, he arranged his public services to achieve the maximum effect on his audiences. He had an heraldic device made and bells rung frequently to attract listeners and increase the tension. Seven to him was a number filled with magical significance as it had been to the Kabbalists of old. He arranged his disciples and followers in sevens to kneel in rows of seven behind him. They sang to the accompaniment of the bells and when the spirit moved them they leapt up to give ecstatic personal testimonials of their faith in Smohalla, the prophet.

A cataleptic, the prophet would emerge from his fits claiming that he had had vision in which he had communicated with Tah-Mah-Ne-Wes, the Great Spirit. "Men who work cannot dream," he told his people, "and wisdom comes to us in dreams." His followers consequently became generally known as the "Dreamers", and though their strange religion did not spread much beyond the north-west, it still survives, over a century later.

So, too, does another messianic movement begun in the last years of the eighteenth century by Wodziwob of the Paviotsos who lived between Nevada and California.[15] Wodziwob prophesied that a great cataclysm would shake the world; the earth would open up and swallow the white man, leaving his buildings, goods and tools for the Indian to use. All Indians would also disappear into the earth, but those belonging to the religion of Wodziwob would return to a life of peace and happiness. The followers danced around a totem pole to songs composed and taught to them by their messiah. The Ghost Dance, as it was known, spread across the north-west and even some white Mormons became addicted to its hypnotic spell.

In 1886, during a high fever, John Wilson, or Wovoka, the Cutter,[16] who had been born in Nevada and raised by a white farmer named Wilson, had a vision in which he heard the Great Spirit command him to establish a new Ghost Dance religion. Through him the movement revived and spread even further afield. He, too, prophesied the end of the world as the Indian knew it. The white man would be taken away in a high wind; the buffalo, with whom the Indian had a very special relationship from birth till death, would return so that the Indian's old ways as a hunter not farmer would also come back. There would be no more hunger because the buffalo would feed the Indian; no more disease because the buffalo would provide medicine for him.

The Ghost Dance itself symbolized the destruction of the world and the spiritual redemption of the Indian people. Ghost Dancers clad themselves in white Ghost Shirts, decorated with feathers, bones, arrows, birds, suns and stars. They also painted their bodies with symbols to show the revelations they had received during the Dance. Arranged in concentric circles, they would begin to sing and move in response to an invocation to the dead by the prophet. The rhythm of the Dance and its incessant motion was designed to bring the Dancers into a state of trance. By the end of a Dance they would be shouting, stamping their feet, contorting their bodies and crying out, "Father, Mother, Brother, here I come!" After a rest, the Dance would start up again and a ceremony could last in this way for four or five days.

The Red Indians still await the Day of Judgment on the white man who killed the buffalo and destroyed their way of life. In anticipation of that day, the Ghost Dance continues to be performed on their reservations in the north-west.

Wherever the European has colonised, he has brought with him his superior technology against which most indigenous cultures have been no match. The inferior status of the people of the country in every sphere—cultural, economic and social—has been aggravated by exploitation and oppression. Unable to drive the colonisers out by force of arms, disturbed by the sudden and overwhelming disruption in their cultural life, deprived of any legitimate way in which to express their confusion and resentment, the colonized have resorted to ecstatic religions. Through these they have been able to give vent to their frustration. Through the messiahs who have led them they have sought otherworldly solutions to problems which are very much of this world.

The "cargo cults" of Melanesia have been influenced by messianism in this way. They, too, are an expression of resistance to the technologically superior civilization of the white man which came and took over their own culture and religion, leaving them without a sense of natural continuity of tradition. They, too, yearned for a return to the past, for a restoration of their glorious dead who would rise to witness the expulsion of all whites from their territories. In 1914 three "generals" from Saibai in the Torres Straits prophesied that a large vessel would reach the island and that in it would be the spirits of the dead.[17] They would bring with them money, clothing, flour, axes and knives. These articles in turn would help create a world in which equality and justice would rule supreme. The "generals" told their people to stop working and to visit the cemeteries to pray to the dead to help them achieve the new era.

Tokerau, a Melanesian messiah, said that in the New Year of 1893 there would be terrible volcanic eruptions, earthquakes and floods which would destroy all but those who believed in his religion.[18] After this, peace would reign for him and his believers. A ship bearing the dead to visit their living relatives would arrive in port, and all would live again in a land rich in food and fruit and good things. It was taboo, however, to touch anything connected with the white invader whose technology was wholly rejected.

Brazil has had centuries of contact with Christianity. It is therefore not surprising that messianism has been used to express the longing of the poor and the deprived who would otherwise have no outlet for their feelings. As far back as 1539 the Tupinambas left their settlements on the Brazilian coast to go in search of a "Holy Land", "a Land of Immortality and Perpetual Rest".[19] For nine years these intrepid seekers after Paradise travelled across the widest area of the vast interior of the continent to arrive in Peru on the west coast. Throughout the voyage they were led by their priests who promised them food and water and protection from their enemies. The Spaniards who met them wanted to know what they were searching for and from their answers came the legend of the fabulous but elusive City of Gold, El Dorado. The Tupinambas did not, of course, find their Immortal Land. Some returned to Brazil; others stayed and settled in Peru.

Another prophet arose and gathered thousands of Indians from the neighbourhood of Rio de Janeiro to lead them on a trek to a Promised Land. They were stopped by the local tribes and allowed to starve to death. The prophet, half Indian, half Portuguese, who claimed to have been born from the mouth of God, also perished.[20]

Thanks to the combination of grinding poverty and intense religiosity that exists side-by-side in Brazilian society, numerous messianic movements have arisen in modern times. Perhaps the most celebrated was that of a Catholic priest, Father Cicero, who started a movement in Joazeiro which was motivated both by religious fervour and social improvement.[21] Father Cicero had the reputation of being a healer and a prophet, and he attracted a huge following. Appointing his own officials, he ruled his New Jerusalem, Joazeiro, like a state within a state, and he was able to resist the challenge of the governor. He preached the return of the monarchy as the symbol of the Golden Age, but his social policies were comparatively forward-looking and enlightened.

The Virgin Theodora[22] was the leader of a sect that had been begun in the late nineteenth century by Joao Martin, a mysterious "monk" who disappeared in 1908 but whose memory was held dear by his followers. They believed he would return and Theodora claimed to be receiving orders direct from him. The authorities tried to put down the movement and only after a long struggle lasting four years did they succeed. This was in 1916.

Space, unfortunately, does not permit me to examine in detail Muslim, Buddhic and Hindu messianism. The subject requires a book of its own.[23] In all three religions there are variations on the belief in a future saviour who will arise after a period of universal upheaval to bring peace and happiness to the world. Muslims of the Shi-'a sect look to the coming of the Mahdī, the twelfth in the line of Imãms, "the rightly-guided one" to restore Islam to its original purity and, through divine catastrophe, to bring about its final world victory.[24] "Never relax in your determination to seek and find Him who is concealed behind the veils of glory," wrote Kazim, a Muslim mystic, in the first half of the nineteenth century.[25] He predicted that the Imãm Mahdī would come soon. One of his disciples, Husain of Bushire, set out in search of him and met Ali Muhammad of Shiraz, in Persia.

Ali, born in 1821, inherited his father's merchant business, but also devoted himself to religious studies. By nature he was inclined towards mysticism and asceticism and he practised various forms of self-discipline, including sitting and staring into the sun for hours at a time.[26] He received instruction from the Shaikhis, an order of Sufi mystics, and experienced ecstatic visions through which he came to believe that the Spirit of God had taken possession of his soul.

When Ali met Husain, so the legend goes, he asked him how he would recognize the expected Imãm Mahdī. Replied Husain: "The man must be of pure lineage, over twenty years of age but less than thirty, filled with intuitive knowledge, and free from bodily defects." Ali said: "Behold, all these signs are manifest in me!"[27]

Husain was not prepared to take his word for it until he had put further tests to him. For this he had prepared a treatise on the mystic, Kazim's, teachings, full of obscure references and allusions. Could Ali unravel these? Husain asked. And could he also compose a commentary on one of the sacred books of Islam? Ali managed both in a matter of hours and Husain was not only convinced but also, there and then, committed to Ali as his most faithful disciple and prophet. "Until now I have been feeble, dejected and timid," he said. "Now I am possessed of such courage and power that were the whole world with its peoples and potentates to rise against me, I would face them undaunted."[28]

Ali then declared to him that he was the Bab, meaning "the Gate", an old symbolic name for the "gateway" through which divine truth is revealed. Husain soon made the claim known and began to collect followers. Apostles were appointed to spread the Bab's teachings and the sect grew quickly in number. The Bab taught simple virtues. All prophets were One, he said. One Universal Intelligence spoke to mankind through a succession of agents; he was the latest but not the last.[29] Man's primary duty was to live in peace and harmony with his fellow-man. Women were to be raised in status; polygamy was to be abolished; so, too, concubinage. Kabbalistic numerology played a rôle in his system. Nineteen was the significant number because it was the numerical value of the Arabic word for "existence". There were nineteen months to the year, nineteen days to the month, and nineteen was the number of members required to regulate the new community of Babis.[30]

At first protected by the civil authorities and treated with respect, the Bab's movement, as it grew in strength, began to displease them and the persecution started. Ali was placed under arrest and confined in the remote fortress of Maku in western Persia where he spent his time composing religious works. Husain was also arrested. His nose was pierced, and threaded with a cord by which he was led through the streets of the city. Some of his followers came out in protest and there were riots. Clashes between the authorities and the Babis were frequent and the Shah of Persia eventually referred the matter to the military since the Babis had built a fort to protect themselves.

In December 1848 the Shah's army attacked Husain and the main body of Babis. Husain was shot dead two months later, and in May 1849, after besieging their fortress, the army persuaded the Babis into giving themselves up on the promise of a free pardon. When they left the fort, they were cut down mercilessly. Those who escaped were later captured and treated with horrible cruelty before being despatched—in some cases by being pushed down a cannon and then blasted to bits.

The Bab was brought to Tabriz by the Governor who had doctors of divinity and holy men sent for to examine him. He was asked who he claimed to be. "I am, I am, I am the Promised One," he said. "I am the One whose name you have for a thousand years invoked, at whose mention you have risen, whose advent you have longed to witness, and the hours of whose Revelation you have prayed to God to hasten."[31]

He was asked for proof, and the reply he gave might stand as a memorial for all would-be messiahs of all religions: "The most convincing evidence of the truth of the Mission of the Prophet of God", he said, "is admittedly his own word. He himself testifies to this truth."[32]

To that there was no answer except punishment. The Bab was bastinadoed, a particularly painful form of retribution used in the East by which the soles of the feet are beaten continuously with sticks. He was then let free, but his followers continued to cause unrest and his execution was ordered. No one wanted the responsibility of killing the holy man until the colonel of a Christian regiment undertook the task. On 9 July 1850, when the Bab was still only 30, he was brought before a firing squad with one of his young disciples who begged to die with him. The first volley only tore off their bonds; but the next cut them to pieces. The Bab's body was thrown into the town ditch where it lay until rescued by his faithful.

He was buried in Teheran for 29 years then finally laid to rest in Haifa. His remains now lie at peace beneath the golden dome of a temple on Mount Carmel. This is the centre of the religion of the Bahais who developed the Bab's teachings and spread them all around the world.

The British were the Babylonians of the nineteenth century as far as their colonies were concerned. British traditions, so strange and different from those of the people they ruled, meant separation from the old ways of life, a disruption and an upheaval. Like the Jews of old the colonized longed for their independence, for the future time when they could reassert their national identity and their sovereignty. In Africa, the Judaeo-Christian tradition, added to African religious beliefs, helped to appease this longing. In India the Muslim tradition of the Imãm Mahdī was incorporated into liberation movements as were Hindu and Buddhic ideas about the coming of a powerful saviour who would remove the yoke of oppression from the shoulders of the people.

Mirza Ghulam Ahmad tried to combine aspects of most of these beliefs by claiming to be at the same time the Christian messiah, the Imãm Mahdī, and an *avatar* or reincarnation of the Hindu deity, Vishnu, who, it was held, would destroy all evil in great cosmic battles, reinstate the old order, then depart to live in a forest, leaving the world in peace and security.[33]

Born of a family of Sūfi mystics in the Punjab in 1839, Ahmad compared the Indians under the British rule with the Jews under their oppressors. He said that he was like Jesus, a man of peace, and that it would be through peaceful methods and not through a Muslim *jihad*, or holy war, that his people would be freed. While adopting the messianic traditions of these different religions, Ahmad attacked them in his many writings and in two papers he edited. Christianity, he said, was spiritually dead, and for proof he pointed to the way its people were behaving towards those they ruled over. The story that Christ had died on the cross was a lie. He claimed that Jesus had only fainted. He was later taken down, revived, and brought to Kashmir where he found the Ten Lost Tribes with whom he lived and to whom he preached. Islam, Ahmad said, was also in decline and he advocated reforms which, together with his self-deification, caused him to be dismissed from the Muslim brotherhood.

Ahmad earned a reputation as a prophet; he was accurate about the deaths of individuals, not so accurate with births. He also became known as a miracle-healer. In 1898 he "invented" a "cure" for the bubonic plague which, he said, had also revived and cured Jesus. Sale of this Ointment of Jesus, as it was called, was banned by the government. He claimed that he and his followers were immune from the many diseases that attacked other Indians, but in 1908 he contracted one of the most deadly and most common, cholera, and died from it.

His sect, the Ahmadiyans, survived his death and grew in strength, making its centre at Quadian where Ahmad was born.

Through enthusiastic missionary work in India and abroad in Africa and Europe, the sect gained thousands of new converts. In 1947, when India and Pakistan were partitioned, the centre was sacked, but there are still many who believe that Mirza Ghulam Ahmad was the messiah. Like many other messiahs, to those who believe in him, he is immortal.

PART THREE

The End and the Beginning

CHAPTER FIFTEEN

PORTRAIT OF A MESSIAH

THIS CHAPTER OUGHT, perhaps, more accurately be called "preliminary sketches for a portrait" since the many different aspects which make up the personality of the messiah cannot possibly be captured in a single life-like, photographic image. He (or she) has a curious habit of shifting out of focus whenever one tries to fix him in place.

The messiah lives in a world of his own, within his own reality. We know about him from his own writings, from the records of his followers, but mainly from hostile chroniclers who exist far outside his reality. These sources make him appear larger-than-life, grotesque: a distorted reflection in a "magic" fairground mirror. He defies and yet at the same time demands understanding and if no more than a few revealing images are glimpsed at, fixed and held, the effort, I feel, is worthwhile. From and through him so much more of ourselves can be discovered.

The messiah has two births: his natural birth and his spiritual birth. Of the first we know far less than the second, mainly because it is usually so ordinary. Sometimes, for this reason, it is shrouded in mystery or linked to some auspicious occurrence in the natural world, like the appearance of a comet. The date, if not the circumstances, may be changed to fit into a significant event in religious history. Sabbatai Zevi, for instance, was traditionally supposed to have been born on the ninth day of Ab, the day on which the Temple in Jerusalem was destroyed and which is still among some very orthodox Jews a day of solemn fasting. Margaret Peter was actually born at Christmas and this gave her a place of great importance in her family from the beginning, one which she held until she destroyed them.

The messiah's relationship with his parents is also usually kept secret. The parents seem hardly to exist in his life. As a young man Jesus rejected his mother with the words: "Woman, what have I to do with thee? Mine hour is not yet come."[1]

And to his disciples he said: "I am come to set a man at variance against his father, and the daughter against her mother".[2] Because of this eagerness to dismiss his parents or at least a reluctance to talk about them, we know little about them. They and the life they represent are cast aside when the messiah enters into the most crucial stage of his life—his second birth. Till then, he lives in a state of suspension.

His early years are undistinguished. In only a few instances is the messiah remarked upon before his rebirth and the discovery of his mission. Jesus at the age of twelve was found in Jerusalem "sitting in the midst of the doctors, both hearing them, and asking them questions. And all that heard him were astonished at his understanding and answers".[3] Henry Niklaes was supposed to have been a brilliant youth, expounding the Scriptures at the age of eight and asking leading questions about the meaning of religious experience that puzzled his elders. At nine he was already having visions by which he felt himself "invaded" by the Holy Spirit. These, however, are exceptions.

The few conclusions one can draw about the messiah's background are tentative and imprecise. He is not of the very rich nor of the very poor. He is by nature bright and intelligent; by nurture indifferently treated. His schooling is probably perfunctory but, because of his innate ability, he is able to pick up with amazing speed subjects which most interest him, discarding everything else that seems irrelevant or of no immediate purpose. His understanding is seldom deep. He is not an intellectual, nevertheless he is articulate and has more than average command of language. He is adept at using theological themes and the vocabulary of messianism in order to further his own claims, but he is seldom an original thinker. Instead, he will probably be gifted with remarkable prophetic insight and an intuitive understanding of the wellsprings of human nature, and his utterances on these subjects sustain his reputation in the minds of his followers. He is fortunate if, like Sabbatai Zevi or Jan Bockelson, he has a prophet and publicist to do most of his real thinking for him, Nathan of Gaza for the former, Bernard Rothmann for the latter.

In some cases the messiah is born into, or very early on brought into, an existing sect which he then takes over and makes over in his own image. The Russian messiah, Peter Vasilevich Verigin was trained for the leadership of the Doukhobors by the woman ruler of the sect, Lukeria Gubanova. He was of Doukhobor nobility since he was directly related to one of the original founders. He later followed the sect when it emigrated to Canada and continued to lead it there as "Saviour" and "Door to the Kingdom" until his death by assassination in 1924.[4]

From a psychological point of view it may be a mistake to pass over so quickly these formative years. However, with so few hard facts available, to do more would be merely to speculate. We know that Sabbatai Zevi and Sir William Courtenay were strongly attached to their mothers, more so than to their fathers; we know that Jan Bockelson was the bastard son of a rich merchant and a peasant woman. But do these scraps of evidence help us to understand why they wanted to lead their people to the Promised Land? In order to make valid connections I think we would have to know much more.

The event which overshadows the messiah's natural birth and early upbringing, at least in his own mind, is his spiritual rebirth. This critical moment, usually followed soon after by a "call" to begin his mission as a messiah, lends itself equally to psychological and theological interpretation. The Bible speaks of the Spirit of the Lord coming upon Saul and of his being "another man" with "another heart" after his anointment by Samuel.[5] When Jesus was baptized by John in the River Jordan, he saw "the Spirit of God descending like a dove, and lighting upon him". He heard the "call", the voice of God from Heaven, saying, "This is my beloved Son, in whom I am well pleased".[6]

Henry Niklaes, when he underwent his second "birth", ceased calling himself by his name, but used only his initials which, he said, now stood for *Homo Novus*, the new man.

Rebirth is invariably preceded by great upheaval in the personal life of the individual. This can be of such magnitude that he ceases to know exactly who he is since his whole world appears to be collapsing around him. At the same time, and to confound his confusion, he begins to have intimations that he has been specially chosen by God to perform some important task. The Ranter prophet, Abiezer Coppe, recorded his experience of rebirth in stunning prose that well became his qualification as an Oxford scholar.[7] "First of all my strength, my forces were utterly routed, my house I dwelt in fired, my father and mother forsook me, the wife of my bosome loathed me, mine old name was rotted, perished; and I was utterly plagued, consumed, damned, ramned, and sunke into nothing."

In similar if more prosaic terms, Anton Boisen, a Christian minister and a psychologist, has described the reactions of "excited schizophrenics" under his care. "Such a patient does not know what to believe. There is utter perplexity regarding the very foundations of his being. 'Who am I? What is going to happen?' become for him questions of life and death to which he seeks new answers."[8]

After the crisis and the sudden terrible loss of identity comes the growing knowledge of a new identity, but first the individual must "die" to his old self. Boisen recorded: "The patient sees no way out. The situation seems to him utterly hopeless. He himself must therefore die; perhaps he is already dead with nothing to hope for but rebirth."[9] Coppe expressed it thus: "And while lying there I heard with my outward eare a most terrible thunder-clap, and after that a second and saw a great body of light, red as fire in the forme of a drum. I lay trembling, sweating and smoaking, and at length, with a loud voyce I inwardly cryed out, Lord what wilt thou do with me?"[10]

Rebirth and baptism are also psychologically and theologically connected. "Except a man be born of water and of the Spirit," said Jesus, "he cannot enter into the kingdom of God."[11] Paul wrote of "the washing of regeneration".[12] The psychiatrist, August Hoch, noted that in the minds of patients with schizoid symptoms the idea of being dead was linked to being underwater. "A theoretically important group is that which includes the patients who, in addition, speak of being in situations such as underwater or underground, which we have mythological and psychological evidence to believe are formulations of a rebirth fantasy."[13]

The old life is not merely washed away in baptism; it dies. "It is," concluded Hoch, "the psychology of wiping the slate clean for a fresh start."[14] The idea, expressed theologically, is to become like Melchisedec, the priest who typifies the Christ-figure: "Without father, without mother, without descent, having neither beginning of days, nor end of life".[15]

The stages of development into the new identity may not be as clearly marked out as I have indicated, but they usually follow this pattern: crisis, interlude of apathy and dejection, followed by visions and dreams of death, possibly by drowning, the hearing of a command to take up a new identity, and finally a "call" to reveal this new identity and the mission that accompanies it to the whole world.

On a very much smaller scale most of us undergo similar progressions in the course of our lives, sometimes quite frequently. When faced with what appears to be an insurmountable problem we go into a state of depression and apathy. We may lie down or sleep to escape the problem. In the course of our "stupor" we may experience a feeling of "dying away" from what we were, "a retirement psychologically from the world",[16] after which we "hear" a "call", an answer to our problem and an urgent desire to get up and act. Awaking or recovering refreshed, we are able to tackle our lives with renewed vigour and, in all likelihood, solve whatever was troubling us. Certainly artists, writers and scientists, people engaged on creative tasks, have found that continual "rebirth" is a necessary part of their lives.

The new life into which the messiah is reborn is not without problems and difficulties, but these seem no longer insoluble because the central problem of identity is, or is about to be, solved. After Abiezer Coppe had called on God to give him a direction, "my most excellent majesty and eternal glory (in me) answered and sayed, Fear not, I will take thee up into mine eternal Kingdom". He then had visions and revelations from God which were "stretched out upon me" for four days, ending finally with God's voice commanding him to "go up to London, to London, that great city, and write, write, write". Coppe did what he felt himself ordered to do. His problem was solved, and, as he concluded his account, "behold, I writ".[17]

No longer does the messiah feel alone, isolated, or to use the modern term, "alienated". He is now "at one" with God. Once again theology has anticipated psychology. Man's inner experiences have not changed over the centuries, merely the way he expresses them. In psychological terms the individual has achieved "problem-solving insight". In theological terms he experiences the unity with God that many mystics strive for. As did Jacob Boehme, the highly influential German mystic of the early seventeenth century. After years of search and meditation, "suddenly my spirit did break through the Gate, not without the assistance of the Holy Spirit, and I reached to the innermost Birth of the Deity and there I was embraced with love as a bridegroom embraces his bride". He went on to say, "My triumphing can be compared to nothing but the experience in which life is generated in the midst of death or like the resurrection from the dead".[8]

Once the union with God is achieved then all is revealed. "I knew God—who He is, how He is, and what His will is", Boehme wrote.[19] Henry Prince, the messiah of the Abode of Love, said, "I am utterly absorbed and swallowed up in God".[20] The messiah who has achieved this unity feels that everything he now does is by the command of God—the books he writes, the prophecies he makes, every decision right down to the smallest is at the prompting of the Almighty or the Holy Spirit. He cannot refuse. Prince told the writer, Dixon, "The Holy Spirit entered me, died in me, and gave me a new birth. After this I wanted to be without personal wish or desire, to yield myself up entirely to guidance from above." If he was going out for a walk, he would enquire from God whether it would rain. If he wanted a chair in his room, he would ask leave of the Spirit to buy one.[21] "No pronouncement of a prophet is ever his own," said the first-century Jewish philosopher, Philo. "He is an interpreter prompted by Another in all his utterances." According to Philo, "reason withdraws and surrenders the citadel of the soul to the new visitor and tenant, the Divine Spirit".[22]

This state of being "invaded" by the spirit of God is, according to the evidence of those who have experienced it, tremendous and overwhelming. Only those who have gone through it can know its power and the strength it imparts to the individual. The messiah has experienced it: most of his followers experience it —or say they have. Those of us who have not can only accept their word for what takes place. As the Muslim mystic of the eleventh century, Al-Ghazzali, commented, "A blind man can understand nothing of colours save what he has learned by narration and hearsay".[23]

It is during the "transport", the "illumination" that the messiah *knows* that he is the messiah. While filled with the guiding spirit who tells him that he is "my beloved Son" or allows him to feel that he has been anointed with holy oil, the messiah declares his mission. At this point he feels all-powerful; he senses that he will succeed in whatever task he sets his mind. Should he wish to lead the Jews back to the Holy Land, the waters will part for him and he and his people will step forth and across to safety. Should he shake his arms at the invading enemy—as did Thomas Müntzer—he will catch their shot in his sleeve, or if he fires his pistol at the heavens—as did Sir William Courtenay—he will bring down the stars. This is the strength that allows a despised Jew to demand an audience with the Pope and then to ask him for aid to free the Holy Land for the Jews—as did David Reubeni. Or to stand on the steps of a suburban church and declare to the congregation that, "it is not as pastor of this church that I stand before you, but as the Son of Man himself come to give everlasting life to all flesh," as did John Smyth-Piggott in Clapton.[24]

The question that the messiah may have to face, especially after the intoxication of the experience has temporarily subsided, is whether his actions were at God's bidding or his own. Jan Bockelson, who, wielding his sword of Justice as King of the New Jerusalem of Münster, struck off the head of one of his favourites, Elizabeth Wandtscherer, for wishing to leave the city, then danced with his queens around her corpse, may afterwards have wondered if such an act was dictated by his own sadistic desire to inflict horrible punishment on a helpless victim or whether it was an action dictated by God. The conflict, if allowed to persist unresolved, will ultimately destroy the messiah. He has to find a solution.

Sometimes the more extreme and "out of character" the act seems after the period of "illumination" is over, the easier it is for him to ascribe it to the Holy Spirit or whatever form the outside guidance assumes in his mind. "Would I have acted in this way," he is able to say to himself, "unless I *was* divinely inspired?" If this fails, then he is still not without a remedy, as we have seen with Joanna Southcott. She began to doubt that she, a virgin of 64 could actually be carrying the divine child as the Spirit had told her. Her followers came to her rescue. They reassured her. They eased her mind and told her that she *was* going to have the child and thereby, of course, relieved any doubts they may have had. Sabbatai Zevi had his loyal and loving prophet, Nathan of Gaza, to support him when he wavered in his resolve to be the messiah of the God of Jacob, the King of Kings, and to explain to him that his "strange acts" were proof of his messianic claims.

Ultimately, however, it is faith in himself that saves the messiah from doubt. Reason has nothing to do with it. Most messiahs have been contemptuous of intellectual argument and rational discussion. Even "book-learning" has been spurned in spite of the fact that they have themselves relied a great deal for their themes and their ideas on books they have read. Danilo Filippov was a Russian messiah of the seventeenth century, a deserter from the army who became a hermit and spent his life in studying the Bible and teaching it to the peasants who came to see him. Then one day he decided that all books were useless. The truth, he said, was in the *living* book, the Holy Spirit, and this Spirit was in every man. Thereupon he put his library in a sack and threw it into the Volga.[25]

Jacob Boehme, though he did not throw his books in the river, was equally scathing about intellectualism. "I have continually written as the Spirit dictated and have not given place to reason", he boasted in a letter to a friend. In his *Epistles* he wrote, "I am only a layman, I have not studied and yet I bring to light things which all the High Schools and Universities have been unable to do".[26] His understanding of nature, he maintained, enabled him to grasp the greatest mysteries without having to learn anything. "As for human learning," John Robins, the Shaker god admitted, "I never had any; my Hebrew, Greek, and Latine come by inspiration."[27] And H.N. declared that the true Light consisted "not in knowing this or that, but in receiving and partaking of the true Being of the Eternal Life".[28]

The source of the messiah's power lies in inner certainty. Self-conviction is the flame that first attracts the followers who then continue to hover about like moths, feeling its warmth, being dazzled by its light. Appearance helps and many messiahs have been endowed with striking looks. The Russian, Verigin, like the Englishman, Courtenay, was tall, broad-shouldered, deep-chested, built like an athlete, with clear eyes and full black beard. Had he been a clerk instead of the leader of a sect he would still have stood out in a crowd. Jan Bockelson was fair-haired and handsome; Jacob Naylor and Henry Prince were of middle stature but both had faces of great sweetness and were graceful and elegant in their movements.

Charisma,* the power of attraction which the messiah possesses to a high degree, cannot be explained by appearance alone for if so it would have been impossible for someone like John Wroe[29] to have gathered together a following of thousands of hard-headed Lancastrians, who, at his bidding, submitted to circum-

* The word originally meant a gift or talent which, appropriately enough in the case of the messiah, was granted by God.

cision, grew long beards, learnt Hebrew, and went about in clothes the colour of claret. Wroe was a hunchback of great ugliness, born in 1782, who took over the leadership of the Southcottians, the followers of Joanna, in the Midlands. He was strongly Judaistic in his beliefs and, by sheer force of his personality, turned his followers into strange, bearded, kosher-meat-eating Christian Israelites. Wroe adopted his theology from another messiah, a woman this time, also, curiously enough, of outstanding hideousness. She was Mary Boon, a Devon peasant woman, who had only one eye and a hare-lip so large that it divided her nose into two.[30] Smohalla, the prophet of the Nez Perces, was described as "large-headed" and "hump-backed".

Thought not ugly, neither Joanna Southcott nor Ann Lee were women of great beauty and yet the devotion they inspired in their followers was total. Both were on the short side, both stout, but both had a clear, penetrating gaze and, Lee especially, a beautiful voice. Said a disciple of her: "She came singing into the room where I was sitting, and I felt an inward evidence that her singing was the gift and power of God".[31]

Almost without exception, the one feature that all messiahs seem to have in common is this: a strong, compelling voice and, in addition, the ability to express themselves articulately. Zevi's singing was a delight to himself and to all his people who loved to hear him chant his favourite prayers in the synagogue. Courtenay, speaking from his balcony at The Rose in Canterbury, attracted large crowds in the street below. Naylor was well known for his eloquence and compelling oration years before his emulation of Jesus at the gates of the city of Bristol.

Power is personality and personality power. Messiahship depends on the strength of the leader's personality, which, in turn, depends on his inner conviction, on the ability to answer, as did the Bab when asked who he believed he was, "I am, I am, I am the Promised One".[32] Or as Jesus said to the woman when she told him she knew the messiah was coming, "I that speak unto thee am he".[32] But because inner conviction is not always "on tap" and readily available, it is sometimes necessary for the messiah to provide his followers with outward displays, the "bread and circuses", to keep their interest alive and their attention held. Bockelson, in order to defeat the enemy outside the walls and to maintain a high level of excitement and active participation in the Anabaptist revolution he was intent on creating in Münster, was acutely aware of the need for ceremony. This he provided daily with the elaborate procession to the seat of power in the city square, with the beautiful clothes worn by him and his sixteen wives, the bejewelled regalia, the commemoration medals stamped with his handsome head, the bodyguard mounted on the finest horses in the city. Henry Prince, to stir up excitement among the members of his Agapemone, appeared at the Great Exhibition in London in a magnificent coach and horses. Jacob Frank, the strange messiah of nihilism who took command of the Polish followers of Sabbatai Zevi in the eighteenth century, lived in "oriental splendour" in the drab midst of Catholic Poland. He went about with a large retinue dressed in uniforms and bearing swords. In this style he was received with honour by the Empress of Austria and her son in March 1775, and when he died in Offenbach near Frankfurt in December 1791, his funeral, attended by hundreds of his followers, rivalled that of a sultan's.

St Paul when writing to Timothy, Bishop of Ephesus, warned against certain kinds of men who, in the last days, will "creep into houses and lead away captive silly women laden with sins and diverse lusts. Ever learning, and never able to come to the knowledge of the truth."[34] Many of the messiahs whose life-stories have been recounted in this book would, in his view, be guilty of acting in such a way. The conclusion cannot be avoided that the sexuality of the messiah plays a large part in his relationship with his women followers and, moreover, without it he would probably have no followers at all. It is no coincidence that the *Song of Solomon*, that exquisitely erotic love poem, was the favourite reading of at least two messiahs, Zevi and Prince, both of whom had more women followers than men.

Freud, in talking about the hypnotist and his subject, spoke of "the unlimited devotion of someone in love, but with the sexual satisfaction excluded".[35] This neatly sums up the relationship between the messiah and the members of his sect which, at the extreme, is not dissimilar to that of the hypnotist and his subject. For his female followers the messiah offers spiritual love and, in addition to this, unrequited love in the physical sense though, as we have seen, he occasionally requites them in both senses. He also appears to offer them power and the chance otherwise denied them to express their personalities in the full. This power, as I shall discuss further in the next chapter, is usually more illusory than real and the women find themselves very often more oppressed and singled out purely as sexual objects than ever they were in ordinary society.

The messiah is not by nature a democrat. He rules "with a rod of iron". He will brook no insubordination. The greatest sin his followers can commit is to disobey him. Schisms so frequently occur in sects because the spirit of compromise and the Holy Spirit do not dwell harmoniously within the messiah. Henry Prince's people, according to Dixon, "lie under bonds, and only act and speak in each other's presence".[36] When Bockelson was anointed King of Münster and handed the sword of Justice by the elders, "and therewith the power to bring all the people on earth under thy authority", he executed his rule over Münster with little mercy. It is true that he was at war, but even so his acts strike one as peculiarly cruel and arbitrary. When a soldier refused to convert to Anabaptism he had him killed on the spot. He was also supposed to have hanged a child of ten for stealing turnips and decapitated a woman for spitting at a preacher.[37] John Wroe, the Bradford Southcottian, was said to have walked with a real rod of iron in his hand. He kept his "Joannas" in place with corporal punishment administered by Twelve Heads of Women specially appointed for the task. He also used authoritarian methods of spying and mutual betrayal to maintain his power.[38]

In spite of this authoritarianism, or perhaps because of it, the messiah is never harmed by his devoted followers. It is society that eventually brings him down. If not tortured or killed, the messiah is usually treated as mad. Certainly some of the acts of the messiah would commonly be regarded as those of a madman. But as Christopher Hill has written, "Lunacy, like beauty, may be in the eye of the beholder".[39]

"Everything is equivocal", R. D. Laing said unequivocally. "Our sanity is not 'true' sanity. Their madness is not 'true' madness."[40] He was talking about schizophrenics in particular and from a clinical point of view it may be said that the messiah sometimes displays some of the classic symptoms of the "disease". He, too, experiences auditory hallucinations, that is, hearing voices which speak in the third person to him or comment upon his thoughts and actions.[41]

Joanna Southcott, for one, was in constant touch with "the

Spirit of the living God". A disciple described the process whereby she and the Spirit got into touch with each other.

> When the Spirit is about to impart some communication, Joanna feels an agitation within; then the Prophetess, her secretary, and the witnesses, range themselves in one group. After this the Spirit begins to speak, addressing himself not to the witnesses, nor the secretary, but to Joanna within so that our Prophetess has simply to sit down and talk to herself![42]

In schizophrenia, the patient's perception may be disturbed; he "believes that everyday objects and situations possess a special, usually sinister, meaning for him".[43] This would, to some extent, describe the circumstances in which the messiah makes his prophetic utterances. He sees "signs" in events and occurrences that everyone else takes for granted. Thunder to most of us is thunder, but to Richard Brothers,

> The very loud and unusual kind of Thunder that was heard in the beginning of January 1791, was the voice of the Angel mentioned in the Eighteenth chapter of the Revelation, proclaiming the judgment of God, and the fall of Babylon the great. The Lord God was so exceeding angry at the time of the loud thunder that he determined to leave his other Judgments unfulfilled relative to London, and burn her immediately with fire from heaven.[44]

He who is of mystical inclination—and most messiahs are—is always looking for the meaning behind the meaning, for the invisible behind the visible.[45] That is why he finds the books of *Daniel* and *Revelation* such fruitful sources of material. They, too, possess special, perhaps sinister, meanings for those who wish to seek them. St John the Divine had visions and hallucinatory experiences of such amazing vividness that, if described to a psychologist, would be categorized as "deluded" and "abnormal". For instance: "And the beast which I saw was like unto a leopard, and his feet were as the feet of a bear, and his mouth as the mouth of a lion".[46] "And I heard the voice of harpers harping with their harps."[47] Commentators may say that the visions are no more than symbolic. As we now know, all dreams are symbolic; but the very force of St John's visions persuades the reader to believe that he actually experienced them and did not merely think them out as an intellectual exercise in allegory.

The meaning that the messiah finds in whatever he reads, whether it be the Bible or the daily newspaper, and for those modern messiahs the radio and television, accords with his own view of reality. That the meaning is the same for others, for his followers who avidly read his interpretations of the events, has a significance which cannot be ignored even though it cannot readily be explained. Richard Brothers regarded thunder as the voice of the Angel and so, too, did his disciple, the brilliant Mr Halhed, who was prepared to give up his enviable reputation in the community to prove that Brothers was neither an impostor nor a madman, in spite of his being locked up in an asylum. Why should he do this? Reason says he had nothing to gain from it, neither wealth nor fame. But then, as the philosopher, William James, pointed out: "if we look on man's whole mental life as it exists, on the life of men that lies in them apart from their learning and science, and that they inwardly and privately follow, we have to confess that the part of it which rationalism can give an account is relatively superficial".[48]

In addition to having the vivid dreams and visions of the schizophrenic, the messiah also displays on occasions behaviour which has been categorized in psychological terms as manic-depressive. As we have seen, Sabbatai Zevi went from extremes of apathy to elation. During his latter periods he was given to carrying out acts which afterwards would shame and perplex him, such as, for example, standing up in the synagogue and crying out the forbidden Tetragrammaton, the Name of God. In his periods of dejection he would retire from all human contact and struggle in solitude with the powers that he felt were demonic and which took control of him.

James Naylor, during his ride into Bristol, seemed from all accounts to be in a state amounting almost to stupor. He was hunched low over the reins which he held loosely in his hands, and whereas his ecstatic followers were happily plunged up to their knees in mud, crying, "Holy, Holy, Holy", he was still and silent. And even when they arrived at the inn and warmed themselves before a fire, he said nothing. It was only when he was brought to the Bristol magistrates and later his judges in London that he seemed to have recovered from his apathy and, refreshed, met their questions with his accustomed wit and eloquence. Joanna Southcott, in the course of one of her "trials", which she recognized were not satisfactory tests of her prophetic powers, was seen to have "suffered a depression" and gone to bed. But soon after she came back quite happily to be with her people. Dr Reece, her consultant, noted that on his crucial visit when she announced that "all appears delusion", she appeared "exhausted, low and dejected, and unable to speak her mind". But as soon as her followers had reassured her that she was the "favoured woman of God who would produce the promised Child", the scene of crying "was changed with her to laughter".[49]

The fact that messiahs may exhibit some of the symptoms of mental illness does not necessarily mean they are mad. It is instructive to compare even the oddest of them with those officially classified as insane. These patients claiming to be messiahs have not been the leaders of sects, no matter how small, have not had their prophecies recorded and avidly read, but have lived their lives out in anonymity in insane asylums, put there, not by a vengeful society, but by bewildered relatives unable to cope with them.

Some years ago at Ypsilanti State Hospital in Michigan, Dr Milton Rokeach conducted an interesting experiment, the purpose of which was "to explore the processes by which their [the patients'] delusional systems of belief and their behaviour might change if confronted with the ultimate contradiction conceivable for human beings: more than one person claiming the same identity".[50] Three patients, all diagnosed as "schizophrenic, paranoid type", believed they were Christ. Rokeach and his assistants brought them together and allowed them to talk to each other, occasionally prompting discussion with questions.

Of the three only the youngest, Leon Gabor, aged 38, showed more than average intelligence. The other two, Clyde Benson, aged 70, and Joseph Cassel, 58 (all pseudonyms), were mostly inarticulate and less able to intellectualize their situation. Gabor, with his clear and eloquent speech, his tall, lean figure and ascetic appearance enhanced by a beard, the more to resemble Christ, was the only one who might possibly have made public his claim to messiahship and attracted a few followers. He was a war veteran and, like Richard Brothers, refused to collect his accumulated pension. He called himself Dr Domino Dominorum et Rex Rexarum, Simplis Christianus Pueris Mentalis Doktor—

Lord of Lords, and King of Kings, Simple Christian Boy Psychiatrist.[51]

In the course of the experiment which lasted just over two years the men went through different crises of identity but all were reluctant to give up the one they had chosen for themselves. When Gabor announced his title to the others on their first meeting, Cassel objected. "I'm God, Christ, the Holy Ghost, and if I wasn't by gosh, I wouldn't lay claim to anything of the sort." All three denied the claims of the other two. Cassel pointed out that he had to be the only God because Clyde and Leon were patients in a mental hospital which proved they were insane.

Clyde announced, "You ought to worship me, I'll tell you that!" Whereupon Leon shouted, "I won't worship you. You're a creature!"[52]

As the weeks passed so their quarrels grew more fierce. Leon claimed to be able to perform miracles like lifting tables. When Dr Rokeach questioned his power to do this, Leon offered to show him. He pointed to a massive table in the room and in a loud voice commanded it to rise. Nothing happened. "I don't see the table lifting," Rockeach said. Gabor's reply was worthy of the best (or worst) mystic: "Sir, that is because you do not see cosmic reality".[58]

Clyde slept in a dormitory with fifteen other patients. One night the air shook with snoring. At last an exasperated voice called out: "Jesus Christ! Quit that snoring." Clyde, rising in his bed and to the nocturnal challenge, shouted back, "That wasn't me snoring," and pointing to another patient, "it was him!"[54]

None of the three men adequately solved the identity problem. Instead, they worked out for themselves explanations for the claims of the other two and avoided stressful situations where they might have to discuss the subject. Leon Gabor concluded: "I won't deny that you gentlemen are instrumental gods—small 'g'. But I'm the one who was created before time began."[55] Clyde Benson said the others were dead with machines inside them doing the talking. Joseph Cassel was satisfied with a simple denial of their claims. The two older men ceased to think about it; Leon is still groping for an answer.

Had these men not been in a mental hospital but living in the outside world, would they have attracted a following? The answer, I feel, must be no, with the exception, perhaps, of Leon in the early days of the experiment when he was confident in his identity. Within the hospital they were alone; outside of it they would have been even more so. All were concerned with their delusion, their own identity. They did not go out to persuade others; but rather, like a child with a newfound toy, hid their identity away from others and exposed it only when required to do so. Their attitude was: why risk arguments or, worse still, ridicule by saying who I know I am when it is safer and less stressful to keep the secret to myself. Apart from this claim to be Christ or God they had nothing, they saw nothing. They had retired into a tiny world of their own where in solitary rumination they could confirm again and again their identity. And this, I think, is where they differed most markedly from the messiahs in this book, who, if nothing more (and many of them had a great deal more), had the courage to go out into the world and proclaim their divinity for all to hear.

The messiah may suffer from what others call delusions. He may hear voices and see visions; he may interpret as signs of the Day of Judgment what to others are perfectly natural phenomena. He may suffer from attacks of melancholy and apathy followed by periods of elation during which he performs "strange acts" and makes extraordinary claims for himself, but, and this is a big "but", he does so with a purpose. He is concerned not so much with identity—as were the three Christs of Ypsilanti—but with his mission, his message. Thus, for all his play-acting, he resembles more the artist than the actor.

The messiah has something to tell the world. He sees society in a special way and he is concerned to tell as many as will listen what he has seen. Gifted with intuition, he senses that beneath the surface of society, beneath the tangible manifestations of poverty or economic upheaval or social injustice, lie intangible but deep-seated yearnings to which he alone can respond, and which he alone can satisfy—or so he believes. His mission is, therefore, both a critique of society and a response to individual needs and longings. The strength of his inner conviction conveys itself to others, and they, his followers, then lend their support to this conviction. Why they might do this is considered in the next chapter.

CHAPTER SIXTEEN

THINGS NEW AND OLD

IN AUGUST 1969 the bodies of five people were found in a house in Hollywood, Los Angeles. The day after, in another house five miles away, two more bodies were found. All seven had been horribly murdered. All were wealthy and some were also celebrities. All had been either shot, stabbed or both. In the first house, the police counted 102 stab wounds in the two dead women and three men. One of the five victims in the one house and both victims in the second house had their heads hooded. Words like "Death to pigs", and "Pig" were scrawled in the blood of the victims on parts of the houses.[1] The killings appeared to be senseless and meaningless: "seven people whose lives were snuffed out by total strangers for motives which may remain known only to them", summed up the judge at the trial of their murderers nearly two years later.[2]

The orgy of killing was the climactic Armageddon prophesied by and instigated by 34-year-old Charles Manson who believed himself to be both Jesus Christ and Satan. Though he was not present at the killings, he was charged and found guilty of first-degree murder with four others who belonged to his "family", a nomadic tribe of hippies to whom the crimes were linked as a result of one of them talking to an outsider. They lived in California's remote Death Valley, travelling about in stolen vehicles known as "dune buggies". When rounded up by the police in October 1969, the "family" numbered 27 adults and eight children, among them babies suffering from malnutrition.[3] The women outnumbered the men by about four to one and were mostly naked or wearing the lower halves of their bikinis. Some of them and all the men bore sheath knives.

They spoke of Manson as God. They were his slaves, willing to do his bidding without question. When arrested, one of the girls said that "Charlie" was "a very beautiful man. We belonged to him, not to ourselves".[4] At his command, so it later came out in court, one man, Charles Watson, and three girls had dressed in black "witchy" clothes, motored many miles across the desert to the home of the actress, Sharon Tate, cut the telephone and electricity lines, and after gaining entrance through a window, caught the victims by surprise, attacking each one in turn, and slaying them. Their trial lasted over seven months; all those charged were found guilty. Other crimes were later attributed to them, including the killing of a musician named Gary Hinman, and of a movie stunt man, both of whom had been associated with the "family". The guilty though sentenced to death are still in gaol.

When Manson's "family" first gathered together in the late 1960s its members were regarded by those who saw them travelling about in a gaudily-decorated minibus as "neat, orderly and clean" if somewhat bizarre.[5] No one took much notice of them because that was a time for bizarre "happenings". Young America, especially on the West Coast, resembled a latter-day seventeenth-century England with numerous small sects and families roaming about the country in search of peace, harmony and freedom from what they regarded as the evil corruption of conventional society. Some of the modern sects, like the Diggers, were even modelled on those of the past. They espoused similar anarchical and pacifist views and tried by living outside society, by being self-sufficient and self-supporting, to reach beyond the present into a Golden Age of innocence and plenitude.

Manson himself might have fitted equally well—or badly—into the England of the seventeenth century. His "theology" was also compounded of the very newest and the most ancient of beliefs. Though poorly educated, he read or had read to him the works of modern writers on psychiatry and hypnotism, and one of his favourite novels was a science-fiction tale of a messiah of the future. He also borrowed ideas from the modern cult of Scientology. At the same time his greatest interest lay in the Bible and, needless to say, the Book which most attracted him was St John's *Revelation*, especially chapter nine, with its apocalyptic visions of "locusts" and "scorpions" scouring the earth.

He and his "family" came to believe that they were these locusts who, in St John's vision, were commanded "that they should not hurt the grass of the earth, neither any green thing, neither any tree; but only those men which have not the seal of God in their foreheads". Their "dune buggies" were the "breastplates of iron and fire" with which the "locusts" ventured forth "unto battle".[6]

From an old Hopi Indian legend Manson borrowed the idea of The Hole, a place from which the Hopi nation was said to emerge to live on the earth. He connected this with "the bottomless pit" of *Revelation*, nine, in which ruled the king of the locusts. He actually found a huge hole in the desert which he believed might be the very place he had heard about. It was filled with water and he went as far as obtaining an estimate to have it drained.[7]

Manson developed a theory from this admixture of new and old that the end of the world was approaching and would finally be brought about in a battle between the whites and the blacks. The blacks would conquer the whites; they would kill off all the wealthy Christian Americans, the "pigs", except for the "family" who, though also white, Christian, and in the case of one or two of them, wealthy, were those things by birth and not by choice. They, the new elect, would remain safe in The Hole during Armageddon. This Manson called Helter Skelter, borrowing this time from a song by the Beatles whose work had for him the force of Scripture and whom he likened to the four avenging angels of *Revelation*, nine.

After the blacks had conquered the whites, they would rule the world until it was revealed to them that Manson still lived and, recognizing their natural inferiority and his superiority, they would hail him as the king of the world. In that way he would "pull off" the Second Coming.[8]

Towards the Armageddon, Manson began assiduously to work. The sect, echoing his every word with a fervent, "Amen, Amen," came more and more to accept him as the Christ. From a neighbouring desert sect, The Fountain of the World, they borrowed a crucifixion ceremony which they re-enacted at regular intervals. Manson would be strapped to an old cross while the others acted out their rôles either as the mocking crowd or as the worshipping followers. One of the girls, a different one each time, was appointed as Mary and dressed in a cloak to sit at the foot of the cross, weeping. The ceremony would end with a "resurrection" and this would be followed by an orgy of intercourse and other sexual acts involving Manson and the others.[9] At their trial, a brief version of this ceremony was performed with Manson and the others charged with him assuming poses, arms extended and heads bowed. The police quickly put a stop to it.[10]

Association with "bikers", groups like the Straight Satans, who rode about on their motorbikes in search of trouble, and the introduction of elements of devil-worship and satanism accompanied by horrible sacrifices of living animals changed the character of the "family". The time sought by all messiahs for the final confrontation with authority was approaching. Manson taught his people how to throw knives; he told them again and again of the impending End of the World. They were always on the look-out for Black Panthers and other black militants whom they believed would bring the end about.

Then, in July 1969, a musician by the name of Gary Hinman, who had known the "family" well and was thought to be about to expose them, was killed. In an attempt to defend himself, he had shot at Manson. Manson had left the musician's apartment where the incident had taken place, and returned later with a sharp sword with which he sliced off one of Hinman's ears. Other members of the "family" later finished Hinman off after one girl tried to sew on the severed ear with dental floss. In court the same girl said, "This whole thing that I'm in this courtroom for . . . started when I killed Gary Hinman because he was going to hurt my love [Manson]".[11] Only a few weeks later the seven victims were stabbed, shot and bludgeoned to death. Helter Skelter had begun. Fortunately, the timely arrest of those responsible prevented it from continuing.

Charles Manson and his "family" were not unique in the history of messianic movements, not even in their bloodthirstiness. The messiahs of the Brethren of the Free Spirit claimed that it was more sinful to disobey them than to murder. Jacob and his Pastoureaux, dressed like shepherds and armed with pitchforks and other weapons, roamed the streets of French towns in the thirteenth century, burning, killing and looting as their moods or their needs dictated. Margaret Peter, a plain Swiss farmer's daughter, stirred her family into such a frenzy of violence that they crucified her after killing her sister. The Skoptsy of the nineteenth century were a Russian messianic sect, distantly related to the hermit messiah Filippov who threw his books into the Volga. To enter the sect a man had to submit to castration by the women—of penis and scrotum to earn the "great seal", of testicles only for the "lesser seal". The women would work up an atmosphere of hysteria and when this reached its peak would perform the operation on the initiate, using knives, razors, and even pieces of iron, tin or glass. Once castrated the initiate believed himself to be "saved" and to be more powerful than other men.[12]

In Manson's "family", as in other sects before it, the women outnumbered the men. Their relationship gives an insight into the inner workings of such a sect; how it gains adherents and holds them. The messiah comes first. He is the magnet. One of Manson's girls said, "Charlie is a man, and we were all looking for a man who would be at our feet with his life but wouldn't let us step on him".[13] Manson made the girls, most of them still under twenty, feel simultaneously under his protection and in fear of him. They felt secure with him, knowing he would do all in his power to help and protect them and in return were willing to give themselves up to him physically and mentally as and when he demanded they do.

Once he had established a small coterie of disciples, it was not difficult to expand and extend the membership. The girls attracted new men to the sect and encouraged other girls to join by the way they talked about their "god", their "Jesus". Manson's fame as a lover was enough to attract some of the girls, but something more was necessary. They also needed to feel that he was going to provide them with the sense of security that the loved one feels in a close relationship. He had to give more than just sex which, after all, they could get from other men. He had to be for them husband and father, the father who took them in when their real fathers had kicked them out.

The men who were attracted to the "family" were free to share Manson's "harem", but as the girls were regarded by him as his property, once the men lay with them, they also became Manson's property. In this way he gained male adherents and kept control over them. He also used the girls for another purpose. If he took a dislike to one of the men, the girls did not have to be told but would automatically cut the offending male out of the "family" by denying him what was freely available to the others. In a promiscuous and polygamous structure, this is the ultimate sanction, and the rejected man would soon leave. "That way," said a 50-year-old handyman who joined briefly after the slayings and in innocence of what had happened, "the women were the key to everything."[14]

This power, this being "the key to everything", otherwise denied to them by society, is still one of the most important factors in attracting women to messianic sects like Manson's so easily and in such numbers. The messiah releases them not only from their families, but also from the restrictions imposed on them by society. In particular, they are liberated sexually from the restriction that they be chaste, a demand not made on men. In conventional relationships between men and women, more so in the past than today, women were required to give of themselves to their husbands on demand, to their husbands only, and to expect no sexual satisfaction in return. For a woman to enjoy sex was wrong. Even in the latter half of the twentieth century guilt still operates to inhibit sexual relationships and the goal of equal satisfaction for both partners remains a wish rather than a fact.

Where, therefore, guilt is deliberately expunged, where it is considered a positive virtue to do what in ordinary society is regarded as sin, women have more to gain than men. Where free and unlicensed relationships are encouraged—as they were in Manson's "family", as they were in the sects of the Brethren of the Free Spirit, in the Familists of the sixteenth century, the Ranters of the seventeenth century, the Sabbataians of Turkey and Poland who followed the radical teachings of Sabbatai Zevi into the eighteenth and nineteenth centuries—women seem from the outside looking in to be as free as men in every respect.

The freedom, however, is more apparent than real. The power they exercise through the sexual license they enjoy has a price, and the price is high. The women have to be prepared to submit to a subjection far in excess of anything demanded of them by the conventional society they have rejected. The Münster messiah, Jan Bockelson, who—like other messiahs—owed his success to his fervent women supporters, made restrictive laws which forced them into marriage with whosoever chose them. The laws also required them, on pain of death, to give themselves wholly to their husbands and to address them as "master". The young virgin whom Brother Henry Prince took in public to reveal the Spirit in the flesh was taken "with power and authority as flesh that belonged to God; and it was at His absolute disposal; so that in taking of it He left it no choice of its own". In the case of the Death Valley "family", the girls were required to yield to Manson or to any man he picked for them in any way and at any time without question. They were "slaves" not permitted to ask "why" of anything; the word itself was taboo.[15]

Manson's girls prepared food for the men but could not eat until they had first fed everyone including the animals kept by the "family". Childhood was regarded as the perfect state by the messiah. Men could talk to the children; the girls who looked after them were only allowed to speak to them in gibberish. If one of the "harem" seemed ready to rebel, she was threatened with dire punishments, like having her breasts cut off.[16]

The girls did not rebel. They remained faithful to their messiah to the end. They might have feared him, but it was more than fear that kept them in submission. When the trial took place they were not even allowed by their lawyers to give evidence; it was felt that they would admit their guilt in an attempt to exculpate Manson. The lawyers were probably correct in their surmise because when eventually the girls were permitted to speak, in an effort to change the death sentence against Manson to one of life imprisonment, they talked their heads off, assuming as much of the guilt as possible.

That the girls, were, according to one report, "apparently wholesome, normal young people" shocked the public almost as much as the terrible deaths of the victims. Most came from middle-class backgrounds; their parents were engineers, teachers and the like. One of the girls used to sing in a church choir, loved pets and wanted to be a teacher; another was her hometown's festival princess and a Girl Guide. One girl not implicated in the killings was actually permitted, if not encouraged, by her parents to join the "family" though later they tried without success to get her back.

Why then did these "normal young people" leave the warmth and security of their homes and take to the nomadic, often dangerous, seemingly always insecure life of a member of Manson's "family"? To take the question further, what makes any woman, or man for that matter, leave the apparent safety of conventional society to become the disciple of a messiah?

In the messiah men and women seek certainty, seek direction and purpose. Freud likens him to "the dreaded primal father".[17] He demands absolute authority but in return he will transform the world for them and, more important, he will ensure that they occupy a privileged place in the new world. From the messiah they seek freedom from doubt and constant reassurance. He might, in the metaphors of the apocalyptic books of the Bible, tell them that things will get worse before they get better, but the main point of his message is that things *will* improve, for them, for his own "family", for "the elect", if for no one else.

The frustrated and the dissatisfied will seek in a messiah a way of overcoming the difficulties that block achievement or satisfaction. The Africans who joined Simon Kimbangu in the Congo were frustrated because they were discriminated against in their own country. The Red Indians of the American north-west who joined Wovoka's Ghost Dance movement were dissatisfied with their position as an exploited and oppressed minority. Yet not all Congo Africans nor all American Indians joined these movements though, doubtless, all were equally oppressed, exploited and discriminated against. Not all *felt* the dissatisfactions and the frustrations to the same extent and, moreover, not all were also psychologically prone to seek the absolute answers that their messiahs offered.

Some individuals more than others even in the same social situations need to know absolutely that they are right and good and virtuous whatever they do or say or think for the very reason that they belong to a group that is right and good and virtuous. They also have to know absolutely that there are others, the wicked, the unrighteous, the "pigs" who are wrong, bad and sinful. They have to know absolutely that because they are right they will ultimately triumph over the wrong. This need for rightness—expressed by them as righteousness—is projected on to their messiah, the perfect one, who is perfectly willing to assume the rôle thrust upon him. He knows he is right. His very existence is based on this self-conviction, as we have seen. Consequently, his followers' need to be right, in a world that seems hopelessly and, by ordinary human means, irretrievably wrong, meets in his self-certainty. From this meeting is derived a new and deeper certainty for both messiah and followers, a conviction of certitude that they use as a shield against the threatening chaos around them. It is to this certainty as much as to the messiah himself that they submit themselves.

To enter into this state of rightness is to be reborn. Like their messiah, the followers have, each one, to experience a second birth after which the Holy Spirit, or however they describe the force, enters into them so that they now know intuitively and without the help of books or reason that they have chosen the right path.

As with their messiah, the rebirth is preceded by a state of apathy, a sense of rejection and dejection when nothing matters any more. Transfixed by anxiety and by despair, they feel that time has come to a halt. There is no future. Nothing will improve; nothing will change. Hope is gone. John Bunyan described such a state of mind in *Grace Abounding*. He said he felt he was "both a burthen and a terror to myself . . . weary of my life, and yet afraid to die".[18] The philosopher, Kierkegaard, called the state "Despair", the "sickness unto death". He wrote: "When existence begins to totter, then too does despair manifest itself as that which was at the bottom".[19]

Despair is created by the apparent or real inability of the individual to solve personal problems or problems posed by his society. As in the messiah-to-be, a sudden disaster like the death of a loved one or the collapse of a business, the onset of war or economic upheaval may also bring about in the follower-to-be a state of apathy. Unable to find meaning in the event the individual tells himself that there is no meaning. All is chaos. The cosmic "birth pangs" which Jewish and early Christian apocalyptic literature described with such force is experienced by the individual within himself. He feels cast off, alienated, in exile. Then comes the person who offers him comfort, security, and freedom from fear, who takes him in when—as he feels—everyone else has thrown him out.

The real core of the religious problem, according to William James, could be summed up in two words, "Help! Help!"[20] A woman patient of the psychiatrist, Dr Rollo May, described how she was in a crowd of people. "They had no faces; they were like shadows. It seemed like a wilderness of people. Then I saw someone in the crowd who had compassion for me."[21] One of Manson's young girls who had left her home after a row with her parents said: "I was sitting down in the street crying and a man walked up and said, 'Your father kicked you out', and that was Charlie".[22]

The messiah presents the lost and anxious individual with a meaningful world-picture in which he can see that his sufferings and his problems have nothing to do with his own inadequacies or with the failure of social institutions, but are part of a vast plan laid down in the distant past to be carried out—through the agency of the messiah—in the near future. Suddenly time starts again. The world seems new because the individual is reborn into a new and different reality. No longer is he alone and isolated. Others also believe in the messiah and the messiah's message. Together they form a tightly-knit group, exclusive, cut-off, self-helping, mutually dependent. To each other they give, from each other they take, be it bread, wine or sex. They make their own rules, or the messiah makes rules for them and no matter how severe the rules are they accept them. To do otherwise is to destroy their new-found reality. One of Mother Ann Lee's Shakers said that "believers", that is, the Shakers, were held together by "a golden chain". If any of them broke their laws, which to them were no less than direct orders from God, then they broke that chain. "But while you are careful to keep the gifts and orders of God, you are surrounded by this golden chain, and are secure from all evil."[23]

Nothing can now harm or touch them so long as they do not "go out among the world", "shake hands with the world", or "blend with the world", as the Millennial Laws of the Shakers decreed. The world that has rejected them is in turn rejected by them. Their messiah has given them the strength and confidence to do so. The question is: for how long?

In some ways Jan Bockelson was fortunate. He had the world represented by the Bishop and his army actually hammering at the gates of his New Jerusalem, trying to get in and destroy him. Every day he and his Münster Anabaptists were in confrontation with the outside, literally not figuratively. Other messiahs have had to exaggerate or invent confrontation in order that their sect maintain its cohesion. Time is the enemy. Followers must always be made to feel separate from the world. Once the world accepts or ignores the messiah, there is danger that his people will be lost to him because the vitality, the excitement he offered them gradually evaporates and with it the sense of drama and purpose. Henry Prince's Agapemone, after the Great Manifestation of the Holy Ghost in the flesh of a young virgin, ended up as little more than a private club for elderly gentlefolk playing billiards.

The messiah knows and his people sense that unless their lives are continually made to feel purposeful, unless they have a goal to aim for in the near future, they will go back to being what they were before they became "the elect". So excitement is created. A confrontation is sought. The Gentiles must be reminded that "the elect" live. In Manson's farmyard world, the "pigs" had to be made aware of the "locusts" in the most hideous way possible.

The more outrageous the confrontation, the fiercer the reaction of the Gentiles. The elect, the righteous, must do battle with the wrongdoers and defeat them before they can inherit the world. The fight must be to the finish, the Armageddon, the Helter Skelter to which most messianic sects are ultimately directed. The scenario was laid down in the Bible and the apocalyptic books written during the terrible days when Judea was being crushed out of existence by the Romans, when Judaism in exile and the new religion of Christ were beginning their separate lives. But the scenario is never completed because the world wins in the end. The future promise remains for ever unfulfilled.

Every messiah is broken. His people watch as he faces his accusers. Will he stand up to them and, if they kill him, will he rise again as he promised? Solomon Molcho went to the stake, refusing the Emperor's offer of mercy in return for a recantation. Jan Bockelson and the two elders with him suffered the most horrible tortures before dying, but they did not go back on what they held to be true. James Naylor was whipped through the streets of London and Bristol and burnt through the tongue without him uttering a word of reproach against anyone or denying the truth of his mission.

Not all messiahs have had this courage. Faced with the choice of martyrdom or freedom, some, like William Franklin, recant, apologize to their accusers and give up their claims. Often the greater the bluster at the start the more abject the humility at the end. Manson said at the beginning of his trial: "The courtroom is like unto an old useless mannequin smelling with lies, deceit and the strings of graft and corruption. Mr and Mrs America, you are wrong. I am not the King of the Jews, nor am I a hippy-cult leader. I am what you have made me."[24] At the end, when sentenced to death, he uttered with head bowed: "I have always lived in the truth of your courtroom. I have always done what I was told. Sir, I invented this courtroom . . . I accept this court as my father."[25]

What of the followers? Most escape punishment, but they have a more difficult problem to face than even the anger of the Gentiles. Hatred they can cope with because they are prepared for it, but they are not prepared for their messiah failing them. Faced with this, they can either accept that they made a mistake and try to go back to what they had been before their messiah came to them, or they can try to explain away his recantation. If the Gentiles have killed him and he does not rise again, they have to find new reasons why this should be so to justify their continued belief in his promise.

In the 1880s a young American girl became the disciple of a middle-aged man who claimed to be the "father of Christs" and was made pregnant by him. She came from a respectable, church-going family and she was faced with a choice: either she had been tricked by a lecherous seducer or he was what he had told her, the man specially ordained by God to be the father of a race of Christs. One who knew her described her agonizing conflict, the same that takes place in the minds of all followers when they are threatened suddenly with a new reality.

"She dared not admit the idea that it was a delusion, for her whole spiritual life seemed to depend upon believing that she had been rightly guided; for if she could think that in the most solemn moments of consecration the Lord could allow her to be so deceived, she would feel that she could never trust Him again." The outcome of her agony was that "she clung with a deathlike grip to the belief that it was Divine guidance, and that she was greatly favoured to be allowed to be the mother of one of these wonderful children". Never did she lose this grip. Many years later she wrote to her friend who had not been convinced by the "father of Christs", saying that the way was still open for her, the friend, "to give up *her self-will** and consent to be guided as the Lord led".[26]

The end of the messiah is not always the end of his sect. Sometimes it is the beginning of an elaborate theology and the foundation of a church in his name. The followers who remain faithful desperately need the support of an unbreakable system of beliefs, more sound and impervious to attack than anything they had prior to their messiah's defeat or defection at the hands of the Gentiles. They also need as many new converts to these beliefs as possible because conviction now depends on numbers as much as, if not more than, on depth and strength.

When Joanna Southcott failed to deliver the Shiloh to her

* Italics added.

disciples, they did not abandon their faith in her. Instead it grew, was taken up by other messiahs like John Wroe and John Ward, who developed Southcottian theology and carried it far beyond its humble beginnings to America, Canada and Australia. More than two centuries later it is dormant but not dead. There are still many who hold that "There is One God and Joanna is His Prophet".[27]

"No doubt of it," sighed Ronald Knox, the orthodox Catholic writer, in despair, "sects die hard."[28]

When Sabbatai Zevi was given the alternative of death or conversion to Islam he chose the latter although to Jews this is the ultimate betrayal. Yet his prophet, Nathan of Gaza, who remained a Jew, and others who came after him, had little difficulty in finding justification for their master's apostasy. They could not deny that he had changed his religion; that was a fact and could not be contradicted; but they could explain to the satisfaction of his followers that what he had done was *part of his mission*. They said that Sabbatai had to go into the "kingdom of impurity", to dwell "in the realm of the strange god" whom he would only appear to worship, to bring about the long-awaited Redemption. Through impurity, through sin would goodness come. Everyone who believed in Sabbatai was urged to follow him. "Let us cram the maw of impurity with the power of holiness until it bursts from within", wrote one of his theologians.[29]

Soon after Sabbatai's conversion, hundreds of Turko-Jewish families who had followed him became Muslims, in name if not in deed. They were called the Donmehs, literally, the apostates. For two and a half centuries in deep secret they continued to worship Sabbatai as the "true King messiah". "I believe with perfect faith that Sabbatai Zevi is the true messiah," read one of their Articles of Faith, "and that he will gather together the dispersed of Israel from the four corners of the Earth."[30]

The Donmehs were ruled by a series of so-called "reincarnations" of Sabbatai, each one more radical and anarchical than his predecessor. They were also politically active and some Donmehs found a place in the organization of Young Turks which originated in Salonika where they had their centre before they took over the government of the country. Djavid Bey, a minister in the first Young Turk government, was a leader of one of the Donmeh groups and was also the direct descendant of one of their messiahs, Baruchya Russo.[31]

Russo, called by his worshippers, O Senor Santo, was regarded as the reborn Sabbatai and God Incarnate. He preached a religion that was almost anti-religious, but even he did not go as far as the last of the Sabbataian messiahs who ruled the Polish contingent of the movement with a rod of iron, Jacob Frank. Frank has been called "one of the most frightening phenomena in the whole of Jewish history".[32] Like Sabbatai, he became an apostate in 1759 when he and many of his followers converted to Catholicism. His baptism was under the patronage of no less a person than the King of Poland and the ceremony was conducted with all the trappings of royalty.

Frank took over Sabbataian theology and turned it into a prescription for almost total anarchy. He loved power and once said of Zevi, "If he had to taste everything in this world, why did he not taste the sweetness of power?"[33] Mosaic Law, he said, was wrong; only the law of the Sabbataians was perfect. He believed that he was going one step further than Christ who had come to redeem the world from the devil. He, Frank, had come to redeem it from all laws and customs. It was his task to annihilate law *in toto* so that what he called "the Good God" could reveal himself. "I came into this world to destroy and annihilate", he told his followers. "I did not come to lift you up but rather to cast you down to the bottom of the abyss." From the bottom of that abyss would "holy knowledge" emerge.[34]

The followers of Charles Manson in California, if they had heard of Frank and had read his "theology", would have found much in it to their liking. In both the Polish nihilist and his Death Valley counterpart was revealed the terrible paradox of messianism: that the concept of a perfect man whose task it is to bring about universal peace, justice and harmony can give rise to men whose characters, beliefs and actions are diametrically opposed to these ideals. The ancient Hebrews looked forward to a man like King David upon whom, long after he was dead, they projected all the attributes of the ideal king. From him they expected that, "He shall judge thy people with righteousness, and thy poor with judgment; save the children of the needy, break in pieces the oppressor, and, in his days shall the righteous flourish and abundance of peace so long as the moon endureth".[35]

What a distance there is between that ideal and the messianic megalomania or malevolence of a Frank or a Manson; between the Righteous King of the World and, say, the Führer of Nazi Germany who also put on the mantle of the messiah and used messianic terminology when it suited him and the cause of Nazism. It was no accident, for example, that Adolf Hitler said his Reich would last for one thousand years, that his rally in Nuremberg had the atmosphere of a religious festival and that during it his worshippers would buy portraits of their Führer, haloed with Christ's face.[36] Or that his Minister for Church Affairs could declare to the German people: "There has arisen a new authority as to what Christ and Christianity are—and that is Adolf Hitler. Adolf Hitler . . . is the true Holy Ghost".[37]

The very worst as well as the very best claimants to the role of the messiah all want to be like a King David and more, like God Himself. They understand that the messianic ideal is realizable only through the agency of someone greater than all men, the perfect being. Between the idealization to which they all aspire and the objective reality of living as a man or woman in this world lies a chasm as deep as St John the Divine's "bottomless pit". It is to this that all messianic claimants—the best and the worst—are drawn because it yawns invitingly between the possible and the impossible. They want to leap over it, they *have* to leap over it, in order to become like God, omnipotent enough to bring about the new heaven and new earth which they have promised their followers. Alas, it is into this they all fall, the best and the worst, because would-be messiahs are human, not God. They cannot achieve the impossible. For all their boating, for all their play-acting, their good deeds and noble sentiments, they remain human, fixed in and by their human condition. They cannot bring about the Millennium. It eludes them as it eludes all of us. The ideal, though, remains, and men and women continue to seek it and to follow those who promise it.

Hardly a year goes by without the announcement somewhere of a new messiah or a new church or sect prophesying the End of Days, waiting anxiously for someone to lead humanity out of present chaos into a timeless time when there will be "neither labour, nor sickness, nor humiliation, nor anxiety, nor need, nor violence, nor night, nor darkness, but great light".[38]

Plain Truth, a popular magazine with a world circulation of nearly 3 million, invites its reader in a recent issue to attend a series of lectures answering "the big question: Is This The End of Time?" "Where's it all going to end?" "What sort of a world *will* our children inherit? Or will there be a world LEFT to inherit?"[39]

Moses David, the Prophet of the sect calling itself The Children of God, had a vision "that this was the last dark hours of this world in the days of terror ahead". He saw in his vision a drugstore which was "The Church", "the visible but drugged organized church". Beneath it, however, was a "happy hippie underground beehive of activity . . . brilliantly lighted and enlightened . . . very wide awake and busy and stripped of the things and hypocrisy of this world". And in that "underground Hippie Heaven", "in a totally free and sinless heavenly society created by God in the spirit world", all went about "naked and unashamed".[40]

Recently *The Times* published a story under the headline: Duke found in Car waiting the End of the World. In Italy, an Italian duke and duchess joined the sect of a former Catholic priest who calls himself, "Christ on Earth". With them they travelled all over Europe, staying at the best hotels on the duke's money until their funds ran out. For months they had taken up residence in the car park of the Geneva airport, waiting for the world's end. When they were found, one of their members had been dead for five days.[41]

The Reverend Sun Myung Moon is a Korean businessman with a following—so it is claimed—of some 600,000. They look upon him as the messiah or the Lord of the Second Advent. He says that at the age of sixteen Jesus appeared to him and commanded that he "carry out my undone task". He established the Unification Church and he preaches that Jesus died on the cross before he could marry and produce a race of "perfect" children to purify the world. As Henry Prince did on a very modest scale, so Sun Myung Moon has done on a vast scale. In Seoul, South Korea, Moon married nearly 800 couples at one mass wedding, all of them members of his sect.[42]

The *Lightning from the East* is the "biography of an Easterner chosen by the Lord Jesus Christ to be His Son".[43] Published by the Wings of Life in Tennessee, U.S.A., the book records the life and teachings of Brother R. Paulaseer Lawrie of South India whom his disciples refer to as "the Man, the Son of Man, and the Son of God". The facts of his life and his ministry are supposed to parallel those of Jesus according to the biography except that they have been somewhat up-dated.

The moment of his rebirth took place in Chicago when he was on an American preaching tour. "We were preaching in the Life Tabernacle for three days and three nights," he recalled, "and on Moonlanding day I had a small television set in front of me. As man was about to land on the moon . . . I could see the sky open and a terrific power come into my heart." Immediately, Brother Lawrie felt himself changed into two people—one Jesus Christ, the other himself. The two were fused within him. He heard them in conversation, the one to the other, and eventually when he came out of this "glorious oneness with Jesus", he announced to those gathered around him: "I will not die".[44]

Once more the very new and the very old are brought together in a potent and inspiring message for those who believe and who desire a new reality; and this is the only reason for mentioning him in this book. Lawrie was born in 1921 on a tea estate in South India. His forebears were "of Jewish stock—a splinter group of the Israelites scattered all over the world, and of the tribe of Judah in the lineage of Nathan".[45] He took part in the anti-British campaign in the early 1940s, but gave up his interest in politics for the sake of his religious vocation. As a young man he cured a girl possessed by demons and brought a dead woman to life; these and other "miracle cures" earned him the reputation of a great faith healer.

Today Brother Lawrie, the "Second Coming of Jesus Christ in person", is a happily married man living with his wife, children and grandchildren in his Ashram which his followers from all over the world regard as the New Jerusalem and to which they make pilgrimage. His followers say that "the destruction of the world order is predicted for the year '77 or before", but those who believe Brother Lawrie is "that Christ (anointed one) Jesus" will be saved. Their names will be recorded on a list and instructions will be sent to them "how to escape the terror of tribulation". In this way they will be able gradually to prepare themselves for "the third coming of the Lord Jesus in all majesty and glory on the Mount Olives in Israel . . . which will conduct over into the Millennium".[46]

It would seem that no matter how successful or otherwise our social, political, economic or religious institutions have been, are now, or will be, there are always men and women in doubt and despair, anxious, uncertain, without a sense of the future, alienated from others and from the centre of their own being; in exile. Some languish in this condition and accept it as their lot, if, indeed, they ever think about it. Others realize their deep fears and discontent and find answers in themselves alone or through the help of priests or doctors. A third group of people, smaller than the other two, seek and find their answers in an individual whose needs are as their own. They call him messiah.

To the unbelievers he is "false" because they say he leads his followers astray. But to those who believe in him he is "the Truth". He encloses the world for them, makes it smaller, less terrifying, more understandable. Through metaphors as fresh now as they were when first written 2,000 and more years ago, he shows how the world has come to be in such a turmoil, how its past and present are no more than a preparation for a glorious future. He reassures them, his elect, that they have a special, secure place in that future—so long as they continue to believe in him. From their Exile of uncertainty, fear and anxiety, he promises them a certain Return to Jerusalem of the quiet mind which will endure for ever. And they follow. . . .

Notes

Bibliography

Index

NOTES

Chapter One: From King to Messiah

1. 1 Sam. 9:2.
2. 1 Sam. 24:14.
3. John Cournos, *A Book of Prophecy* (Charles Scribners Sons) New York, 1942, p. 22.
4. Sir James George Frazer, *The Golden Bough* (Macmillan & Co. Ltd) London, 1936, pp. 390–1.
5. Ibid. 380.
6. Ibid. 385.
7. Ibid. 396.
8. Ibid. 401.
9. 1 Sam. 27:7.
10. 1 Sam. 16:13.
11. 1 Chron. 29.
12. Is. 9:6.
13. Is. 11:4.
14. Is. 11:10.
15. Is. 10:6.
16. Is. 11:6.
17. Martin Buber, *The Prophetic Faith* (Harper & Bros) New York, 1949, p. 149.
18. Sigmund Mowinckel, *He That Cometh*, tr. G. W. Anderson (Basil Blackwell) Oxford, 1956, p. 157.
19. Is. 53.
20. Is. 42:1 and 52:13.
21. Is. 49:7.
22. Zech. 9:9–10.

Chapter Two: Exile and the Last Days

1. Jer. 52.
2. Hag. 2:23.
3. Zech. 6:12.
4. Zech. 6:13.
5. Zech. 4:9.
6. Zech. 6:15.

7. Zech. 12.
8. Zech. 14:11.
9. Mowinckel, p. 256.
10. 1 Macc. 4:28–59. See Emily Solis-Cohen Jr., *Hanukkah, The Feast of Lights* (The Jewish Publication Society of America) Philadelphia, 1945, pp. 127–30.
11. Jubillees 31:18–20. See *The Apocrypha and Pseudepigrapha of the Old Testament* (Ed.) R. H. Charles (Oxford University Press) Oxford, 1913, pp. 1–82.
12. Dan. 7:8.
13. Dan. 9:24.
14. Dan. 9:25.
15. Dan. 7:25.
16. Dan. 12:7.
17. Dan. 7:18.
18. Dan. 7:8.

Chapter Three: Simon, Judah and Joshua

1. *The Works of Flavius Josephus* (Ed.) William Whiston, London, 1825, pp. 66 ff.
2. *Encyclopaedia Judaica* (Keter Publishing House Ltd) Jerusalem, 1971, Vol. 11, cols. 1418–27 at 1421.
3. *Josephus*, pp. 66 ff.
4. Ibid.
5. Ibid. 281 ff.
6. Ibid. 125.
7. Matt. 3:4.
8. John 3:28.
9. H. Graetz, *Popular History of the Jews* (Hebrew Publishing Company) New York, 1930, Vol. 2, pp. 70 ff.
10. Matt. 1:1–16.
11. Luke 3:23–38.
12. John 2:4.
13. Luke 18:29.
14. Luke 14:26.
15. Matt. 3:16–17.
16. John 1:13.
17. John 3:4–5.
18. August Hoch, *Benign Stupors* (Cambridge University Press and Macmillan & Co.) New York, 1921, p. 240.
19. John 6:1–11.
20. Matt. 10:34.
21. Matt. 17:9.
22. Matt. 17:22–3.
23. Is. 53.

24. Matt. 16:21.
25. Matt. 26:64 and Luke 22:70.
26. Mark 14:62.
27. Mark 15:2.
28. Graetz, Vol. 2, pp. 70 ff.
29. Acts 2:44–6.
30. Rom. 10:12–13.
31. James Hastings, *Dictionary of the Bible*, Second Edition, revised by Frederick C. Grant and H. H. Rowley (T. & T. Clark) Edinburgh, 1963, pp. 849–50.
32. Rev. 16:15.
33. Rev. 20.
34. Rev. 21:1–4.

Chapter Four: Creation to Adam + X Years = Messiah

1. Moses Gaster, *Studies and Texts in Folklore, Magic &c.* (Maggs Bros) London, 1925–8, Vol. 1, pp. 147–8.
2. 1 Thess. 5:5–8.
3. Abba Hillel Silver, D.D., *A History of Messianic Speculation in Israel* (Macmillan Co.) New York, 1927, p. 195.
4. Norman Cohn, *The Pursuit of the Millennium* (Secker & Warburg) London, 1957, p. 14.
5. James Black, D. D., *New Forms of the Old Faith* (Baird Lecture 1946–7) (Thomas Nelson & Son Ltd) Edinburgh, 1948, pp. 236–7.
6. 2 Pet. 3:3–4.
7. Emile Gebhart, *Mystics and Heretics in Italy* (George Allen & Unwin) London, 1922, p. 89.
8. Silver, p. 34.
9. Ibid. 71.
10. Ibid. 250.
11. Ibid. 251.
12. Abraham Aboulafia, "Every Man His Own Messiah" in *Memoirs of My People* (Ed.) Leo W. Schwarz (Rinehart & Co. Inc.) New York, 1943.
13. Ibid. 22.
14. Ibid. 23.
15. Ibid. 25.
16. Ibid. 26.
17. Silver, p. 90.
18. Graetz, Vol. 3, pp. 370 ff.
19. Silver, pp. 100–1.
20. Ibid. 117.
21. Isaac E. Barzilay, *Between Reason and Faith* (Columbia University Press) New York, 1967, p. 123.

22. Deut. 4:19.
23. Silver, p. 256.
24. Ibid. 256.
25. Nathaniel Brassey Halhed, M.P., *A Calculation on the Commencement of the Millennium,* London, 1795, p. 12.
26. Clara Endicott Sears, *Days of Delusion* (Houghton Mifflin Co.) Boston and New York, 1924, p. 28.
27. Ibid. 35.
28. Ibid. See Appendix.
29. Ibid. 122.
30. Ibid. 203.
31. Ibid. 237.
32. Ibid. 242.
33. Ibid. 248.

Chapter Five: Messiahs of the First Millennium

1. Num. 24:17.
2. Gaster, p. 672.
3. *Judaica,* Vol. 4, cols. 228 ff.
4. Ibid. 228 ff.
5. Ibid. 228 ff.
6. Silver, p. 199.
7. *Judaica,* Vol. 11, cols. 1418–27.
8. Sir Hamilton A. R. Gibb, *Mohammedanism* (The New American Library) New York, 1955, p. 13.
9. Frank Kobler (Ed.) *Letters of Jews Through the Ages* (Ararat Publishing Society) London, 1952, Vol. 1, p. 70.
10. Silver, p. 55. See also *Judaica,* Vol. 11, col. 1422.
11. Silver, p. 57.
12. Silver, p. 52.
13. Rev. 20 and 21.
14. Richard Lewinsohn, *Prophets and Prediction* (Secker & Warburg) London, 1958, p. 78.
15. Maurice H. Krout, *Introduction to Social Psychology* (Harper & Bros) New York, 1942, p. 712.
16. Lewinsohn, p. 78.
17. Cohn, pp. 35 ff.
18. Jer. 31:7–13.
19. Silver, p. 58.
20. Ibid. 59.
21. Ibid. 78. See also, Moses Maimonides, "Logbook of a Physician" in *Memoirs of My People,* p. 17.
22. Maimonides, p. 17.
23. Silver, p. 78.
24. Maimonides, p. 17.

25. Gershom G. Scholem, *The Messianic Idea in Judaism* (George Allen & Unwin Ltd) London, 1971, pp. 28–9.
26. *Judaica*, Vol. 11, col. 1423.
27. Silver, pp. 79–80.
28. Benjamin Disraeli, *Alroy, A Romance*, in Collection of British Authors, Vol. Cl. (Bernhard Tauchnitz) Leipzig, 1846.
29. Ibid. 67.

Chapter Six: Every Man His Own Messiah

1. 2 Cor. 3:17.
2. Robert E. Lerner, *The Heresy of the Free Spirit in the Later Middle Ages* (University of California Press) Berkeley and Los Angeles, p. 21. See also, Howard Kaminsky, "The Free Spirit in the Hussite Revolution" in *Millennial Dreams in Action* (Ed.) Sylvia Thrupp (Society for the Comparative Study of Society and History) (Mouton & Co.) The Hague, 1962, pp. 166–86.
3. Lerner, p. 109.
4. Ibid. 151.
5. Ibid. 30.
6. See Cohn, particularly Chapters VII and VIII for a detailed discussion of Free Spirit ideology.
7. Lerner, p. 151.
8. Cohn, p. 182.
9. E. Belfort Bax, *Rise and Fall of the Anabaptists* (Swan Sonnenschein) London, 1903, p. 35.
10. Claus-Peter Clasen, *Anabaptism, A Social History 1525–1618* (Cornell University Press) Ithaca and London, 1972, pp. 137–9.
11. Gershom G. Scholem, *Major Trends in Jewish Mysticism* (Thames & Hudson) London, 1955, pp. 316 ff.
12. Ibid. 316 ff.
13. Scholem, *Messianic*, pp. 130 ff.
14. William Hepworth Dixon, *Spiritual Wives* (Hurst & Blackett) London, 1868, pp. 317–8.
15. Adolf Hitler, *Mein Kampf* quoted Walter C. Langer, *The Mind of Adolf Hitler* (Secker & Warburg) London, 1972, pp. 190 ff.
16. *Judaica*, Vol. 7, cols. 55 ff.
17. Scholem, *Messianic*, p. 158.

Chapter Seven: David and Solomon

1. Cohn, pp. 82 ff.
2. Deut. 28:64–6.
3. Philip Zeigler, *The Black Death* (Collins) London, 1969, p. 270.

4. James Parkes, *A History of the Jewish People* (Penguin Books) London, 1964, p. 85.
5. Salo Wittmayer Baron, *A Social and Religious History of the Jews* (Columbia University Press) New York, 1957, Vol. III, pp. 121 ff. and 172.
6. Ibid. Vol. IV, p. 132.
7. Ibid. Vol. IV, p. 132.
8. Cecil Roth, *A History of the Marranos* (Meridian Books Inc. and The Jewish Publication Society of America) New York, 1959, pp. 14–16.
9. Ibid. 7 ff.
10. Henry Charles Lea, *A History of the Inquisition of Spain* (Macmillan & Co.) New York, 1906, Vol. 1, pp. 114 ff.
11. Don Isaac Abravanel, "Twilight of Spanish Glory" in *Memoirs*, pp. 43–7.
12. Ibid. 146 n.
13. Baron, Vol. XIII, pp. 44 ff.
14. Lea, Vol. 1, pp. 114 ff.
15. Baron, Vol. XIII, p. 79.
16. Ibid. 82.
17. Ibid. 47.
18. Lea, Vol. 3, pp. 551 ff.
19. Roth, *Marranos*, pp. 168 ff.
20. David Reubeni, "The Road to Rome" in *Memoirs*, pp. 48–61.
21. Elkan Nathan Adler, *Jewish Travellers* (George Routledge & Sons Ltd) London, 1930, pp. xxi-xxii.
22. David Reubeni, "Visit to the Pope" in *The Jewish Caravan* (Ed.) Leo W. Schwarz (Rinehart & Co. Inc.) New York, 1935, pp. 265–71.
23. Ludwig Pastor, *The History of the Popes* (Ed.) Ralph Kerr (Routledge & Kegan Paul Ltd) London, 1950, Vol. IX, p. 242.
24. Graetz, Vol. 4, pp. 338 ff.
25. Pastor, p. 242.
26. Graetz, Vol. 4, pp. 338 ff.
27. Reubeni, *Caravan*, p. 267.
28. Ibid. 268.
29. Ibid. 270.
30. Graetz, Vol. 4, p. 341.
31. David Reubeni in *A Golden Treasury of Jewish Literature* (Ed.) Leo W. Schwarz (Arthur Barker Ltd) London, 1937, p. 304.
32. Adler, p. 288.
33. Graetz, Vol. 4, p. 342.
34. Adler, p. 303.

35. Ibid. 293.
36. Ibid. 303.
37. Silver, p. 146.
38. Adler, p. 322.
39. Silver, pp. 148–9.
40. Solomon Molcho, "Pope, Emperor, and the Inquisition" in *Memoirs*, pp. 62–7.
41. Morris S. Goodblatt, *Jewish Life in Turkey in the XVIth Century* (Jewish Theological Seminary of America) New York, 1952, p. 8.
42. Pastor, p. 400.
43. Kobler, Vol. 2, p. 335.
44. Molcho, *Memoirs*, p. 65.
45. Ibid. 66.
46. Ibid. 66.
47. Ibid. 67.
48. Graetz, Vol. 4, p. 354.
49. Ibid. p. 353.
50. Mannheim, p. 196.

Chapter Eight: Wars and Rumours of Wars

1. Judg. 7.
2. Ps. 18.
3. Rev. 16:14, 16.
4. See Norman Cohn, "Medieval Millenarism" in *Millennial Dreams in Action*, pp. 35–8.
5. Rev. E. Gordon Rupp, M.A., D.D., *Thomas Müntzer, Hans Huth and the 'Gospel of All Creatures'* (The John Rylands Library) Manchester, 1961, pp. 493–4.
6. Cohn, *Pursuit*, pp. 251–71.
7. Rupp, pp. 495–7.
8. Cohn, *Pursuit*, p. 268.
9. Ezek. 34:23–8.
10. Matt. 24:29–30.
11. Cohn, *Pursuit*, p. 268.
12. Heinrich Bullinger (1560) quoted Clasen, p. 6.
13. Bax, p. 63.
14. Ibid. 28–9.
15. R. J. Smithson, *The Anabaptists* (J. Clarke & Co.) London, 1935, p. 14.
16. Bax, pp. 67 ff.
17. Ibid. 28–9.
18. Ibid. 67 ff.
19. Smithson, p. 133.
20. Bax, pp. 118–9.

21. Ibid. 117.
22. S. Baring Gould, *Historic Oddities and Strange Events* (Methuen & Co.) London, 1891, p. 221.
23. Bax, p. 158.
24. Gould, p. 264.
25. Ibid. 256.
26. Ibid. 265.
27. Ibid. 266.
28. Ibid. 276.
29. Bax, p. 153.
30. Ibid. 152.
31. Ibid. 195.
32. Ibid. 163–4.
33. Harry C. Schnur, *Mystic Rebels* (The Beechhurst Press) New York, 1949, p. 126.
34. Gould, p. 301.
35. Bax, p. 215.
36. Ibid. 225; Gould, p. 316.
37. Bax, p. 222.
38. Ibid. 189–90.
39. Gould, p. 301.
40. Ibid. 306.
41. Ibid. 317.
42. Ibid. 317.
43. Ibid. 327.
44. Ibid. 310–11.
45. Ibid. 331.
46. Ibid. 343.
47. Ibid. 341.
48. Schnur, p. 142.
49. Bax, pp. 316–17.
50. Ibid. 318–19.

Chapter Nine: A Profusion of Messiahs

1. Rufus M. Jones, *Studies in Mystical Religion* (Macmillan & Co.) London, 1909, p. 437.
2. Rufus M. Jones, *Mysticism and Democracy in the English Commonwealth* (Harvard University Press) Cambridge, Mass., 1932, p. 123.
3. Christopher Hill, *The World Turned Upside Down* (Temple Smith) London, 1972, pp. 21 ff.
4. Pagitt, *Heresiography*, pp. 91–7.
5. Ibid. 91–7.
6. Anon, *The Devil of Delphos, or, The Prophets of Baal*, London, 1708.

7. Ibid.
8. *Calendar of State Papers*, Domestic Series, 1648–9 (Ed.) Mary A. E. Green (Longman, Green, Longman, Roberts and Green) London, 1864, pp. 425–6.
9. Pagitt, pp. 91–7.
10. Ibid. 91–7.
11. Ibid. 91–7.
12. Keith Thomas, *Religion and the Decline of Magic* (Weidenfeld & Nicolson) London, 1971, p. 133.
13. Ibid. 133–5.
14. Ibid. 133–5.
15. Ibid. 133–5.
16. Ibid. 144.
17. Ronald Matthews, *English Messiahs, 1656–1927* (Methuen & Co.) London, 1936, p. xiv.
18. *Calendar of State Papers*, Domestic Series, 1591–4, pp. 75–6.
19. Thomas, p. 134.
20. *Calendar*, pp. 75–6 .
21. Ibid. 75–6.
22. Ibid. 75–6.
23. N. Spinckes, *The New Pretenders to Prophecy Examin'd*, London, 1709, p. 370.
24. Victor Harris, *All Coherence Gone* (University of Chicago Press) Chicago, 1949, p. I.
25. Mal. 3 :5, and 4 :1.
26. *Reports of Cases in the Courts of Star Chamber* (Ed.) Samuel Rawson Gardiner, London, 1886, p. 188.
27. *Calendar*, 1636–7, pp, 459–460.
28. Ibid, 487–8.
29. Ibid, 1637, p. 66.
30. See Humphry Ellis, *Pseudochristus*, London, 1650, pp. 6–51.

Chapter Ten: Shaking, Ranting and Quaking

1. Theodorus Verax (Clement Walker), *Anarchia Anglicana, or, The History of Independency*, London, 1649, pp. 152–3.
2. Mabel Richmond Brailsford, *A Quaker from Cromwell's Army: James Naylor* (The Swarthmore Press) London, 1927, p. 15.
3. Ibid. 74.
4. Dan. 2 :44.
5. Theaurau John (Thomas Tany) *Proclamation*, London, 1650. See also, W. H. G. Armytage, *Heavens Below (Utopian Experiments in England 1560–1960)* (Routledge & Kegan Paul Ltd) London, 1961, p. 16.

6. *The Weekly Intelligencer of the Commonwealth*, London, 1655. Monday, 24 September.
7. Gen. 14:18.
8. Heb. 7:1–3.
9. John Robins, *The Declaration of John Robins, the false prophet, otherwise called the Shakers God, and Joshua Beck, and John King, the two false Disciples, with the rest of their Fellow-Creatures now prisoners in the New-prison at Clerkenwell, by G.H., an Ear-witness*, London (2 June), 1651.
10. Ibid. 5.
11. Hill, p. 160.
12. Ibid. 162.
13. Jones, *Mysticism*, p. 132.
14. Theaurau John, *His Aurora in Tranlagorum in Salem Gloria, or, The discussive of the Law and the Gospell betwixt the Jew and the Gentile in Salem Resurrectionem*, London, 1655.
15. Hill, p. 168.
16. Ibid. 165.
17. S. S. Gent (Samuel Sheppard), *The Joviall Crew, or, The Devill turn'd Ranter*, London, 1651.
18. Hill, p. 250.
19. Brailsford, p. 94.
20. Ibid. 35.
21. Ibid. 85.
22. Ibid. 94 and 97.
23. Ibid. 98.
24. Ibid. 98.
25. Ibid. 106.
26. Ibid. 110.
27. William Grigge, *The Quaker's Jesus, or, The Unswadling of that Child James Nailor, which a wicked Toleration hath midwiv'd into the world*, London, 1658.
28. For a discussion on this, see Hill, pp. 199 ff.
29. Brailsford, p. 133.
30. Ibid. 134.
31. For a transcript of Naylor's trial, see *The Harleian Miscellany*, Vol. VI, London, 1810, pp. 424–38.
32. Ibid. 424–38.
33. Ibid. 424–38.
34. Brailsford, p. 138.
35. Ibid. 142–3.
36. Ibid. 149.
37. Ibid. 192.

Chapter Eleven: Sabbatai Zevi

1. Rabbi Nathan Hannover, *Abyss of Despair*, tr. Abraham J. Mesch (Bloch Publishing Co.) New York, 1950, see Introduction.
2. Ibid. 43.
3. Ibid. 53.
4. Ibid. 50.
5. *Judaica*, Vol. 5, cols. 480–3.
6. Ibid. col. 480.
7. For a full discussion of the Kabbalah and its relationship to messianic thought, see Scholem, *The Messianic Idea in Judaism*, and *On the Kabbalah and its Symbolism* (Routledge & Kegan Paul Ltd) London, 1965.
8. Ariel Bension, *The Zohar in Moslem and Christian Spain* (George Routledge & Sons Ltd) London, 1932, p. 180.
9. Thomas, p. 270.
10. Silver, p. 156 n.
11. Goodblatt, pp. 111 ff, for the situation of the Marranos generally in Turkey.
12. Gershom G. Scholem, *Major Trends in Jewish Mysticism* (Thames & Hudson) London, 1955; see, Eighth Lecture, "Sabbataianism and Mystical Heresy", pp. 287 ff. and 290.
13. *Judaica*, Vol. 14, cols. 1219–54.
14. Joseph Kastein, *The Messiah of Ismir, Sabbatai Zevi*, tr. Huntley Paterson (John Lane, The Bodley Head) London, 1931, p. 99.
15. Song of Sol. 4:12, 16; 5:1–8.
16. Kobler, Vol. 2, p. 524.
17. Scholem, *Trends*, p. 295.
18. J.E. (John Evelyn), *The History of the Three Late Famous Impostors*, London, 1669, p. 60.
19. Kastein, p. 124.
20. Ibid. 197.
21. *The Diary of Samuel Pepys, F.R.S.* (George Routledge & Sons Ltd) London, 1906. Entry for February 19th, 1665.
22. *Impostors*, p. 65.
23. *A True and Exact Account of a Famous New Prophet Now Residing at Alkair, a City in Egypt. Sent in a Letter to a Friend in London*, London, 1687.
24. Jacob Emden, "Defeat of Satan" in *Memoirs of My People*, p. 131.
25. Kobler, Vol. 2, p. 528.
26. Impostors, p. 93.
27. Ibid. 73.

28. Scholem, *Messianic*, p. 74.
29. *Impostors*, p. 77.
30. Kastein, pp, 189 ff.
31. Ibid. 151.
32. Ibid. 294.
33. Ibid. 304–5.
34. Ibid. 304–5.
35. *Impostors*, p. 52.

Chapter Twelve: In the Female Line

1. *Devil of Delphos*, p. 16.
2. Hannah Whitall Smith, *Religious Fanaticism* (Ed.) Ray Strachey (Faber & Gwyer) London, 1928, p. 148.
3. Ibid. 48.
4. Ronald A. Knox, *Enthusiasm* (Clarendon Press) Oxford, 1950, p. 167.
5. Smith, p. 48.
6. For my main sources I have relied on Edward Deeming Andrews, *The People called Shakers* (Oxford University Press) New York, 1953; and Clara Endicott Sears, *Gleanings from Old Shaker Journals* (Houghton Mifflin Co.) Boston and New York, 1916.
7. Andrews, p. 11.
8. Sears, p. 65.
9. Ibid. 68.
10. Ibid. 108.
11. Ibid. 109.
12. Andrews, p. 244.
13. Sears, p. 158.
14. For Margaret Peter I have relied solely on S. Baring Gould, *Historic Oddities and Strange Events*, pp. 1–38.
15. Secondary sources : G. R. Balleine, *Past Finding Out* (S.P.C.K.) London, 1956; and Ronald Matthews, *English Messiahs*, pp. 45–84.
16. Joanna Southcott, Various tracts in the British Library collection.
17. Balleine, p. 12.
18. Rev. 12 : 1–2.
19. Southcott, *Advertisement in The Times*, 28 October 1813. Various tracts.
20. Southcott, *The Trial of Joanna Southcott during seven days at the Neckinger House, Bermondsey*, London, 1804.
21. Southcott, *Joanna's Dispute with Satan—A dispute between the Woman and Darkness*, London, 1813.

22. *The Life of Joanna Southcott the Prophetess, Containing an Impartial Account of her wonderful and astonishing Writings, her Miraculous Conception, the coming of Shiloh, and of the numerous presents sent to her Preparatory to Her Accouchement, particularly the Superb Crib!!*, London, 1814.
23. Ibid.
24. Ibid.
25. P. Mathias, Surgeon and Apothecary, *The Case of Joanna Southcott*, London, n.d.
26. Richard Reece, M.D., *A Correct Statement of the Last Illness and Death of Mrs Southcott*, London, 1815.
27. Ibid.
28. Ibid.
29. Mathias, *Case of Southcott.*
30. Balleine, p. 68.
31. Southcott, *Elegy, by a Believer*, Various tracts.

Chapter Thirteen: Rebels and Billiard Players

1. Richard Brothers, *A Revealed Knowledge of the Prophecies and Times. Wrote under the Direction of the Lord God, And publish'd by his Sacred Command; It being the first sign of warning for the benefit of all Nations. Containing, With other great and remarkable Things, not revealed to any other Person on Earth, The Restoration of the Hebrews to Jerusalem by the year of 1798, under their revealed Prince and Prophet*, Dublin, 1795.
2. G. M. Trevelyan, *A Shortened History of England* (Penguin Books) London, 1960, p. 384.
3. For the facts on which this account is based I have relied on Ronald Matthews, *English Messiahs*, pp. 87–125; and Cecil Roth, *The Nephew of the Almighty* (Edward Goldston Ltd) London, 1933.
4. Brothers, *Revealed*, p. 30.
5. Ibid. 26.
6. Roth, *Nephew*, p. 46.
7. *The Times*, 4 March 1795.
8. Roth, p. 60.
9. Matthews, p. 109.
10. *Dictionary of National Biography*, Vol. 24, pp. 41–2.
11. Nathaniel Brassey Halhed, M.P., *Testimony of the Authenticity of the Prophecies of Richard Brothers*, published with A Revealed Knowledge, 1795.
12. Ibid. 19.
13. Halhed, *A Calculation of the Millennium*, 1795.

14. *A Description of Jerusalem: Its Houses and Streets, Squares, Colleges, Markets, and Cathedrals, the Royal and Private Palaces, with The Garden of Eden in the Centre, by Mr Brothers who will be revealed to the Hebrews as their King and Restorer*, Printed for George Riebau, Bookseller to the King of the Hebrews, London, 1801, p. 158.
15. Ibid. 168.
16. Ibid. 27.
17. Ibid. 43.
18. Ibid. 47.
19. David Levi, *Letters to Nathaniel Brassey Halhed, M.P., in answer to his Testimony of the Authenticity of the Prophecies of Richard Brothers, And his pretended Mission to Recall the Jews*, London, 1795.
20. Secondary sources: Ronald Matthews, *English Messiahs*, pp. 129–59; and P. G. Rogers, *Battle in Bossenden Wood* (Oxford University Press) London, 1961.
21. Matthews, p. 132.
22. Sir William Courtenay (John Tom), Various tracts. British Library collection.
23. *The Lion*, No. 6.
24. *The Lion*, No. 4.
25. Ibid.
26. *The Lion*, No. 6.
27. Rogers, p. 210.
28. Courtenay, Various tracts.
29. Trevelyan, pp. 457–8.
30. Jam. 5.
31. Matthews, p. 152.
32. Rogers, p. 113.
33. *The Globe*, 2 June 1838.
34. Ibid.
35. Matthews, p. 159.
36. Courtenay, Various tracts.
37. Rogers, p. 221.
38. Ibid. 221.
39. Br. Henry Prince, *The Testimony; The Little Book Open*, London, 1856.
40. Secondary sources: Matthews, *Messiahs*, pp. 163 ff.; William Hepworth Dixon, *Spiritual Wives* (Hurst & Blackett) London, 1868.
41. Dixon, p. 274.
42. Matthews, p. 171.
43. Dixon, p. 300.

44. Ibid. 300.
45. Ibid. 315.
46. Prince, *Little Book.*
47. Ibid.
48. Ibid.
49. Dixon, p. 321.
50. Prince, *Little Book.*
51. Dixon, p. 319.
52. Prince, *Little Book.*
53. Dixon, p. 233.
54. See Matthews, *Messiahs*, pp. 179–95.
55. Ibid. 187.
56. Ibid. 190.

Chapter Fourteen: Full Circle

1. Hos. 8 :14.
2. Joel 2 :25–6.
3. Joel 2 :31.
4. Jer. 23 :5.
5. Mic. 4 :1,3.
6. Bengt G. M. Sundkler, *Bantu Prophets in South Africa* (International African Institute, Oxford University Press) London, 1961, pp. 323–37.
7. Vittorio Lanternari, *The Religions of the Oppressed* (MacGibbon & Kee) London, 1963, pp. 11–14.
8. Ibid. 11–14.
9. Ibid. 11–14.
10. George Shepperson, "Nyasaland and the Millennium" in *Millennial Dreams in Action*, p. 148.
11. Sundkler, pp. 323–37.
12. Ibid. 323–37.
13. Lanternari, pp. 88 ff.
14. Helen Addison Howard and Dan L. McGrath, *War Chief Joseph* (University of Nebraska Press) Lincoln, pp. 82–4.
15. Lanternari, p. 131.
16. Ibid. 133 ff.
17. Ibid. 205 ff.
18. Ibid. 205 ff.
19. Ibid. 173.
20. Ibid. 175.
21. Ibid. 192.
22. Ibid. 194.
23. See, for example, Stephen Fuchs, *Rebellious Prophets* (Asia Publishing House) London, 1965.
24. Gibb, *Mohammedanism*, p. 101.

25. Sir Francis Younghusband, *Modern Mystics* (John Murray) London, 1935, pp. 97–142.
26. *The Encyclopaedia of Islam* (Luzac & Co.) London, 1913, Vol. 1, p. 544.
27. Younghusband, pp. 98 ff.
28. Ibid. 98 ff.
29. Ibid. 98 ff.
30. *Encyclopaedia of Islam*, p. 544.
31. Younghusband, pp. 98 ff.
32. Ibid. 98 ff.
33. Fuchs, pp. 198–203.

Chapter Fifteen: Portrait of a Messiah

1. John 2:4.
2. Matt. 10:35.
3. Luke 2:46–7.
4. George Woodcock and Ivan Avakumovic, *The Doukhobors* (Faber & Faber) London, 1968, pp. 81 ff.
5. 1 Sam. 10:6, 9.
6. Matt. 3:16–17.
7. Abiezer Coppe, *A Fiery Flying Roll: A Word from the Lord to all the Great Ones of the Earth whom this may concerne: Being the last Warning Piece at the dreadfull day of JUDGEMENT*, London (in the beginning of that notable day, wherein the secret of all hearts are laid open; and wherein the worst and foulest of villanies are discovered, under the best and fairest outsides), 1649.
8. Anton T. Boisen, *Religion in Crisis and Custom*, p. 58.
9. Ibid. 61.
10. Coppe, *Flying Roll.*
11. John 3:5.
12. Tit. 3:5.
13. August Hoch, *Benign Stupors*, p. 240.
14. Ibid. 234.
15. Heb. 7:1–3.
16. Hoch, p. 243.
17. Coppe, *Flying Roll.*
18. Rufus M. Jones, *Spiritual Reformers in the 16th and 17th Centuries* (Macmillan & Co. Ltd) London, 1914, p. 160.
19. Ibid. 160.
20. Matthews, p. 171.
21. Dixon, p. 272.
22. *Judaica*, Vol. 14, col. 366.
23. William James, *The Varieties of Religious Experience* (Longmans, Green & Co.) London, 1902, 1929, p. 404.

24. Matthews, p. 190.
25. Woodcock, p. 260.
26. Jones, *Reformers*, p. 152.
27. Robins, *Declaration*, p. 6.
28. Jones, *Mystical Religion*, p. 435.
29. Balleine, pp. 83 ff.
30. Ibid. 70.
31. Sears, *Gleanings*, p. 66.
32. Younghusband, pp. 98 ff.
33. John 4:26.
34. 2 Tim. 3:6.
35. Sigmund Freud, *Group Psychology and the Analysis of the Ego*, Complete Works, Vol. XVIII (The Hogarth Press) London, 1935, p. 115.
36. Dixon, p. 233.
37. Gould, p. 315.
38. Balleine, pp. 88–9.
39. Hill, p. 13.
40. R. D. Laing, *The Politics of Experience* (Penguin Books) London, 1967, p. 118.
41. *Encyclopedia of Psychology* (Search Press) London, 1972, Vol. 3, p. 175.
42. *The Life of Joanna Southcott.*
43. *Encyclopedia of Psychology*, Vol. 3, p. 175.
44. Brothers, *Revealed Knowledge*, p. 26.
45. Jones, *Reformers*, p. 171.
46. Rev. 13:2.
47. Rev. 14:2.
48. James, p. 73.
49. Reece, *A Correct Statement.*
50. Milton Rokeach, *The Three Christs of Ypsilanti* (Arthur Barker Ltd) London, 1964, p. 4.
51. Ibid. 5.
52. Ibid. 56.
53. Ibid. 75.
54. Ibid. 105.
55. Ibid. 315.

Chapter Sixteen: Things New and Old

1. *The Times*, 9 August 1969.
2. Ibid. 20 April 1971.
3. Ed. Sanders, *The Family* (Panther Books Ltd) London, 1973, p. 13.
4. *The Times*, 9 December 1969.
5. Sanders, p. 41.

6. Rev. 9:4, 9.
7. Sanders, p. 99.
8. Ibid. 116.
9. Ibid. 86.
10. *The Times*, 16 June 1970.
11. Ibid. 12 February 1971.
12. Egon Larsen, *Strange Sects and Cults* (Arthur Barker Ltd) London, 1971, p. 53.
13. Report by Michael Knipe, Los Angeles, *The Times*, 4 February 1971.
14. *The Times*, 6 December 1969.
15. Sanders, p. 161.
16. Ibid. 162.
17. Freud, p. 127.
18. James, p. 158.
19. Søren Kierkegaard, *The Sickness Unto Death*, tr. Walter Lowrie (Doubleday & Co. Inc.) New York, 1954, p. 177.
20. James, p. 162.
21. Rollo May, Ernest Angel, Henri F. Ellenberger (Eds) *Existence* (Basic Books Inc.) New York, 1958, 1960, p. 42.
22. Michael Knipe, *The Times*, 4 February 1971.
23. Andrews, *The People Called Shakers*, pp. 289 and 244 ff.
24. *The Times*, 22 January 1971.
25. Ibid. 20 April 1971.
26. Smith, *Religious Fanaticism*, pp. 182 ff.
27. Balleine, p. 112.
28. Knox, p. 574.
29. Abraham Miguel Cardozo (1627–1706) quoted Scholem, *Messianic*, p. 108.
30. Ibid. 157.
31. Ibid. 158.
32. Ibid. 126.
33. Scholem, *Mysticism*, p. 336.
34. Scholem, *Messianic*, p. 130.
35. Ps. 72:2–7.
36. Langer, *Hitler*, p. 54.
37. Ibid. 56.
38. 2 Enoch 65:8. See, *The Apocrypha and Pseudepigrapha of the Old Testament*.
39. *Plain Truth*, Vol. XXXIX. No. 8 (Ambassador College Press) California, September, 1974.
40. Moses David, "The Drugstore" in *The Green Door* (Children of God) London, September, 1973, p. 2.
41. *The Times*, 17 October 1974; *International Herald Tribune*,

19 and 20 October 1974.

42. *Sunday Times*, 16 June 1974; 17 November 1974. *Sunday People*, 2 December 1973.
43. L. D. Dale, *The Lightning from the East* (Wings of Life) Tennessee, n.d.
44. Ibid. 76.
45. Ibid. 18.
46. Ibid. 124.

BIBLIOGRAPHY

ADLER, Elkan Nathan, *Jewish Travellers* (George Routledge & Sons Ltd) London, 1930.

ANDREWS, Edward Deeming, *The People called Shakers* (Oxford University Press) New York, 1953.

ANON, *The Devil of Delphos, or, The Prophets of Baal*, London, 1708.

ANON, *The Life of Joanna Southcott, the Prophetess*, London, 1814.

ANON, *A True and Exact Account of a Famous New Prophet*, London, 1687.

ANON, *A Sad and Dismal Year*, London, 1655.

ARMYTAGE, W. H. G., *Heavens Below (Utopian Experiments in England 1560–1960)* (Routledge & Kegan Paul Ltd) London, 1961.

BALDWIN, R. A., *The Jezreelites* (The Lambarde Press) Kent, 1962.

BALLEINE, G. R., *Past Finding Out* (S.P.C.K.) London, 1956.

BARON, Salo Wittmayer, *A Social and Religious History of the Jews* (Columbia University Press) New York, 1957.

BARZILAY, Isaac E., *Between Reason and Faith (Anti-rationalism in Italian Jewish Thought 1250–1650)* (Near and Middle East Studies) (Columbia University Press) New York, 1967.

BAX, E. Belfort, *Rise and Fall of the Anabaptists* (Swan Sonnenschein) London, 1903.

BENSION, Ariel, *The Zohar in Moslem and Christian Spain* (George Routledge & Sons Ltd) London, 1932.

Berkeley, Hume and Kant. Philosophers Speak for Themselves (Eds) T. V. Smith and Marjorie Grene (University of Chicago Press) Chicago, 1958.

BLACK, James, D. D. *New Forms of the Old Faith* (Baird Lecture 1946–7) (Thomas Nelson & Son Ltd) Edinburgh, 1948.

BLUNT, John Henry, *Dictionary of Sects, Heresies, etc.* London, 1874.

BOISEN, Anton T., *Religion in Crisis and Custom* (Harper & Bros) New York, 1944–5.

BONNER, Hypatatia Bradlaugh, *Penalties upon Opinion* (Watts & Co.) London, 1912.

BRAILSFORD, Mabel Richmond, *A Quaker from Cromwell's Army: James Naylor* (The Swarthmore Press) London, 1927.

BROTHERS, Richard, *A Description of Jerusalem*, London 1801.

BROTHERS, Richard, *A Revealed Knowledge of the Prophecies and Times*, Dublin, 1795.

BROWN, Louise Fargo, *The Political Activities of the Baptists and Fifth Monarch Men in England during the Interregnum* (American Historical Association) Washington, 1912.

BUBER, Martin, *The Prophetic Faith* (Harper & Sons) New York, 1949.

Calendar of State Papers, Domestic Series, 1591–4; 1636–7; 1648–9; 1665–6 (Ed.) Mary A. E. Green (Longman, Green, Longman, Roberts and Green) London, 1864.

CHARLES, R. H., (Ed.) *The Apocrypha and Pseudepigrapha of the Old Testament* (Oxford University Press) Oxford, 1913.

COHN, Norman, *The Pursuit of the Millennium* (Secker & Warburg) London, 1957.

CLASEN, Claus-Peter, *Anabaptism, A Social History, 1525–1618* (Cornell University Press) Ithaca and London, 1972.

COPPE, Abiezer, *A Fiery Flying Roll*, London, 1649.

COURNOS, John, *A Book of Prophecy* (Charles Scribners' Sons) New York, 1942.

COURTENAY, Sir William (John Tom) Various Tracts in the British Library, circa 1832–1838.

DALE, L. D., *The Lightning from the East* (Wings of Life) Tennessee, n.d.

DAVID, Moses, *The Green Door* (Children of God), London, 1973.

DAVIES, A. Powell, *The Meaning of the Dead Sea Scrolls* (The New American Library) New York, 1956.

A Dictionary of Comparative Religion (Ed.) S. G. F. Brandon (Weidenfeld & Nicolson) London, 1970.

Dictionary of National Biography, Volume 24.

DISRAELI, Benjamin, *Alroy. A Romance* (Bernhard Tauchnitz) Leipzig, 1846.

DIXON, William Hepworth, *Spiritual Wives* (Hurst & Blackett) London, 1868.

ELLIS, Humphry, *Pseudochristus*, London, 1650.

The Encyclopaedia of Islam (Luzac & Co.) London, 1913.

The Encyclopaedia of the Jewish Religion, London, 1967.

Encyclopaedia Judaica (Keter Publishing House Ltd) Jerusalem, 1971.

Encyclopedia of Psychology (Search Press) London, 1972.

FESTINGER, Leon; Riecken, Henry W.; Schachter, Stanley; *When Prophecy Fails* (Harper Torchbooks) New York, 1956.

FLUSSER, David, *Jesus* (Herder & Herder) New York, 1969.

FRANKFORT, Henri, *Kingship and the Gods* (University of Chicago Press) Chicago, 1948.

FROMM, Erich, *Psychoanalysis and Religion* (Victor Gollancz) London, 1951.

FROMM, Erich, *The Fear of Freedom* (Kegan Paul, Trench, Trubner & Co. Ltd) London, 1942.

FRAZER, Sir James George, *The Golden Bough* (Macmillan & Co. Ltd) London, 1936.

FREUD, Sigmund, *Group Psychology and the Analysis of the Ego*. Complete Works, Volume XVIII (The Hogarth Press) London, 1955.

FUCHS, Stephen, *Rebellious Prophets* (Asia Publishing House) London, 1965.

GASTER, Moses, *Studies and Texts in Folklore, Magic &c.* (Maggs Bros.) London, 1925–8.

GEBHART, Emile, *Mystics and Heretics in Italy* (George Allen & Unwin) London, 1922.

GENT, S. S. (Samuel Sheppard) *The Joviall Crew, or, The Devill turn'd Ranter*, London, 1651.

G. H., See Robins, John.

GIBB, Sir Hamilton A. R., *Mohammedanism* (New American Library) New York, 1955.

GLASSON, T. Francis, *The Second Advent* (The Epworth Press) London, 1963.

GOLUB, Jacob S., *In the Days of the First Temple* (Union of American Hebrew Congregations) Cincinnati, 1931.

GOODBLATT, Morris S., *Jewish Life in Turkey in the XVIth Century* (Jewish Theological Seminary of America) New York, 1952.

GOULD, S. Baring, *Historical Oddities and Strange Events* (Methuen & Co.) London, 1891.

GRAETZ, H., *Popular History of the Jews* (Hebrew Publishing Co.) New York, 1930.

GREENSTONE, Julius H., *The Messiah Idea in Jewish History* (The Jewish Publication Society of America) Philadelphia, 1906.

GRIGGE, William, *The Quakers' Jesus*, London, 1658.

HALHED, Nathaniel Brassey, *A Calculation on the Commencement of the Millennium*, London, 1795.

HANNOVER, Rabbi Nathan, *Abyss of Despair*, tr. Abraham J. Mesch (Bloch Publishing Company) New York, 1950.

The Harleian Miscellany, Volume VI, London, 1810.

Harris, Victor, *All Coherence Gone* (University of Chicago Press) Chicago, 1949.

Hastings, James, *Dictionary of the Bible*, Second Edition revised by Frederick C. Grant and H. H. Rowley (T. & T. Clark) Edinburgh, 1963.

Hill, Christopher, *The World Turned Upside Down* (Temple Smith) London, 1972.

Hirsch, S. A., *The Cabbalists and other Essays* (William Heinemann) London, 1922.

Hobsbawm, E. J., *Primitive Rebels* (Manchester University Press) Manchester, 1959.

Hoch, August, *Benign Stupors* (Cambridge University Press) (Macmillan Co.) New York, 1921.

Howard, Helen Addison, and McGrath, Dan L., *War Chief Joseph* (University of Nebraska Press) Lincoln, 1945.

I.R., *The Displaying of an Horrible Secte*, London 1578.

Israel, Joseph ben, *The Converted Jew*, London 1653.

James, William, *The Varieties of Religious Experience* (Longmans, Green & Co.) London, 1902, 1929.

J.E., *The History of the Three Late Famous Impostors*, London, 1669.

The Jewish Expositor, Volume IV, London, 1819.

John, Theaurau (Thomas Tany), *His Aurora in Tranlagorum in Salem Gloria*, London, 1651, 1655.

John, Theaurau (Thomas Tany), *Proclamation*, London, 1650.

Jones, Rufus M., *Mysticism and Democracy in the English Commonwealth* (Harvard University Press) Cambridge, Mass., 1932.

Jones, Rufus M., *Spiritual Reformers in the 16th and 17th Centuries* (Macmillan & Co. Ltd) London, 1914.

Jones, Rufus M., *Studies in Mystical Religion* (Macmillan & Co.) London, 1909.

Josephus, Flavius, see Whiston, William.

Kastein, Joseph, *The Messiah of Ismir, Sabbatai, Sabbatai Zevi*, tr. Huntley Paterson (John Lane, The Bodley Head) London, 1931.

Kierkegaard, Søren, *The Sickness Unto Death*, tr. Walter Lowrie (Doubleday & Co. Inc.) New York, 1954.

Klausner, Joseph, *The Messianic Idea in Israel* (George Allen & Unwin Ltd) London, 1956.

Knox, Ronald A., *Enthusiasm* (Clarendon Press) Oxford, 1950.

Knox, Ronald A., and Cox, Ronald, *Waiting for Christ* (Burns & Oates) London, 1960.

Kobler, Franz, (Ed.) *Letters of Jews Through the Ages* (Ararat Publishing Society) London, 1952.

KROUT, Maurice H., *Introduction to Social Psychology* (Harper & Bros) New York, 1942.

LAING, R. D., *The Politics of Experience* (Penguin Books) London, 1967.

LANGER, Walter C., *The Mind of Adolf Hitler* (Secker & Warburg) London, 1972.

LANTERNARI, Vittorio, *The Religions of the Oppressed* (MacGibbon & Kee) London, 1963.

LARSEN, Egon, *Strange Sects and Cults* (Arthur Barker Ltd) London, 1971.

LEA, Henry Charles, *A History of the Inquisition of Spain* (The Macmillan Co.) New York, 1906.

LERNER, Robert E., *The Heresy of the Free Spirit in the Later Middle Ages* (University of California Press) Berkeley and Los Angeles, 1972.

LEVI, David, *Letters to Nathanial Brassey Halhed M.P.*, London, 1795.

LEWINSOHN, Richard, *Prophets and Prediction* (Secker & Warburg) London, 1958.

LINDZEY, Gardner, and Aronson, Elliot, (Eds) *The Handbook of Social Psychology* (Addison-Wesley Publishing Co.) Massachusetts 1954, 1969.

LIVER, J., "The Doctrine of the two messiahs in sectarian literature in the time of the Second Commonwealth", *The Harvard Theological Review*, Vol. LII, No. 3 (1959).

MACKAY, Charles, *Memoirs of Extraordinary Popular Delusions* (National Illustrated Library) London, 1852.

MADDI, Salvatore R., The Existential Neurosis. *Journal of Abnormal Psychology*, Vol. 72, No. 4 (1967).

MANNHEIM, Karl, *Ideology and Utopia* (Routledge & Kegan Paul Ltd) London, 1936, 1960.

MATHIAS, P., *The Case of Joanna Southcott*, London, poss. 1815.

MATTHEWS, Ronald, *English Messiahs 1656–1927* (Methuen & Co. Ltd) London, 1936.

MAY, Rollo; Angel, Ernest; Ellenberger, Henri F.: (Eds) *Existence* (Basic Books Inc.) New York, 1958, 1960.

MOWINCKEL, Sigmund, *He That Cometh*, tr. G. W. Anderson (Basil Blackwell) Oxford, 1956.

NETANYAHU, B., *The Marranos of Spain, from the late XIVth to the early XVI century, according to contemporary Hebrew sources* (American Academy for Jewish Research) New York, 1966.

The New Standard Jewish Encyclopedia (Eds) Cecil Roth and Geoffrey Wigoder (W. H. Allen) London, 1970.

Notes and Queries, Vol. 175. 1938.

Nuttall, Geoffrey, *James Naylor, a fresh approach* (Friends Historical Society) London, 1954.

Pagitt, E., *Heresiography—a description of the hereticks and sectaries of these latter times*, London, 1646.

Parkes, James, *A History of the Jewish People* (Penguin Books) London, 1964.

Pastor, Ludwig, *The History of the Popes* (Ed.) Ralph Kerr (Routledge & Kegan Paul Ltd) London, 1950.

Pepys, Samuel, *Diary* (George Routledge & Sons Ltd) London, 1906.

Pines, Shlomo, *The Jewish Christians of the Early Centuries of Christianity according to a new source* (Israel Academy of Sciences and Humanities) Jerusalem, 1966.

Plain Truth, Vol. XXXIX, No. 8 (Ambassador College Press) California, September 1974.

Prince, Br. Henry, *The Testimony; the Little Book Open*, London, 1856.

Reece, Richard, M.D., *A correct statement of the last illness and death of Mrs Southcott*, London, 1815.

Reports of Cases in the Courts of Star Chamber (Ed.) Samuel Rawson Gardiner, London, 1886.

Robins, John, *The Declaration of John Robins, the false Prophet*, by G. H., London, 1651.

Roger, P. G., *Battle of Bossenden Wood* (Oxford University Press) London, 1961.

Rokeach, Milton, *The Open and Closed Mind* (Basic Books Inc.) New York, 1960.

Rokeach, Milton, *The Three Christs of Ypsilanti* (Arthur Barker Ltd) London, 1964.

Roth, Cecil, *A History of the Marranos* (Meridian Books Inc. and The Jewish Publication Society of America) New York, 1959.

Roth, Cecil, *The Nephew of the Almighty* (Edward Goldston Ltd) London, 1933.

Rupp, E. Gordon, *Thomas Müntzer, Hans Huth and the 'Gospel of All Creatures'* (The John Rylands Library) Manchester, 1961.

Sanders, Ed., *The Family* (Panther Books Ltd) London, 1973.

Sargant, William, *Battle for the Mind* (Pan Books) London, 1957.

Schechter, S., *Studies in Judaism*, Second Series (The Jewish Publishing Society of America) Philadelphia, 1908.

Schnur, Harry C., *Mystic Rebels* (The Beechhurst Press) New York, 1949.

Scholem, Gershom G., *Major Trends in Jewish Mysticism* (Thames and Hudson) London, 1955.

SCHOLEM, Gershom G., *On the Kabbalah and its Symbolism* (Routledge & Kegan Paul Ltd) London, 1965.

SCHOLEM, Gershom G., *The Messianic Idea in Judaism* (George Allen & Unwin Ltd) London, 1971.

SCHOLEM, Gershom G., *Sabbatai Zevi: the mystical Messiah 1626–1676* (Routledge) London, December 1973, in "The Written Library of Jewish Civilization" (a Routledge series).

SCHWARZ, Leo W. (Ed.) *A Golden Treasury of Jewish Literature* (Arthur Barker Ltd) London, 1937.

SCHWARZ, Leo W. (Ed.) *The Jewish Caravan* (Rinehart & Co. Inc.) New York, 1935.

SCHWARZ, Leo W. (Ed.) *Memoirs of My People* (Rinehart & Co. Inc.) New York, 1943.

SEARS, Clara Endicott, *Days of Delusion* (Houghton Mifflin & Co.) Boston and New York, 1924.

SEARS, Clara Endicott, *Gleanings from Old Shaker Journals* (Houghton Mifflin Co.) Boston and New York, 1916.

SHAW, George Bernard, *Prefaces* (Odhams Press Ltd) London, 1938.

SILVER, Abba Hillel, D. D., *A History of Messianic Speculation in Israel* (Macmillan Co.) New York, 1927.

Slotki, Judah J., *Menasseh ben Israel, his life and times* (Jewish Religious Educational Publications) London, 1951.

SMITH, Hannah Whitall (Ed.) Ray Strachey, *Religious Fanaticism* (Faber & Gwyer) London, 1928.

SMITHSON, R. J., *The Anabaptists* (J. Clarke & Co.) London, 1935.

SOLIS-COHEN, Emily, *Hanukkah, The Feast of Lights* (The Jewish Publication Society of America) Philadelphia, 1945.

SOUTHCOTT, Joanna, *Joanna's Dispute with Satan—A dispute between the Woman and Darkness*, London, 1813.

SOUTHCOTT, Joanna, Various tracts in the British Library, London, 1804, 1813, 1814.

SPINCKES, N., *The New Pretenders to Prophecy Examin'd*, London 1709.

SUNDKLER, Bengt G. M., *Bantu Prophets in South Africa* (International African Institute and Oxford University Press) London, 1961.

SZASZ, Thomas S., *Ideology and Insanity* (Penguin Books) London, 1974.

SZASZ, Thomas S., *The Myth of Mental Illness* (Secker & Warburg) London, 1961.

TANY, Thomas, see John, Theaurau.

TAYLOR, Gordon Rattray, *The Angel-Makers: A Study in the Psychological Origins of Historical Change, 1750–1850* (Heinemann) London, 1958.

T.H., *A True Discourse of the Two Infamous Upstart Prophets*, London, 1636.

THOMAS, Keith, *Religion and the Decline of Magic* (Weidenfeld & Nicolson) London, 1971.

THRUPP, Sylvia L. (Ed.) *Millennial Dreams in Action* (Society for the Comparative Study of Society and History) (Mouton & Co.) The Hague, 1962.

TOBIAS, *Mirabilis opera Dei, Certaine wonderfull works of God which hapned to HN*, London, 1575.

TOM, John, see Courtenay, Sir William.

TREVELYAN, G. M., *A Shortened History of England* (Penguin Books) London, 1960.

TUVESON, Ernest Lee, *Millennium and Utopia* (University of California Press) Berkeley and Los Angeles, 1949.

TUVESON, Ernest Lee, The Power of Believing, *Comparative Studies in society and history*, Vol. 5, No. 1, October 1962.

Universal Jewish Encyclopedia (Ed.) Isaac Landman (The Universal Jewish Encyclopedia Inc.) New York, 1942.

VERAX, Theodorus (Clement Walker), *Anarchia Anglicana, or, The History of Independency*, London, 1649.

VERMES, G., *The Dead Sea Scrolls in English* (Penguin Books) London, 1962, 1966.

WALLIS, Wilson D., *Culture and Progress* (McGraw-Hill Co.) New York, 1930.

WALKER, D. P., *The Decline of Hell* (Routledge & Kegan Paul Ltd) London, 1964.

WARD, John, *Letters, Epistles and Revelations of Jesus Christ*, London, 1831.

The Weekly Intelligencer of the Commonwealth, 1655.

WHISTON, William, *The Works of Flavius Josephus*, London, 1825.

WILSON, Bryan R., *Sects and Society* (William Heinemann) London, 1961.

WISCHNITZER, Rachel, *The Messianic Themes in the paintings of the Dura Synagogue* (University of Chicago Press) Chicago, 1948.

WOODCOCK, George, and Avakumovic, Ivan, *The Doukhobors* (Faber & Faber) London, 1968.

YOUNGHUSBAND, Sir Francis, *Modern Mystics* (John Murray) London, 1935.

ZANGWILL, Israel, *Dreamers of the Ghetto* (William Heinemann) London, 1898.

ZIEGLER, Philip, *The Black Death* (Collins) London, 1969.

INDEX

Jews easily duped
— Abbott p. 61

<u>False Prophets</u>

Jes. 9/15 Ez 13/3

Jer. 5/31. 14/14.15. 23/25. 27/14

Lam. 2/14.

---

pp. 227. 247